The
Reference Shelf®

Campaign Trends and Election Law

The Reference Shelf
Volume 88 • Number 5
H.W. Wilson
A Division of EBSCO Information Services, Inc.

Published by
GREY HOUSE PUBLISHING
Amenia, New York
2016

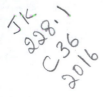
The Reference Shelf

The books in this series contain reprints of articles, excerpts from books, addresses on current issues, and studies of social trends in the United States and other countries. There are six separately bound numbers in each volume, all of which are usually published in the same calendar year. Numbers one through five are each devoted to a single subject, providing background information and discussion from various points of view and concluding with an index and comprehensive bibliography that lists books, pamphlets, and articles on the subject. The final number of each volume is a collection of recent speeches. Books in the series may be purchased individually or on subscription.

Publisher's Cataloging-In-Publication Data
(Prepared by The Donohue Group, Inc.)

Publisher's Cataloging-In-Publication Data
(Prepared by The Donohue Group, Inc.)

Names: H.W. Wilson Company.
Title: Campaign trends and election law / [compiled by] H. W. Wilson, a division
    of EBSCO Information Services.
Other Titles: Reference shelf ; v. 88, no. 5.
Description: Amenia, New York : Grey House Publishing, 2016. | Includes
    bibliographical references and index.
Identifiers: ISBN 978-1-68217-067-0 (v. 88, no. 5) | ISBN
    978-1-68217-062-5 (volume set)
Subjects: LCSH: Political campaigns--United States. | Election law--United
    States. | Campaign funds--United States. | Social media--Political aspects--
    United States.
Classification: LCC JK2281 .C36 2016 | DDC 324.70973--dc23

Contents

Preface   ix

1

Election Laws, Redistricting, Campaign Financing, Corporate Fundraising

Cash and Constituency: Campaign Financing and Partisan Electoral
    Manipulation   3

Drawing the Line: How Redistricting Turned America From Blue to Red.   8
By Elizabeth Kolbert *The New Yorker*, June 27, 2016

What is Political "Dark Money"—and Is It Bad?   15
By Michael Beckel The Center for Public Integrity, January 20, 2016

How "Ghost Corporations" Are Funding the 2016 Election   19
By Matea Gold and Anu Narayanswamy *The Washington Post*, March 18, 2016

Why Redistricting Threatens Democracy   23
By John Nichols *The Nation*, February 20, 2012

Voting Rights Become a Proxy War in the 2016 Presidential Election   26
By Frank Askin *The Conversation*, July 8, 2015

How Citizens United Has Changed Politics in 5 Years   29
By Gabrielle Levy *U.S. News and World Report*, January 21, 2015

The Many Sins of "Citizens United"   33
By Senator Sheldon Whitehouse *The Nation*, September 24, 2015

The First Postmodern Political Machine   36
By Walter Russell Mead *The American Interest*, August 21, 2015

2

Election Laws, Redistricting, Campaign Financing, Corporate Fundraising

Political Outsiders: Class, Race, and Gender in the 2016 Election   45

The Woman Card: How Feminism and Antifeminism Created Hillary Clinton
    and Donald Trump   51
By Jill Lepore*The New Yorker*, June 27, 2016

Working-Class Heroes: The 2016 Election Shows That, When Talking About
    Class, Americans and Their Candidates Are Both Out of Practice   61
By Jelani Cobb *The New Yorker* April 25, 2016

Outsiders' Chance   64
The Economist, January 30, 2016

Class, Trump, and the Election   70
By Victor David Hanson *National Review*, May 31, 2016

Race, Class, and the 2016 Election   74
By Keeanga-Yamahtta Taylor *Tikkun*, March 8, 2016

The Great Republican Revolt   80
By David Frum *The Atlantic*, January/February 2016 Issue

Trump's America   92
By Charles Murray *The Wall Street Journal*, February 12, 2016

Identity Heft: Why the Politics of Race and Gender Are Dominating the 2016
    Election   97
By Jeet Heer *The New Republic*, November 18, 2015

The Populists   100
By George Packer *The New Yorker*, September 7, 2015

3

Campaign Issues: Immigration, Trade, the Economy

Identity and Economics: Immigration and Globalization in the 2016 Race   105

The Truth About Trade: What Critics Get Wrong About the Global Economy   110
By Douglas A. Irwin *Foreign Affairs*, July/August 2016

Immigration and the 2016 Election   119
By Victor Agbafe *Harvard Political Review*, January 18, 2016

Even Conservatives Say Trump's Immigration Plan Is Dystopian   122
By Issie Lapowsky *Wired*, May 5, 2016

Supreme Court's Split Elevates Immigration as Election Issue   124
By Mike Dorning *Bloomberg Politics*, June 23, 2016

Simmering for Decades, Anger About Trade Boils Over in '16 Election   127
By Binyamin Appelbaum *The New York Times*, March 29, 2016

Why the Conditions Were Perfect for Bernie's Socialist Crusade   131
By Robert Kuttner *The American Prospect* , March 31, 2016

Election 2016 Is Propelled by the American Economy's Failed Promises   134
By Jon Hilsenrath and Bob Davis *The Wall Street Journal*, July 7, 2016

4

Campaign Messaging: Language, Social Media, Video

News and Information in the 2016 Campaign   143

The Rhetorical Brilliance of Trump the Demagogue   148
Jennifer Mercieca *The Conversation*, December 11, 2015

Who's Influencing Election 2016?   152
By William Powers *Medium,* February 23, 2016

Here's How Social Media Will Impact the 2016 Presidential Election   160
By Rohan Ayyar *Adweek,* February 17, 2016

2016 Presidential Election Circus: Is Social Media the Cause?   164
by Marissa Lang *The San Francisco Chronicle,* April 5, 2016

Digital Video Plays Critical Role in 2016 Election   168
By Philip Rosenstein *MediaPost,* July 8, 2016

Foul-Mouthed and Proud of It on the '16 Campaign Trail   170
Matt Flegenheimer and Maggie Haberman *The New York Times,* November 27, 2015

What Google and Twitter Can Tell Us About 2016   173
By Daniel White *Time,* February 22, 2016

Facebook to Provide "Political Bias" Training for Employees   177
By Rob Bluey *The Daily Signal,* June 22, 2016

The Polls Are All Wrong: A Startup Called Civis Is Our Best Hope to Fix Them 180
Garrett M. Graff *Wired,* August 22, 2016

Bibliography   189
Websites   195
Index   199

Preface

Election 2016: Dissatisfaction and Dissonance

Are Americans fed up with the two party system? Are the Democrats and Republicans out of synch with the priorities of the populace? These were some of the questions asked by analysts and journalists after an unprecedented election season marked by the emergence of an outsider, populist movement, high levels of voter interest, and some of the lowest levels of voter satisfaction in history. The message from voters was clear; the United States has serious issues and neither party has done enough to solve them. In a July 2016 Gallup Poll, 57 percent of voters viewed Hillary Clinton unfavorably while 62 percent viewed Donald Trump unfavorably.[1] Numerous articles characterized the public as feeling as if they were forced to vote for the "lesser of two evils," or to keep the opposing candidate out of office. However, despite low satisfaction, interest remained high as voters prepared to make a historic choice between Hillary Clinton—the first woman nominated by a major party for president—and Donald Trump—the first true political outsider, having had no previous experience in governance, military, or public service—to lead one of the major parties.

The 2016 campaign was also notable for having an especially vehement primary season. In both the Republican and Democratic parties, candidates openly insulted one another's fitness to lead and attacked each other's past political records. Surprisingly, Democratic candidate Bernie Sanders proved difficult to defeat as his campaign, calling on the most progressive faction of the party, hit an important note with a large contingent of democratic voters. Despite Hillary Clinton's lead in winning party delegates, Sanders' campaign seemingly refused to die and some hoped that he would stand as an independent candidate in the election as Clinton clinched the primary vote. On the other side of the divide, Trump mercilessly belittled his fellow Republican candidates and his support within the electorate demonstrated that many Republican voters shared or at least supported his openly hostile attitude. During the course of the primaries, it became clear that the GOP leadership was uncomfortable with Trump as the party's candidate. As other candidates failed to counter his lead, more and more Republican leaders rallied behind him, but Trump remained an outlier in the degree to which Republicans and Republican leaders disapproved of him as a potential president.

The Republican Party

Historical analyses indicate that, whenever one party succeeds in winning two consecutive terms in the White House, the rival party enjoys a major advantage in the subsequent election.[2] Though armed with this advantage, as the election season proceeded, the Republican party appeared to unravel. Unexpectedly little support for mainstream candidates, like dynastic contender Jeb Bush, led to a dramatic internal split with conservative voters displaying a clear preference for billionaire businessman and reality TV star Donald Trump.[3] Trump's success has been attributed to a "populist" swing in the party as Trump's key supporters, predominantly non-college educated white men, reportedly feel alienated and angry at the political and economic establishment. The media referred to Trump's campaign as a "takeover" or "revolution," as both GOP and Democrat politicians expressed bewilderment at the conservative movement behind Trump's controversial candidacy.

Republican political consultant Todd Domke theorized that millions of Americans, having watched Trump on *The Apprentice*, and not fully appreciating that reality television is highly contrived and scripted for entertainment value, had essentially been fooled into believing they had a reliable understanding of Trump as a person from his celebrity persona. Domke further theorized that eight years of conservative media urging listeners to feel the federal government had betrayed them, essentially backfired on the GOP, with millions of conservatives deciding that, if they couldn't trust the system, they should look outside for leadership.[4] Writing in *Slate*, columnist Jamelle Bouie expressed the belief that Trump appealed to an underlying racist sentiment among white men and women opposed to the perceived negative effects of America's diversification, which has gradually eroded the social advantages afforded exclusively to whites.[5] While Bouie's claims may be extreme, a May 2016 study from the Western Political Science Association found that Trump supporters were more than twice as likely as supporters of other Republicans to express negative opinions about Hispanics, Muslims, and African Americans and that 64 percent of Trump supporters believed President Obama was Muslim.[6]

Having never held office or worked in a public service field, Trump has been referred to as the least conventionally qualified individual in history to win a party nomination.[7] Trump's supporters argue that leading a nation is similar to running a corporation, and that Trump's skills as a business leader, as detailed in his self-help book *The Art of the Deal*, qualify him to serve as the nation's chief executive. The degree to which business acumen and political leadership overlap in terms of key skills is a matter of debate, with most analysts believing that the two skillsets are fundamentally different.[8] A Trump victory would therefore provide the first actual test of the theory that business savvy can translate into effective national leadership.

The son of real estate impresario Fred Trump, Donald Trump used his 1974 inheritance of $40 million, and a $1 million loan from his father, to build an estimated $2.9 billion in net worth. While his success is widely acknowledged, especially in marketing and branding, Trump's business record is more controversial. Critics have cited his involvement in 3,500 separate legal actions, a civil racketeering charge brought by New York State for his ownership of a business alleged to have defrauded customers, and six separate bankruptcies for Trump-owned companies, as evidence refuting claims about Trump's business leadership.[9] Writing in the *Washington Post*, journalist Ana Swanson opined that Trump's business record is not as controversial as his most ardent critics have claimed, but also not as impressive as Trump claims. In Swanson's opinion, Trump's primary skill is brand marketing, and it is this skill that has allowed Trump to market himself as a business innovator despite an unexceptional entrepreneurial record.[10]

Political analysts believe that Trump's popularity represents widespread dissatisfaction with the direction of the nation's economic and social evolution. Trump's campaign slogan, "Make America Great Again," encapsulates the view that America, at some unspecified point in the past, had been a great nation, though "greatness" in this characterization is an undefined quality, and that subsequent events (also unspecified) have degraded the nation's greatness. Much of the attention afforded to Trump's campaign was due to the candidate's penchant for igniting controversy with inflammatory rhetoric and unusually personal attacks against his rivals. For supporters, however, Trump's atypical behavior is part of his appeal, demonstrating that Trump is a passionate man too wealthy to be bought by special interests and unwilling to compromise his ideals for the sake of political decorum.

The Democratic Party

The 2016 Democratic Party also experienced an outsider swing behind Vermont Senator Bernie Sanders, a liberal independent turned Democrat who, for years, had been one of the party's most outspoken critics. Sanders, from the outset, echoed the sentiments of the "Occupy Wall Street" movement, promising to make income inequality a priority if elected. Like Trump, Sanders was described as a "populist," reflecting the dissatisfaction and anger of the electorate towards the major parties.[11] In comparing Sanders to rival Hillary Clinton, both candidates supported many of the same goals, while Sanders' proposals were more radical. For instance, on economic issues, Clinton proposed eliminating community college tuition, while Sanders proposed providing grant-funded free tuition at all public universities. Similarly, Clinton proposed a federal minimum wage increase to $12, while Sanders proposed a minimum wage of $15.[12]

After a contentious race, Clinton secured the nomination and Sanders agreed to endorse Clinton and assist in her campaign. However, in the wake of her nomination, Clinton's public approval plummeted. Several controversies, repeatedly cited by opponents, were instrumental in damaging her public image. The most significant was the revelation, in 2015, that Clinton used a personal email server to store later classified documents and communications while she served as secretary of state. The FBI launched an investigation, resulting in the determination that Clinton had been careless with potential state secrets though no charges were filed. Opponents also allege that Clinton is guilty of corruption, with Trump repeatedly referring to her as "Crooked Hillary," and both Trump and Sanders calling attention to Clinton's numerous speeches to big financial institutions, for which she was paid $250,000 each time, as evidence of questionable ethics.[13]

The reasons for Clinton's low approval rating are not entirely clear. By traditional measures, Clinton has been described as one of the most accomplished presidential candidates in history. Having served as a state senator and secretary of state, Clinton, in both positions, accumulated a wealth of accomplishments. As a senator, Clinton pioneered a widely lauded initiative for children's health insurance, and, as secretary of state, Clinton helped negotiate a ceasefire between Hamas and the government of Israel and was the first American politician to speak out in favor of women's rights to the government of China, earning a high public approval rating for her term as secretary.

While detractors frequently accuse Clinton of "lying," the website *Politifact*, which fact checks statements made by politicians, found that Clinton and Sanders told the truth an equal amount of the time and were the two most truthful candidates in the 2016 race. By comparison, *Politifact* estimates that more than 70 percent of Trump's statements were inaccurate.[14] The most reasonable criticism of Clinton comes from those who believe her deep connections to the Democratic party will make her ineffective at stimulating changes for America's downtrodden. Numerous journalists have also called attention to the troubling level of misogyny in public attacks aimed at Clinton. Trump's references to Clinton's role in "enabling" Bill Clinton's infidelity and the frequent use of sexist epithets in social media posts referring to Clinton represent, to some, a disturbing level of sexism among the public with many of the same criticisms having been used to marginalize women taking leadership roles for centuries.

The public familiarity with Clinton, combined with high levels of apathy towards both major parties, and the questions of corruption and scandals that have diminished her popularity, have obscured, to some degree, the historic import of Clinton's campaign. Despite the fact that Trump's colorful, controversial campaign earns far more media attention, Clinton's role in the effort to achieve gender equality is not trivial. Clinton's achievement, whether or not she wins the election, is a symbolic victory for all women struggling within the world's many male-dominated societies. For American women, Clinton's potential presidency represents a milestone in a more than 200-year fight for equality.

Micah L. Issitt

Works Used

Bates, Laura. 'Spanking' Hillary Clinton Is Grotesque Misogyny." *Time*. Time Inc. Feb 8 2016. Web. 19 Aug 2016.

Bouie, Jamelle. "How Trump Happened." *Slate*. Slate Media Group. Mar 13 2016. Web. 18 Aug 2016.

Domke, Todd. "Commentary: How Did Trump Happen?" *WBUR*. WBUR Radio. Jun 28 2016. Web. 18 Aug 2016.

"Favorability: People in the News." *Gallup*. Gallup. Aug 19 2016. Web. 19 Aug 2016.

Frum, David. "The Great Republican Revolt." *The Atlantic*. Atlantic Monthly Group. Jan/Feb 2016. Web. 18 Aug 2016.

Goldberg, Michelle. "The Hillary Haters." *Slate*. The Slate Group. Jul 24 2016. Web. 20 Aug 2016.

Koran, Laura and Ryan Browne. "Can Trump Be the First to Go Directly From Corner Office to Oval Office?" *CNN*. Cable News Network. Aug 12 2016. Web. 18 Aug 2016.

Krugman, Paul. "A Country Is Not a Company." *HBR*. Harvard Business Review. Jan-Feb 1996. Web. 19 Aug 2016.

Matthews, Chris. "Donald Trump Says Hillary Clinton Is Corrupt—Is He Right?" *Fortune*. Fortune Inc. Jun 13 2016. Web. 19 Aug 2016.

McDaniel, Jason and Sean McElwee. "Trump Supporters Have Cooler Feelings Towards Many Groups, Compared to Supporters of Other Candidates." *The New West*. Western Political Science Association. May 16 2016. Web. 19 Aug 2016.

McLaughlin, Dan. "History Is Not on the Democrats' Side in 2016." *The Federalist*. FDRLST Media. Sep 4 2014. Web. 19 Aug 2016.

Parini, Jay. "Why Do They Hate Hillary Clinton So Much?" *CNN*. Cable News Network. Mar 21 2016. Web. 19 Aug 2016.

"Republicans' Early Views of GOP Field More Positive Than in 2012, 2008 Campaigns." *Pew Research*. May 19 2015. Web. 19 Aug 2016.

Robinson, Eugene. "The Rock-Star Appeal of Bernie Sanders." *The Washington Post*. Nash Holdings. Oct 1 2015. Web. 19 Aug 2016.

Sahadi, Jeanne and Tal Yellin. "Hillary vs. Bernie: Their Money…and Yours." *CNN Money*. Cable News Network. Aug 18 2016. Web. 18 Aug 2016.

Swanson, Ana. "The Myth and the Reality of Donald Trump's Business Empire." *The Washington Post*. Feb 29 2016. Web. 18 Aug 2016.

Winter, Tom. "Trump Bankruptcy Math Doesn't Add Up." *NBC News*. National Broadcasting Company. Jun 24 2016. Web. 18 Aug 2016.

Notes

1. "Favorability: People in the News," *Gallup*.
2. McLaughlin, "History Is Not on the Democrats' Side in 2016."
3. Frum, "The Great Republican Revolt."
4. Domke, "Commentary: How Did Trump Happen?"
5. Bouie, "How Trump Happened."
6. McDaniel and McElwee, "Trump Supporters Have Cooler Feelings Towards Many Groups, Compared to Supporters of Other Candidates."
7. Koran and Browne, "Can Trump Be the First to Go Directly From Corner Office to Oval Office?"
8. Krugman, "A Country Is Not a Company."
9. Winter, "Trump Bankruptcy Math Doesn't Add Up."
10. Swanson, "The Myth and the Reality of Donald Trump's Business Empire."
11. Robinson, "The Rock-Star Appeal of Bernie Sanders."
12. Sahadi and Yellin, "Hillary vs. Bernie: Their Money…and Yours."
13. Matthews, "Donald Trump Says Hillary Clinton Is Corrupt—Is He Right?"
14. Parini, "Why Do They Hate Hillary Clinton So Much?"

1
Election Laws, Redistricting, Campaign Financing, Corporate Fundraising

Credit: Paul J. Richards / AFP/Getty Images

Various labor unions and progressive organizations protest on Capitol Hill September 16, 2015, calling for the restoration of the Voting Rights Act struck down by the US Supreme Court.

Cash and Constituency: Campaign Financing and Partisan Electoral Manipulation

Campaign financing and the partisan manipulation of elections are among the most controversial and contested issues in electoral politics. In both cases, electoral policies that are supposed to foster an even field for candidates and ensure that the will of the people is most accurately represented in each election have been manipulated to the advantage of partisan politics and wealthy interest groups. While voters overwhelmingly support policies that reduce corporate/monetary influence and that foster fair, unbiased voting, controversial court rulings have enabled partisan and economic manipulation to continue unabated and, in some cases, have exacerbated existing problems.

Campaign Finance Reform Then and Now

In 1757, seeking election to the Virginia House of Burgesses, George Washington decided to host a campaign event at which he (using his own money) supplied 43 gallons of alcoholic cider and 35 gallons of wine to his supporters. Washington won the election, but the Burgesses were concerned by his strategy. Then, as now, the idea of someone being able to "buy" an election was seen as contrary to the American ideal in which the nation's leaders would be chosen by popular consensus and politicians would represent the people rather than special interests or the economic elite. The House of Burgesses swiftly passed a law prohibiting political candidates from using gifts, rewards, or entertainment to win elections,[1] while, over the next two centuries, achieving the same goal at the federal level proved elusive.

By the early 1900s, the cynical view that economic and special interest groups controlled politics was a familiar part of American political discourse. Famed American writer Ambrose Bierce went so far as to propose a definition of "politics" as: "A strife of interests masquerading as a contest of principles." Theodore Roosevelt tried to eliminate campaign corruption with the 1907 Tillman Act law, which made corporate donations illegal, and the 1910 Federal Corrupt Practices Act, which required all political candidates to disclose their campaign finances. Though well intentioned, interest groups found ways to circumvent Roosevelt's and all subsequent restrictions on campaign donations. After the 1943 Smith-Connally Act prohibited unions from donating to federal candidates, the Congress of Industrial Organizations (CIO) created the first Political Action Committee (PAC) which was not officially part of the union and so was able to donate with impunity.

The 1976 Supreme Court case *Buckley v. Valeo* resulted in the ruling that limiting campaign donations violated First Amendment protections of free speech and

3

expression, thus essentially ruling that political spending was a form of expression. The 2010 case *Citizens United v. Federal Election Commission*, expanded on this, allowing for the creation of Super PACs, committees that do not have to adhere to spending limits, and 501 groups, nonprofits that can donate to candidates without disclosing information about their contributors. As a result, the 2010 congressional election saw a fourfold increase in outside spending from 2006 and a vast increase in "dark money," funds given by unknown donors to nonprofits.

Political reformer Derek Cressman believes that the problem with the *Buckley* and *Citizens United* decisions is not the classification of donations as a form of expression, but rather the rejection of the idea that, "…in order for all voices to be heard in a policy debate, we must limit the amount that each individual can speak." Cressman therefore advocates both the idea that donations are expressions, while still limiting to the level to which corporations or interest groups are allowed to "speak" in support of a candidate.[2] In a 2015 *New York Times* poll, 85 percent of Americans believed the United States needs measures to restrict the influence of wealthy investors, needs to limit the money that can be spent by SuperPACs, and should require public disclosure of all political donations. Specifically, 85 percent believed that at least fundamental changes were needed, while only 13 percent believed the system needed only minor changes.[3] A December 2015 poll by Pew Research found that 84 percent of Democrats and 72 percent of Republicans favor limiting both corporate and individual donations.[4]

While all candidates in the 2016 race echoed public calls for finance reform, Super PACs played a major role in the 2016 electoral season. While Clinton raised $119.7 million from Super PACs, Trump's Super PACs raised only $12 million for his campaign. Trump touted his low level of reliance on PACs as evidence of incorruptibility, and frequently alleged that Clinton was vulnerable to manipulation by her donors. Trump's campaign elicited a different kind of corruption controversy, however, when it was revealed that 17 percent of the funds raised by his campaign were given to companies owned by Trump or his family, with critics accusing him of profiting from his campaign. Along party lines, 57 percent Republican funding came from Super PACs, as compared to 18 percent of Democratic funding. Clinton also raised $62 million in small donations (under $200) compared to Trump's raising $37 million in small donations. Bernie Sanders was an outlier in that most of Sanders' funding came from small donations and his campaign was frequently used to demonstrate the power of grassroots fundraising.[5]

After the primaries, the official party platforms were more diametrically opposed. The GOP platform officially opposed placing any limits on corporate or private donations and opposed any new requirements forcing candidates to disclose the source of donations. The Democratic platform, in sharp contrast, called for an amendment to overturn both *Buckley v. Valeo* and *Citizens United*. The platform also endorsed legislation that would require congressional candidates to use public funds in their campaigns and that would strengthen rules requiring candidates to disclose the source of donations.[6]

Redistricting and Voting Laws

Candidates for both local and federal offices are elected by voters within districts, which are segments of a larger territory. The reasoning behind creating districts is to ensure that citizens are equally represented in the state and federal legislatures. A state or city with a large population, for instance, will be divided into multiple districts with each district electing state and federal representatives. As populations grow and change, redistricting is needed to ensure that the representation for each district reflects changing demographics. According to US law, the nation may only have 435 districts, and so new districts can only be created if other districts are abolished. Every 10 years, when the US Census Bureau completes its decennial survey, politicians decide where new congressional districts should be drawn and where districts should be removed.

In 32 states, redistricting is a partisan process handled by the state legislature where political parties have frequently used redistricting to give their candidates an advantage. This process is called "gerrymandering," a term coined in 1812 when then Massachusetts governor Elbridge Gerry created a new district (which was described as having a "salamander" shape) to benefit his party in an upcoming election.[7] Gerrymandering is not illegal, though many consider it unethical. In California, Hawaii, Idaho, Arizona, Montana, New Jersey, and Washington, the states use independent or bipartisan committees to handle redistricting in an effort to prevent gerrymandering.[8]

Among the most controversial redistricting issues has been the tendency for Republican-controlled legislatures to redraw districts so as to reduce the impact of minority voters, who typically favor Democratic candidates. In a 2016 case in Virginia, courts rejected a redistricting plan that concentrated African-American voters into a single district, thus reducing the impact of the African-American vote in the state legislature.[9] A 2013 study by political science students at Fordham University indicated that 54 percent of Americans don't know how congressional redistricting or gerrymandering occurs.[10] However, when the process is explained, voters do not approve of gerrymandering. A 2014 study by the University of Virginia, for instance, found that 74 percent of state residents favored independent redistricting.[11]

Another important issue in 2016 is a new wave of controversial voting laws that, critics argue, are discriminatory against low-income, minority, and young voters. The Voting Rights Act prohibits states with a history of discrimination from making new voting rules without federal approval. However, in the case of *Shelby County v. Holder,* the Supreme Court ruled that some states, including North Carolina, would be freed from this requirement and that state legislatures would be allowed to enact new voting laws without approval. Shortly after the Supreme Court ruling, the Republican legislature of North Carolina, an increasingly competitive state due to a growing African-American population, enacted new laws that required voters to use state-issued photo IDs and eliminated same-day voter registration. The legislature argued that the new laws were intended to eliminate voter fraud.

A 2011 report from the Brennan Center indicated that only 8 percent of white citizens, but a full 25 percent of African-Americans lack state-issued photo IDs and that many minority individuals relied on alternative IDs such as public assistance cards.[12] The NAACP and other civil rights groups argue that some voting rules, such as the new wave of voter ID laws, were created by Republican legislatures hoping to reduce the impact of African American, young, and low-income voters. In July, three justices in a federal appeals court struck down North Carolina's 2013 voting law after the law had been upheld in a lower court. In a similar decision in Wisconsin, US district Judge James Peterson ruled that the Republican legislature's proposed voter ID law "…demonstrates that a preoccupation with mostly phantom election fraud leads to real incidents of disenfranchisement, which undermine rather than enhance confidence in elections, particularly in minority communities."[13]

Despite widespread concern, numerous studies indicate that the kind of voter fraud that might be hindered by requiring state IDs or restricting late registration is not a significant problem in the United States.[14] Even in cases where judges support state rights to enact voting laws, the seminal argument is that states have the constitutional *right* to combat fraud, and *not* that voting fraud of the type purportedly being addressed is a problem or that the laws in question are an effective measure against fraud. The new wave of voting laws have been proposed in Republican-led legislatures, and this factor, given the Republican Party's historic and current lack of support with any and all minorities, raises concerns about the motivation behind the new wave of voting restrictions.

Micah L. Issitt

Works Used:

Barasch, Emily. "The Twisted History of Gerrymandering in American Politics." *Atlantic*. Atlantic Monthly Group. Sep 19 2012. Web. 15 Aug 2016.

Barnes, Robert and Ann E. Marimow. "Appeals Court Strikes Down North Carolina's Voter-ID Law." *The Washington Post*. Jul 29 2016. Web. 20 Aug 2016.

Blumenthal, Paul. "On Campaign Finance, Republicans and Democrats Could Not Be Further Apart." *The Huffington Post*. Jul 19 2016. Web. 19 Aug 2016.

"Citizens Don't Like Gerrymandering; Study Offers Alternative Redistricting Methods." *UVA Today*. University of Virginia. Weldon Cooper Center for Public Service. Jun 30 2014. Web. 16 Aug 2016.

Confessore, Nicholas and Megan Thee-Brenan. "Poll Shows Americans Favor an Overhaul of Campaign Financing." *New York Times*. New York Times Company. Jun 2 2015. Web. 13 Aug 2016

Cressman, Derek. "End Court-Ordered Corruption." *US News*. U.S. News and World Report. Jan 29 2016. Web. 16 Aug 2016.

Desilver, Drew and Patrick Van Kessel. "As More Money Flows into Campaigns, Americans Worry About Its Influence." *Pew Research*. Pew Research Center. Dec 7 2015. Web. 19 Aug 2016.

Fuller, Jaime. "From George Washington to Shaun McCutcheon: A Brief-ish History of Campaign Finance Reform." *The Washington Post*. Nash Holdings. Apr 3 2014. Web. 15 Aug 2016

Hamilton, Alec. "A Brief History of Campaign Finance (and Why It Matters)." *WNYC*. New York Public Radio. Dec 21 2010. Web. 15 Aug 2016.

Narayanswamy, Anu, Cameron, Darla, and Matea Gold. "Money Raised as of July 31." *Washington Post*. Nash Holdings. Jul 31 2016. Web. 21 Aug 2016.

Nyhan, Brendan. "Voter Fraud Is Rare, but Myth Is Widespread." *New York Times*. New York Times Company. Jun 10 2014. Web. 20 Aug 2016.

Panagopoulos, Costas. "Public Awareness and Attitudes About Redistricting Institutions." *Journal of Politics and Law*. Vol 6, No 3; 2013. Pdf. 15 Aug 2016.

Saad, Lydia. "Half in U.S. Support Publicly Financed Federal Campaigns." *Gallup*. Gallup Inc. Jun 24 2013. Web. 12 Aug 2016.

Scott, Eugene. "Judge Upholds Controversial North Carolina Voter ID Law." *CNN*. Cable News Network. Apr 26 2016. Web. 21 Aug 2016.

Stebenne, David. "Re-mapping American Politics: The Redistricting Revolution Fifty Years Later." *OSU*. Oregon State University. Vol 5, Iss 5, Feb 2012. Web. 15 Aug 2016.

Wasik, John. "Voter Fraud: A Massive, Anti-Democratic Deception." *Forbes*. Forbes Inc. Nov 6 2012. Web. 20 Aug 2016.

Weiser, Wendy R. and Lawrence Norden. "Voting Law Changes in 2012." *Brennan Center*. Brennan Center for Justice. 2011. Pdf. 19 Aug 2016.

Wolf, Richard. "Supreme Court Upholds Virginia Redistricting." *USA Today*. May 23 2016. Web. 15 Aug 2016.

Wolf, Richard and Gregory Korte. "Supreme Court Strikes Blow Against Gerrymandering." *USA Today*. Gannett Company. Jun 29 2015. Web. 15 Aug 2016.

Notes

1. Fuller, "From George Washington to Shaun McCutcheon: A Brief-ish History of Campaign Finance Reform."
2. Cressman, "End Court-Ordered Corruption."
3. Confessore and Thee-Brenan, "Poll Shows Americans Favor an Overhaul of Campaign Financing."
4. Desilver and Van Kessel, "As More Money Flows into Campaigns, Americans Worry About its Influence."
5. Narayanswamy, Cameron, and Gold, "Money Raised As of July 31."
6. Blumenthal, "On Campaign Finance, Republicans and Democrats Could Not Be Further Apart."
7. Barasch, "The Twisted History of Gerrymandering in American Politics."
8. Stebenne, "Re-mapping American Politics: The Redistricting Revolution Fifty Years Later."
9. Wolf, "Supreme Court Upholds Virginia Redistricting."
10. Panagopoulos, "Public Awareness and Attitudes About Redistricting Institutions."
11. "Citizens Don't Like Gerrymandering; Study Offers Alternative Redistricting Methods," *UVA Today*.
12. Weiser and Noren, "Voting Law Changes in 2012."
13. Barnes and Marimow, "Appeals Court Strikes Down North Carolina's Voter-ID Law."
14. Nyhan, "Voter Fraud Is Rare, but Myth Is Widespread."

Drawing the Line: How Redistricting Turned America From Blue to Red

By Elizabeth Kolbert
The New Yorker, June 27, 2016

Sometime around October 20, 1788, Patrick Henry rode from his seventeen-hundred-acre farm in Prince Edward, Virginia, to a session of the General Assembly in Richmond. Henry is now famous for having declared, on the eve of the Revolution, "Give me liberty, or give me death!"—a phrase it's doubtful that he ever uttered—but in the late seventeen-eighties he was best known as a leader of the Anti-Federalists. He and his faction had tried to sink the Constitution, only to be outmaneuvered by the likes of Alexander Hamilton and James Madison. When Henry arrived in the state capital, his adversaries assumed he would seek revenge. They just weren't sure how.

"He appears to be involved in gloomy mystery," one of them reported.

The Constitution had left it to state lawmakers to determine how elections should be held, and in Virginia the Anti-Federalists controlled the legislature. Knowing that his enemy Madison was planning a run for the House of Representatives, Henry set to work. First, he and his confederates resolved that Virginia's congressmen would be elected from districts. (Several other states had chosen to elect their representatives on a statewide basis, a practice that persisted until Congress intervened, in 1842.) Next, they stipulated that each representative from Virginia would have to run from the district where he resided. Finally, they stuck in the shiv. They drew the Fifth District, around Madison's home in the town of Orange, to include as many Anti-Federalists as possible.

An ally of Madison's who attended the session in Richmond wrote to him that while it was unusual for the legislature to "bend its utmost efforts" against a single individual, this was, indeed, what had happened: "The object of the majority of today has been to prevent yr. Election in the house of Representatives." Another friend reported, "The Counties annexed to yours are arranged so, as to render your Election, I fear, extremely doubtful." George Washington, too, was pessimistic; Madison's defeat seemed to him "not at all improbable."

Henry's maneuver represents the first instance of congressional gerrymandering, which is impressive considering that Congress did not yet exist. (One of his biographers has observed that Henry was fortunate that "the wits of Virginia" weren't quick enough to invent the word "henrymandering.") Since then, every party out of power has railed against the tactic. Meanwhile, every party in power has deployed it. The Federalists, when they got their turn, gerrymandered just as energetically as the Anti-Federalists. So did the Whigs, the Democrats, and, once the Whigs collapsed, the Republicans. In the eighteen-thirties, the Anti-Masonic Party briefly came to power in Pennsylvania. The Party used its hour upon the stage to push through a round of gerrymandering.

In contrast to our union, gerrymandering actually has grown more perfect with time. Henry had only his gut to go on, and his gut, it turned out, wasn't that reliable. In spite of his machinations, the Fifth District elected Madison. Today, when party functionaries draw district lines, they have at their disposal detailed census results, precinct-level voter tallies, and a cloud's worth of consumer choices. The result, David Daley argues in *Ratf**ked: The True Story Behind the Secret Plan to Steal America's Democracy* (Liveright), is a system so rigged that it hardly matters anymore who's running for office.

Much of *Ratf**ked* is devoted to a Republican scheme optimistically called REDMAP, for Redistricting Majority Project. REDMAP was created in early 2010, at a point when the country's electoral map was largely blue. In twenty-seven states, Democrats held the majority of seats in both houses of the legislature, and in six more they held a majority in one house. The Presidency, the US Senate, and the House of Representatives were all in Democratic hands. To describe their own party, Republicans were using words like "wounded" and "adrift."

And, as bad as things looked at the time, the GOP's prospects down the road looked even worse. In 2011, new census figures were due to be released, and this would trigger a round of redistricting. Republicans, Daley writes, were facing "a looming demographic disaster."

The idea behind REDMAP was to hit the Democrats at their weakest point. In several state legislatures, Democratic majorities were thin. If the Republicans commissioned polls, brought in high-powered consultants, and flooded out-of-the-way districts with ads, it might be possible to flip enough seats to take charge of them. Then, when it came time to draw the new lines, the GOP. would be in control.

"People call us a vast right-wing conspiracy," Karl Rove told potential donors to the project at an early fund-raiser in Dallas. "But we're really a half-assed right-wing conspiracy. Now it's time to get serious."

Daley conveys what happened next through the example of David Levdansky, a member of the Pennsylvania House of Representatives. Levdansky, a Democrat, had served in Harrisburg for thirteen terms. He was running for a fourteenth in a picnics-and-handshakes sort of way when flyers with out-of-state postmarks started landing in his constituents' mailboxes.

"Stop David Levdansky from increasing taxes by a billion dollars again," one declared.

"David Levdansky voted to waste $600 million taxpayer dollars and build an Arlen Specter library," a second announced.

"$600 million down the toilet just to honor Arlen Specter," a third flyer lamented.

(Specter, then the state's senior U.S. senator, had recently switched his party affiliation from Republican to Democratic.)

Between mid-October and early November, prospective voters in Levdansky's district, south of Pittsburgh, received something like two dozen pieces of negative mail. The mail campaign was reinforced by equally negative cable-TV ads.

Levdansky tried to explain that the information in the flyers was false. The appropriation he'd voted for was to help finance a new library at Philadelphia University, and it amounted to just two million dollars. But the truth was no match for REDMAP. Levdansky lost his seat by a hundred and fifty-one votes.

"The fucking Arlen Specter library," he tells Daley.

Others who found themselves in REDMAP's crosshairs met similar fates. Daley, a journalist who now edits the Web site *Salon*, goes to interview a second former Pennsylvania representative named David Kessler. The two meet in a pizza parlor near Reading.

"I could have been running against that saltshaker and I would have lost," Kessler says. "Because it all came down to those mailers." One flyer sent to Kessler's constituents likened the "$600 million" Arlen Specter library to the Taj Mahal.

This pattern was repeated in normally sleepy legislative districts from North Carolina to Oregon. All told, in 2010 Republicans gained nearly seven hundred state legislative seats, which, as a report from REDMAP crowed, was a larger increase "than either party has seen in modern history." The wins were sufficient to push twenty chambers from a Democratic to a Republican majority. Most significantly, they gave the G.O.P. control over both houses of the legislature in twenty-five states. (One was Pennsylvania.) The blue map was now red.

> **The science of gerrymandering is now so precise that most incumbents' main fear is a primary challenge, and here the best defense is to play to the lunatic fringe. The net result, as many analysts have noted, is increasing polarization.**

Two of the most common gerrymandering techniques are "packing" and "cracking." In the first, the party in charge of redistricting tries to "pack" voters from the rival party into as few districts as possible, to minimize the number of seats the opposition is likely to win. In the second, blocs of opposition voters are parcelled out among several districts, to achieve the same goal.

Both techniques were brought to bear in Pennsylvania. The new Republican majority "packed" blue-leaning voters into a handful of districts around Philadelphia and Pittsburgh. Then it "cracked" the rest into districts that tilted red.

The original gerrymander—named for Massachusetts' ninth governor, Elbridge Gerry—was a sinuous blob that wound around Boston. ("The Gerry-Mander: A new species of Monster" read the headline over a cartoon of the district that ran in the March 26, 1812, edition of the *Boston Gazette*.) Among the misshapen districts to emerge from Pennsylvania's 2011 redistricting plan is one Daley describes as looking "like a horned antelope barrelling down a hill on a sled." Another has been compared to Donald Duck kicking Goofy in the groin. So skillfully were the lines drawn that in 2012—when President Obama carried Pennsylvania by three hundred thousand votes and the state's Democratic congressional candidates collectively outpolled their G.O.P. rivals by nearly a hundred thousand votes—Republicans still won thirteen of Pennsylvania's eighteen seats in the U.S. House of Representatives.

"Arguably the most distorted map in the country" is how one researcher described the Pennsylvania districts. "In Pennsylvania, the Gerrymander of the Decade?" the Web site *RealClearPolitics* asked.

Another REDMAP target was Michigan. In 2010, the project poured a million dollars into legislative campaigns in the state, an expenditure that helped elect Republican majorities in both chambers. When the state's new congressional map was unveiled in 2011, one commentator likened it to a psychedelic confection, "with districts swirling around Southeast Michigan like colors in a Willy Wonka lollipop." *Roll Call* labelled Michigan's revamped Fourteenth District one of the "five ugliest" in the country. The Fourteenth, which starts in Detroit, snakes through eastern suburbs like Grosse Pointe, and then abruptly juts west and north to Pontiac, has an outline that resembles Bart Simpson holding a fishing pole. It became known as "the 8 Mile Mess," after a major thoroughfare that forms one of its boundaries. (Its rivals for the ugliest-district award included North Carolina's Fourth, nicknamed "the Hanging Claw," and Maryland's Third, dubbed "the Pinwheel of Death.")

REDMAP's strategists were so pleased with how the 8 Mile Mess and the lollipop swirls performed in November of 2012 that they boasted about it in an end-of-year analysis. "The 2012 election was a huge success for Democrats at the statewide level in Michigan," they wrote. "Voters elected a Democratic U.S. Senator by more than 20 points and reelected President Obama by almost 10 points." Still, Republicans ended up with the lion's share of the state's congressional seats—nine, to the Democrats' five.

Daley's account of REDMAP's craftiness is compelling—so compelling that it almost undoes itself. If gerrymandering is all-important, it's hard to explain how REDMAP ever got anywhere. In 2010, Republicans were dealing with lines that had, in several key states, been drawn by Democrats. Yet the G.O.P. managed to win control not only of state legislatures but of Congress.

Daley addresses this problem by presenting 2010 as an electoral outlier. First came the unanticipated frenzy of the Tea Party. Then came Citizens United. The Supreme Court's decision turned the usual torrent of campaign cash into Niagara Falls.

REDMAP was funded by a super-PAC-like group called the Republican State Leadership Committee. In the aftermath of Citizens United, the R.S.L.C. raised nearly thirty million dollars. (Altria, the parent company of Philip Morris, contributed $1.4 million; Reynolds American, owner of R. J. Reynolds and the American Snuff Company, kicked in another $1.3 million.) Many of the contributions—roughly eighteen million dollars' worth—were received just weeks before Election Day. To the extent that state lawmakers like Levdansky and Kessler even realized what was going on, they didn't have time to respond.

The blue equivalent of the R.S.L.C. is the Democratic Legislative Campaign Committee. By the logic of *Ratf**ked*, it should have been fighting REDMAP tooth and nail. And yet it seems to have been caught napping. Daley has no real explanation for this, aside from the old Will Rogers joke, "I belong to no organized political party. I am a Democrat." When Daley interviews Representative Steve Israel, of New York, who's in charge of the Democratic Congressional Campaign Committee, Israel tells him, "The Republicans have always been better than Democrats at playing the long game."

Credit for coining the word "ratfuck" is often given to Donald Segretti, one of the dirty tricksters who worked on Richard Nixon's 1972 reëlection campaign. (A typical Segretti "ratfuck" involved composing a letter on Senator Edmund Muskie's letterhead accusing one of Muskie's rivals for the Democratic Presidential nomination, Senator Henry Jackson, of having fathered an illegitimate child.) The term comes in so handy in politics that it could be—and probably is—used all the time. Only rarely, though, does it make it into print, and it's from one of these appearances that Daley draws his title.

As Daley tells it, the story begins in 1989. Lee Atwater, who, a year earlier, as manager of George H. W. Bush's Presidential campaign, had said of Bush's opponent, Michael Dukakis, that he was going to "strip the bark off the little bastard," had just become chairman of the Republican National Committee. The map that confronted Atwater—much like the one that would later confront the R.S.L.C.— was awash in blue. Atwater decided Republicans needed to "do something about redistricting," and he assigned this task to the R.N.C.'s counsel, Ben Ginsberg. The "something" Ginsberg came up with was an appeal to the Congressional Black Caucus.

The caucus didn't have much reason to listen to the R.N.C. At the time, it had zero Republican members (and today it has just one). But Ginsberg argued that when it came to redistricting—or, from another perspective, gerrymandering—the two groups shared a common interest. How about if they collaborated?

The pitch worked. The R.N.C. and the Congressional Black Caucus joined forces to press for the creation of more majority-black districts. These districts were drawn so as to concentrate, or "pack," African-American voters, a move that had a dramatic and possibly permanent effect. Consider the example of Georgia. In 1990, the state sent nine Democrats to Congress. Eight of them were white; the ninth was the civil-rights leader John Lewis. In 1994, the state sent three African-Americans to Congress. The trade-off was that only one white Democrat got elected (and he switched parties five months later). Perhaps not coincidentally, in 1994, Republicans took control of the House. In an interview with this magazine the following year, Ginsberg said he was convinced that the alliance with the Black Caucus had been crucial to the G.O.P.'s victory. Asked if the strategy had had a name, he said no, then jokingly suggested "Project Ratfuck."

Like revolutions, ratfucks often turn on their own. In the case of REDMAP, this may be karmic, or it may simply be mathematical. The science of gerrymandering is now so precise that most incumbents' main fear is a primary challenge, and here the best defense is to play to the lunatic fringe. The net result, as many analysts have noted, is increasing polarization. Daley takes this analysis a half step further, arguing that the control Republicans exercised over the latest round of redistricting is the very reason the Party has lost control over its members. The representatives who make up the House Freedom Caucus—the group that last year forced House Speaker John Boehner to resign—hail from districts so red that the biggest danger they face is being branded insufficiently immoderate. Daley quotes James Huntwork, a Republican election-law expert, who describes a primary campaign in a typically lopsided district as a contest between one candidate who says, "I am completely crazy!" and one who says, "I am even crazier than you!"

What is to be done about all this? Over the past few decades, dozens of lawsuits have been filed to block redistricting plans on the ground that they disenfranchise one party's voters or the other's. A few of these challenges have made it all the way to the U.S. Supreme Court, without much success. (The Court has sometimes intervened in cases of racial gerrymandering, and it recently agreed to hear a challenge to the lines Republicans drew for Virginia's House of Delegates. The suit alleges that the lines reduce the influence of minority voters by "packing" them into too few districts.)

In the meantime, several states, including Iowa and California, have tried to slay the Gerry-Mander by shifting responsibility for redistricting from their legislatures to independent boards. Perhaps the most disturbing chapters of *Ratf**ked* deal with what happens when this sort of civic-minded effort bumps up against the realities of partisan politics. (Think of a small bunny bumping up against a ten-ton truck.)

Daley recounts how, in 2000, Arizona voters opted to turn redistricting over to a board made up of two Democrats, two Republicans, and one independent. The commission's maiden effort, in 2001, was generally regarded as an improvement over previous plans. But by 2011 both Democrats and Republicans had figured out how to game the system, and Arizona's experiment in bipartisanship devolved into ever more devious forms of ratfucking. One of the commissioners was accused of lying about contacts with Democratic Party officials. A group that claimed to be working for "fair" districts turned out to be funded by a Koch-brothers-linked conservative network. The Republican governor tried to oust the commission's chairwoman, charging her with "gross misconduct." The only basis for the charge seemed to be that the governor did not care for the way the new districts had been drawn.

"The closer one looks, the less independent the Arizona Independent Redistricting Commission appears," Daley writes. He finds the situation so disheartening that he proposes the whole election system be revamped. States, he suggests, should return to the multi-member districts that were popular back in Patrick Henry's day. There is no reason to expect this or any other reform to be enacted. Pretty much by definition, gerrymandering suits those in power.

As far as the upcoming election is concerned, a REDMAP victory seems almost guaranteed. In House races in 2012, 1.7 million more votes were cast for Democrats than for Republicans. And still, thanks to the way those votes were packed and cracked, Republicans came away with thirty-three more congressional seats. A

Trumpocalypse, if such a thing is possible, could put seemingly safe districts in play. But few pundits see that as likely.

In preparation for the next census, Democrats have come up with a REDMAP-like plan of their own. They call it Advantage 2020, and say they hope to fund it to the tune of seventy million dollars. Republicans, for their part, have announced REDMAP 2020. Their spending goal? A hundred and twenty-five million dollars.

Print Citations

CMS: Kolbert, Elizabeth. "Drawing the Line: How Redistricting Turned America From Blue to Red." In *The Reference Shelf: Campaign Trends and Election Law*, edited by Betsy Maury, 8-14. Ipswitch, MA: Salem Press, 2016.

MLA: Kolbert, Elizabeth. "Drawing the Line: How Redistricting Turned America From Blue to Red." *The Reference Shelf: Campaign Trends and Election Law*. Ed. Betsy Maury. Ipswitch: Salem Press, 2016. 8-14. Print.

APA: Kolbert, E. (2016). Drawing the line: How redistricting turned America from blue to red. In Betsy Maury (Ed.), *The reference shelf: Campaign trends and election law* (pp. 8-14). Ipswitch, MA: Salem.(Original work published 2016)

What Is Political "Dark Money" — and Is It Bad?

By Michael Beckel
The Center for Public Integrity, January 20, 2016

By now, you've probably heard the phrase "dark money."

Activists use it. Politicians use it. And journalists use it, including here at the Center for Public Integrity.

For some people, it's just another piece of confusing campaign finance jargon. For others, it's a term of art, with a precise definition.

So here are answers to some of the most frequently asked questions about dark money in politics.

What Makes Political Money Dark Money?

The sources behind most of the money raised by politicians and political groups are publicly disclosed. Candidates, parties and political action committees— including the super PACs that are allowed to accept unlimited amounts of money— all report the names of their donors to the Federal Election Commission on a regular basis. Or, to be technical, they regularly disclose the names of all their donors who each give more than $200. But when the source of political money isn't known, that's dark money.

What Does Political Dark Money Look Like?

The two most common vehicles for dark money in politics are politically active nonprofits and corporate entities such as limited liability companies. Certain politically active nonprofits— notably those formed under sections 501(c)(4) and 501(c)(6) of the tax code— are generally not required to publicly disclose their donors. Meanwhile, when limited liability companies are formed in certain states, such as Delaware and Wyoming, they are essentially black boxes; the company's name is basically the only thing known about them. These LLCs can be used to make political expenditures themselves or to donate to super PACs.

How much money are we talking about?

During the 2012 election cycle— the last time the presidency was at stake— dark money groups pumped about $300 million into political messages that called for the election or defeat of federal candidates, according to the nonpartisan Center for Responsive Politics. Additionally, dark money groups spent hundreds of millions of dollars on political advertisements that focused more on issues than candidates. The most notable example? Americans for Prosperity, the flagship nonprofit of the conservative billionaire brothers Charles and David Koch. Also worth noting: Dark money doesn't affect every election. It frequently targets the most high-profile political races.

Do Democrats use Dark Money?

Yes. Neither party wants to be left behind in the political money arms race. The result: Dark money groups are multiplying— and thriving— on both ends of the political spectrum. However, during the 2012 election cycle, conservative dark money groups that reported expenditures to the FEC outspent liberal ones by about 8-to-1, according to the Center for Responsive Politics.

How Does Dark Money Relate to the *U.S. Supreme Court's Citizens United v. Federal Election Commission* Ruling?

The *Citizens United* decision gave the green light to corporations, including certain types of nonprofit corporations, to spend money on political ads that expressly called for the election or defeat of federal candidates. A prior U.S. Supreme Court ruling in 2007, known as *Wisconsin Right to Life v. FEC*, had allowed corporations, including certain types of nonprofits, to spend money on issue ads during the run-up to elections— so long as they did not overtly call for the election or defeat of candidates. The Bipartisan Campaign Reform Act of 2002 had banned both types of corporate spending in politics. Now that these restrictions have been overturned, politically active nonprofit groups are spending more money than ever to directly influence elections.

Are There Other Types of Money in Politics That Come From Unknown Sources?

The names of small-dollar donors who give $200 or less are not publicly disclosed. Some conservative activists and politicians have worried that foreigners, or other illicit donors, might try to exploit this disclosure rule to their advantage. But most election observers can't point to any evidence of widespread abuse.

Why Are So Many People Upset About Dark Money in Politics?

Campaign finance reform activists argue that voters should know who is funding political advertisements. Such information, they assert, is essential to voters' ability to evaluate the merits of political messages— and to know if certain special interests may be trying to curry favor with politicians. Fred Wertheimer, the founder and president of Democracy 21, for one, has said that "history makes clear that unlimited contributions and secret money are a formula for corruption." Likewise, the Campaign Legal Center has called the emergence of dark money a "serious threat to our democracy." In a portion of the controversial *Citizens United* decision, eight of the nine Supreme Court justices agreed that disclosure of money in politics was important because "transparency enables the electorate to make informed decisions and give proper weight to different speakers and messages."

Who Thinks Dark Money in Politics is Good?

Supporters of anonymity in politics frequently note that *The Federalist Papers* and Thomas Paine's *Common Sense* were published anonymously during the country's founding. Lawyers at the Wyoming Liberty Group, for instance, have argued that throughout American history, "anonymous political speech has been the scorn of entrenched powers and the saving balm of emerging voices." Meanwhile, officials at the Center for Competitive Politics have argued that dark money is a "pejorative term" and that its threat is "overblown." The Center for Competitive Politics has further argued that "disclosure comes with a cost," including the potential to chill speech and for donors to be harassed.

> Campaign finance reform activists argue that voters should know who is funding political advertisements. Such information, they assert, is essential to voters' ability to evaluate the merits of political messages— and to know if certain special interests may be trying to curry favor with politicians.

Who Regulates Political Dark Money?

The nation's primary regulator of money in politics is the six-member FEC. However, the FEC's three Republican commissioners and three Democratic ones have significant ideological disagreements about the degree to which dark money is a problem. Meanwhile, the Internal Revenue Service regulates nonprofit organizations and can revoke a nonprofit's tax-exempt status if a group is deemed to not deserve it. But in recent years, only a handful of 501(c)(4) nonprofits— which have the primary purpose of promoting "social welfare"— have had their tax-exempt status revoked because the Internal Revenue Service deemed them to be too political. The Department of Justice can also criminally prosecute "knowing and willful" violations of campaign finance law, although this, too, is rare.

So, Is There Really No Way to Know Who's Behind Political Dark Money?

Over the years, journalists have developed a number of backdoor approaches to follow the money flowing to dark money organizations. But oftentimes, these approaches only yield results long after a dark money spending spree is over.

What Are These Backdoors?

Sometimes dark money groups receive money from other political groups that must disclose their expenditures to either state or federal campaign finance regulators.

Other times, dark money groups receive substantial amounts of money from other nonprofits that must report doling out these grants on their own annual tax filings with the IRS. Similarly, some dark money groups receive money from labor unions, which must report those expenditures on annual reports filed with the Department of Labor. And on rare occasions, corporations voluntarily disclose their contributions to politically active nonprofits. If an individual donates to a dark money group, there is essentially no public paper trail to follow.

Print Citations

CMS: Beckel, Michael. "What Is Political 'Dark Money'—and Is It Bad? Secret Cash Is Influencing Elections: Here's How." In *The Reference Shelf: Campaign Trends and Election Law*, edited by Betsy Maury, 15-18. Ipswitch, MA: Salem Press, 2016.

MLA: Beckel, Michael. "What Is Political 'Dark Money'—and Is It Bad? Secret Cash Is Influencing Elections: Here's How." *The Reference Shelf: Campaign Trends and Election Law*. Ed. Betsy Maury. Ipswitch: Salem Press, 2016. 15-18. Print.

APA: Beckel, M. (2016). What is political "dark money"—and is it bad? Secret cash is influencing elections: Here's how. In Betsy Maury (Ed.), *The reference shelf: Campaign trends and election law* (pp. 15-18). Ipswitch, MA: Salem. (Original work published 2016)

How "Ghost Corporations" Are Funding the 2016 Election

By Matea Gold and Anu Narayanswamy
The Washington Post, March 18, 2016

Two days before Christmas, a trust called DE First Holdings was quietly formed in Delaware, where corporations are required to reveal little about their workings. A day later, the entity dropped $1 million into a super PAC with ties to Jersey City, N.J., Mayor Steven Fulop, a Democrat considering a gubernatorial bid.

The trust, whose owner remains unknown, is part of a growing cadre of mystery outfits financing big-money super PACs. Many were formed just days or weeks before making six-or-seven-figure contributions— an arrangement that election law experts say violates a long-standing federal ban on straw donors.

But the individuals behind the "ghost corporations" appear to face little risk of reprisal from a deeply polarized Federal Election Commission, which recently deadlocked on whether to even investigate such cases.

Advocates for stronger campaign-finance enforcement fear there will be even more pop-up limited liability corporations (LLCs) funneling money into independent groups, making it difficult to discern the identities of wealthy players seeking to influence this year's presidential and congressional contests.

The 2016 campaign has already seen the highest rate of corporate donations since the Supreme Court unleashed such spending with its 2010 *Citizens United v. FEC* decision.

One out of every eight dollars collected by super PACs this election cycle have come from corporate coffers, including millions flowing from opaque and hard-to-trace entities, according to a *Washington Post* analysis of federal campaign finance filings.

So far, 680 companies have given at least $10,000 to a super PAC this cycle, together contributing nearly $68 million through Jan. 31, The *Post* found. Their donations made up 12 percent of the $549 million raised by such groups, which can accept unlimited donations.

That means corporations are on track to far exceed the $86 million they gave to super PACs in the entire 2012 presidential cycle, when such donations totaled 10 percent of the money raised by such groups, according to data from the nonpartisan Center for Responsive Politics.

The FEC just made it easier for super PAC donors to hide their identities

Many corporate givers this cycle are well-established hedge funds, energy companies and real estate firms. But a significant share of the money is coming from newly formed LLCs with cryptic names that offer few clues about their backers.

Among the new players is Children of Israel LLC, a company formed in California last June by Shaofen "Lisa" Gao, a real estate agent in Cupertino, California, whose Happy Realty firm helps Chinese buyers find homes in Silicon Valley.

On a form filed with the secretary of state's office in September, Gao listed Children of Israel's type of business as "Donations," according to a document found by a researcher for End Citizens United, a Democratic PAC that supports candidates in favor of stricter campaign-finance rules.

Weeks after being formed, Children of Israel gave $50,000 to Pursuing America's Greatness, a super PAC supporting the presidential bid of former Arkansas governor Mike Huckabee, FEC records show. In November, the LLC gave the pro-Huckabee group $100,000. And this January, it donated $250,000 to Stand for Truth, a super PAC backing Sen. Ted Cruz of Texas.

> **Several campaign finance watchdog groups have filed complaints with the FEC against the recent pop-up LLCs, but the chances of the agency's looking into the cases appear slim.**

Gao— who has no history of making political contributions in California or at the federal level— did not respond to repeated calls and emails seeking comment.

Valerie Martin, a senior adviser to End Citizens United, said the blatant admission by the company that its purpose is to make contributions underscores the degree to which donors feel emboldened to hide behind such entities.

"This goes to the heart of what's really wrong with the system and how it's broken," she said. "I think it really bothers Americans that people want to influence elections without fingerprints."

Federal law requires political committees to confirm that a donation is legal before accepting it.

Eric Lycan, the attorney for the pro-Cruz Stand For Truth, declined to address specific donations but said in a statement that the super PAC "at all times complied with the law" and investigated any potentially illegal contributions.

"Contributions from an LLC to a super PAC are legal and permissible, and the fact standing alone that a contribution came from an LLC would not be reason to return the contribution," he added.

The Little Rock-based treasurer for the pro-Huckabee super PAC did not respond to a request for comment about whether the group vetted Children of Israel.

Ted Cruz is running a well-organized campaign. His super PACs— not so much.

Some donors who have given through LLCs this year said they did so out of convenience rather than any effort to mask their identities.

Frank VanderSloot, the chief executive of an Idaho nutritional-supplement company, said he used two corporations he owns to give $175,000 to a super PAC supporting Sen. Marco Rubio of Florida in December because the group needed immediate donations to make its year-end deadline.

"It's where I had the cash," said VanderSloot, who also gave the super PAC $150,000 in his own name. "These LLCs have been around forever— they are working operations. It takes 12 seconds to see my name. It doesn't take any great sleuthing."

In other cases, it is much harder to pin down who is behind entities contributing large sums to super PACs.

Little is known about Tread Standard LLC, which gave $150,000 to a super PAC supporting former Florida governor Jeb Bush last June, weeks after an incorporation service set the company up in Delaware.

Equally elusive is Decor Services LLC, which was incorporated in Delaware by a paralegal in a Milwaukee law firm in January— two weeks before donating $250,000 to a super PAC backing New Jersey Gov. Chris Christie.

One of the largest mystery donations this cycle came from DE First Holdings, the trust that gave $1 million to Coalition for Progress, the super PAC allied with Fulop. Neither a spokeswoman for Fulop nor Bari Mattes, the Democratic fundraiser who runs the group, responded to requests for comment.

Several campaign finance watchdog groups have filed complaints with the FEC against the recent pop-up LLCs, but the chances of the agency's looking into the cases appear slim.

Last month, the agency closed a nearly five-year-old complaint about a limited liability company allegedly used to mask a donor's identity— unable to even agree whether it merited investigation. The LLC had been set up in Delaware shortly before making a $1 million donation to a super PAC supporting then-Republican presidential candidate Mitt Romney. A Romney associate later came forward to acknowledge he was the source of the donation.

The FEC's inability to come to a decision "creates incentives for people to take some risks, on the theory that even if some liability materializes, it may not be that serious," said Bob Bauer, a veteran Democratic campaign-finance lawyer.

"It is inconceivable to me that they wouldn't have taken the opportunity to clarify that at a very basic level, a donor cannot set up a LLC for the purpose of making contributions through the LLC and defeating the disclosure requirements," he added.

How much money is behind each campaign?

Jan Baran, a longtime Republican election-law attorney, agreed that there is a need for the commission to weigh in, noting that the FEC has not issued any new rules regarding corporate donations since the *Citizens United* ruling made such spending permissible.

"The agency is just not providing any legal guidance on what the rules are in the aftermath of all these momentous court decisions," he said. "That's the job of the FEC, and it hasn't done its job."

FEC Chairman Matthew Petersen, a Republican appointee to the panel, did not respond to a request for comment.

Ellen Weintraub, one of two Democrats on the FEC's six-member panel, warned that donors who try to hide behind shell corporations should not assume there will be no repercussions.

"The regulation is pretty darn clear, and I think there is potential criminal liability for people who are just flouting a plain-English restriction," she said. "I don't think people ought to take as much comfort as they seem to from the FEC's apparent inability to muster four votes to enforce the law."

Alice Crites contributed to this report.

Print Citations

CMS: Gold, Matea, and Anu Narayanswamy. "How 'Ghost Corporations' Are Funding the 2016 Election." In *The Reference Shelf: Campaign Trends and Election Law*, edited by Betsy Maury, 19-22. Ipswitch, MA: Salem Press, 2016.

MLA: Gold, Matea, and Anu Narayanswamy. "How 'Ghost Corporations' Are Funding the 2016 Election." *The Reference Shelf: Campaign Trends and Election Law*. Ed. Betsy Maury. Ipswitch: Salem Press, 2016. 19-22. Print.

APA: Gold, M., & A. Narayanswamy. (2016). How "ghost corporations" are funding the 2016 election. In Betsy Maury (Ed.), *The reference shelf: Campaign trends and election law* (pp. 19-22). Ipswitch, MA: Salem. (Original work published 2016)

Why Redistricting Threatens Democracy

By John Nichols
The Nation, **February 20, 2012**

Redistricting is fate. It defines the destiny of candidates for Congress, state legislatures and local posts more than campaign finances, Super PACs, political trends or issues. It explains why the vast majority of races are not competitive. Though campaign strategies invariably garner more media attention, they are mere manipulations of the electoral process. Defining that process comes at the start, and it's often made by politicians already in power. "Voters are supposed to choose their political leaders," says Fred Kessler, a former jurist and current Wisconsin state legislator who consults on redistricting. "But in most states the politicians choose their voters." This year national and state parties are pouring tens of millions of dollars into computerized systems and legal teams to redraw the maps in ways that remove even the slightest risk from elections. This, says the Brennan Center for Justice, has created an "epidemic of gerrymandering [that] poses a growing threat to our democracy."

For most politicians, the goal of redistricting is to eliminate competition by pooling voters inclined to back them inside their district lines while isolating voters who might oppose them in electoral wastelands. A decade after census figures are used to draw maps, the partisan lines shape election results; thus, even in "wave" years, when "change" is the watchword, most incumbents retain their seats and most open seats are held by the party of retiring incumbents. In 2010 84 percent of House seats remained in the hands of the party that held them before election day. In many big states, district lines proved to be even more fixed; California Democrats went into the 2010 election with twenty-five State Senate seats and came out with twenty-five; Ohio Republicans started with twenty-one and finished with twenty-three. And that was in a volatile election year defined by economic uncertainty, Tea Party activism and record campaign spending.

"The lack of competition in legislative elections is nauseating," declare election reformers Rob Richie and Steven Hill of FairVote. "Most Americans, most of the time, experience 'no choice' elections for their city council, their state legislature and the US House of Representatives. They live in political monopolies where there is no two-party system, let alone one with viable third parties."

There is a growing movement to address Big Money's manipulation of politics since the Supreme Court's *Citizens United* ruling, and civil rights groups are challenging voter suppression. Meanwhile, redistricting abuse ranks low on the list of democratic concerns. That's a bad oversight, as it is the decennial apportionment process that disenfranchises the most Americans

John Stuart Mill was right when he wrote, "It is an essential part of democracy that minorities should be adequately represented. No real democracy, nothing but a false show of democracy, is possible without it." Consider this: since 1996 Democrats have won every US House race in Massachusetts, despite Republicans' having consistently won more than 35 percent of the vote for most of those seats. In Nebraska, Republicans have not lost a House seat since Ronald Reagan was president, even though over the same period Democrats won a third of the vote and sometimes as much as 40 percent. Fair maps and voting systems would elect Republicans in Massachusetts and Democrats in Nebraska. But that doesn't happen under the current arrangement.

Because redistricting is invariably controlled by party insiders who are close to campaign donors, it tends to punish mavericks and narrow the debate. In Ohio, Republicans barely won 2010 elections for governor and attorney general, thus gaining control of redistricting. Prodded by House Speaker John Boehner, they gerrymandered the maps to lock in GOP gains. Representatives Dennis Kucinich and Marcy Kaptur, stalwart members of the Congressional Progressive Caucus, were thrown into the same district, where they will face each other in a Democratic primary that will eliminate one of the House's two most consistent economic populists. The Ohio map would have been even worse if reformers and labor activists had not threatened to force a "people's veto" referendum on the GOP plan.

The Ohio referendum threat was one of several progressive efforts to challenge GOP abuses. In Texas, where growth in the Hispanic population was largely responsible for the state's gaining four Congressional seats, Governor Rick Perry approved maps that created more districts for white conservatives while limiting prospects for Hispanics. Legal challenges by the League of United Latin American Citizens and the Mexican American Legislative Caucus appear likely to force a less egregious compromise. But for every success in tempering discriminatory plans, there has been a defeat elsewhere.

Groups like Common Cause are right to argue that redistricting decisions should be made by nonpartisan independent commissions. This model has worked reasonably well in Iowa, where it has created more competitive districts. But that's hardly sufficient. Similarly, federal proposals to set some universal standards, such as the Redistricting Transparency Act of 2011, are worthy, but small-d democrats should think bigger. Maryland state senator and constitutional law professor Jamie Raskin, for instance, argues that the best way to end redistricting abuse is to eliminate single-member districts. Raskin proposes that US House members and state legislators be elected from multiple-member "super districts," where proportional representation or ranked-choice voting could give voters more freedom to choose and to have choices matter. This is not a new idea: from 1870 to 1980 Illinois legislators were elected from multimember districts. As Raskin notes, "Nearly every district elected both Democrats and Republicans." In the 1930s and '40s, proportional representation allowed New York City voters to elect Democrats, Republicans, Socialists and Communists to the city council.

Opening up the process will require changing laws and ways of thinking. And it's time. As reformers press for a constitutional amendment to overturn *Citizens United*, they should also seek to end redistricting as we know it.

Print Citations

CMS: Nichols, John. "Why Redistricting Threatens Democracy." In *The Reference Shelf: Campaign Trends and Election Law*, edited by Betsy Maury, 23-25. Ipswitch, MA: Salem Press, 2016.

MLA: Nichols, John. "Why Redistricting Threatens Democracy." *The Reference Shelf: Campaign Trends and Election Law*. Ed. Betsy Maury. Ipswitch: Salem Press, 2016. 23-25. Print.

APA: Nichols, J. (2016). Why redistricting threatens democracy. In Betsy Maury (Ed.), *The reference shelf: Campaign trends and election law* (pp. 23-25). Ipswitch, MA: Salem. (Original work published 2012)

Voting Rights Become a Proxy War in the 2016 Presidential Election

By Frank Askin

The Conversation, July 8, 2015

Republicans – with a helping nudge from the United States Supreme Court's conservative majority (of which more below) – are passing restrictive voting laws in states where they control both branches of government.

Meanwhile, Democrats are expanding voting rights in states where they dominate the governing process. Democrats Senator Patrick Leahy of Vermont and Representative John Lewis of Georgia also introduced a bill in Congress at the end of June that would require states (mostly in the South) to get federal approval for any changes in any statewide voting laws or procedures.

This battle is especially important for a presidential election year, when voter turnout is significantly higher than in midterm elections.

Much of the difference in the turnout is made up of prime Democratic constituencies – the young and minorities – which explains why Democrats are so set on increasing turnout and Republicans would prefer to restrict it.

Under the banner of preventing "voter fraud," GOP lawmakers are making it harder for people to register to vote by requiring photo-ID documents and by limiting early and weekend voting, which is more frequently used by those who find it hard to get to the polls on a Tuesday.

In many inner cities, for example, black churches have run "souls to the polls" caravans on the Sunday before election day.

Republicans in Maine went so far as to repeal their long-standing Election Day Registration law (EDR); however voters reinstated it in 2011 when Democrats managed to place the issue on a referendum ballot.

On the other side of the aisle, Democrats have successfully extended Election Day registration in the blue states of Colorado, Connecticut, Illinois, California and Rhode Island, bringing the number of EDR states to 13 plus the District of Columbia.

GOP Cites 'Rampant Voter Fraud'

Republicans cite rampant voter fraud as the basis for more restrictive voting laws. However, there is scant empirical evidence for such claims.

The risk of prosecution for perjury is a strong disincentive for an ineligible voter to impersonate someone else in order to cast a single ballot. While voter fraud does exist, it is usually committed by election officials who would be unaffected by photo ID laws.

Despite this, Republican lawmakers keep pushing such regulations, which Democrats contend have the greatest impact on segments of the population—racial minorities and young people—who tend to vote Democratic and are less likely to have driver licenses or other acceptable forms of ID.

Tightening Laws in the Red States

Since the 2010 election, 21 Republican-controlled states have enacted laws making it more difficult to register or vote. Among the most draconian of these laws are:

North Carolina: The Voter Information and Verification Act mandates strict identification to cast a vote, and disallows the use of student or public employee IDs. It also cut back early voting days by a week. One study found that 55% of North Carolina Democrats lacked an appropriate state-issued ID.

Ohio: The legislature sharply curtailed early voting, including voting on the Sunday before an election, when historically African-American churches rallied their congregants to go to the polls. It also eliminated Golden Week when citizens could both register and vote on the same day.

Florida: The state is arguably the leader in implementing voting restrictions. It was one of the first states to cut back on early voting, suppress voter registration drives and cut off voting rights for those with former criminal convictions. Some 1.5 million Floridians with criminal convictions are essentially permanently disenfranchised.

> **This battle is especially important for a presidential election year, when voter turnout is significantly higher than in midterm elections.**

Texas: The state's voter ID law is probably the strictest in the country. It allows only a few forms of photo identification, and does not allow student IDs or tribal IDs, although gun permits are acceptable. The law was initially struck down by a federal court, but the US Supreme Court allowed it to go into effect for the 2014 election.

Georgia: The Peach State has one of the most restricting photo ID laws. It does not recognize student ID cards from private colleges or government benefit cards.

Kansas: The Secure and Fair Elections Act of 2011 requires the following in order to vote: (1) show a photo ID at the polling place; (2) voters requesting a mail-in ballot must submit their driver's license number or a copy of a photo ID; and (3) provide proof of US citizenship.

Pennsylvania: In 2012, the legislature passed a law requiring voters to bring a photo ID to the polls. But in 2014, the Commonwealth Court struck down the law, finding it in violation of the State Constitution. The court found that "hundreds of thousands of registered voters lacked the restrictive forms of ID required." And the state had not made it easy to get an ID. The court also found there was no evidence of in-person voter fraud. The state declined to appeal.

More restrictive voting laws were also adopted in the following states: Arkansas (photo ID required to vote—Legislature overrode gubernatorial veto; Indiana (authorized challengers can demand proof of identification); Nebraska (reduced early voting period); North Dakota (required photo ID to vote); Tennessee (more restrictive photo ID requirement); Virginia (required photo ID and restricted third-party voter registration).

Legislative battles continue to rage in many other states over Republican-backed voting restrictions, and court fights continue over many of those already in place.

However, the conservative Supreme Court majority has provided support for many of these laws, first by upholding the Indiana photo ID law a decade ago and then by striking down Section 5 of the Federal Voting Rights Act, which required states with a history of racial discrimination in voting to get pre-clearance for new restrictive voting laws from either a federal court or the US Department of Justice.

Blue States Expand Voting Rights

Meanwhile, blue states have been moving sharply in an opposite direction to expand the right to vote. At the same time, Democrats are challenging voter rights restrictions imposed by Republicans.

A number of states have adopted online voting registration, making it easier for eligible voters to get on the rolls in states like Illinois, Virginia and West Virginia. And Maryland expanded early voting and allowed same-day registration during early voting.

But most significantly, Oregon adopted universal registration of anyone over 18 who does not opt out. This position now seems to be supported by Hillary Rodham Clinton, the Democrats' likely presidential candidate, and will no doubt be endorsed by other Democratic politicians.

The general counsel for Clinton's presidential campaign, Marc Elias, has been leading the charge in filing challenges to voting rules in the key battleground states of Virginia, Ohio and Wisconsin.

The success of those challenges – or the continued ability of Republican legislators to impose voting restrictions – would markedly change the US electorate in the decades to come.

Print Citations

CMS: Askin, Frank. "Voting Rights Become a Proxy War in the 2016 Presidential Election." In *The Reference Shelf: Campaign Trends and Election Law,* edited by Betsy Maury, 26-28. Ipswitch, MA: Salem Press, 2016.

MLA: Askin, Frank. "Voting Rights Become a Proxy War in the 2016 Presidential Election." *The Reference Shelf: Campaign Trends and Election Law.* Ed. Betsy Maury. Ipswitch: Salem Press, 2016. 26-28. Print.

APA: Askin, F. (2016). Voting rights become a proxy war in the 2016 presidential election. In Betsy Maury (Ed.), *The reference shelf: Campaign trends and election law* (pp. 26-28). Ipswitch, MA: Salem. (Original work published 2015)

How Citizens United Has Changed Politics in 5 Years

By Gabrielle Levy

U.S. News and World Report, January 21, 2015

Five years ago Wednesday, the Supreme Court handed down a decision that dramatically reshaped the business of politics in the U.S.

In its *Citizens United v. Federal Election Commission* decision, the court opened the campaign spending floodgates. The justices' ruling said political spending is protected under the First Amendment, meaning corporations and unions could spend unlimited amounts of money on political activities, as long as it was done independently of a party or candidate.

The result has been a deluge of cash poured into so-called super PACs – particularly single-candidate PACs, or political action committees – which are only nominally independent from the candidates they support. What's more, the legal protections for corporations mean much of this spending, known as "dark money," never has to be publicly disclosed.

A recent analysis of the 2014 Senate races by the Brennan Center for Justice found outside spending more than doubled since 2010, to $486 million. Outside groups provided 47 percent of total spending – more than the candidates' 41 percent – in 10 competitive races in last year's midterms.

"The premise that the Supreme Court was relying on, that these groups would be truly independent of the candidates themselves, is very questionable," says Commissioner Ellen Weintraub, one of three Democrats on the six-member Federal Election Commission.

Weintraub, who was appointed by President George W. Bush in 2003, has been a vocal advocate for establishing stronger disclosure rules to straighten out what she says is a contradiction in the court's ruling.

The court effectively has said a donation of $1,000 does not, legally speaking, indicate a stronger association with a candidate than a donation of $10. So even when a candidate is aware of a huge donation to his or her single-candidate PAC, it's not considered a problem.

"Plainly, if you worry about the corrupting influence of somebody making a million-dollar contribution directly to the candidate, the notion that the candidate can't be corrupted by a million-dollar contribution that they know about to a super PAC that's advocating solely on their behalf – it just doesn't make sense to a lot of people," she says.

As the rules are currently written, these PACs are able to circumvent restrictions preventing them from directly coordinating with campaigns, even though they're often run by members of candidates' inner circles. Sometimes those efforts are literally laughable (remember #McConnelling?) as campaigns and PACs hide their unofficial coordination in plain sight, such as through public announcements of their plans for television ad buys or through out-of-the-way Twitter accounts.

Most advocates say the Supreme Court made a good-faith effort to promote transparency and prevent coordination in its Citizens United ruling.

But the contradiction between the court's stated desire for transparency – eight justices joined the portion of Citizens United that upheld federal disclosure requirements – and its definition of corporations as people protected by the First Amendment created a loophole that campaigns and PACs are all too happy to use to their advantage.

As a result, a small group of wealthy donors has gained even more influence on elections, and are able to maintain that influence once candidates take office.

> **A recent analysis of the 2014 Senate races by the Brennan Center for Justice found outside spending more than doubled since 2010, to $486 million. Outside groups provided 47 percent of total spending – more than the candidates' 41 percent – in 10 competitive races in last year's midterms.**

Of the $1 billion spent in federal elections by super PACs since 2010, nearly 60 percent of the money came from just 195 individuals and their spouses, according to the Brennan Center report. Thanks to Citizens United, supporters can make the maximum $5,200 donation directly to a candidate, then make unlimited contributions to single-candidate super PACs.

Campaign reform advocates say the amount of money spent is not inherently a problem; rather, it's the fact that a tiny number of extraordinarily wealthy individuals are bankrolling the majority of that spending.

"We have folks that are essentially using million-dollar megaphones to drown out the voices of ordinary citizens," says Adam Lioz, a senior adviser at the liberal policy group Demos. "These millionaires are kingmakers in our democracy."

A Demos report released last week found winning Senate candidates in the 2014 races had to raise an average of $3,300 per day, every day, for six years (House candidates needed to raise $1,800 a day in their two-year cycle). The pressure to fundraise means candidates focus on those donors who can provide large donations, to the detriment of their less wealthy constituents.

"When you're talking to the same kinds of people for six to eight hours a day, when you do call time and dial for dollars, you begin to believe that their problems are the country's problems," Lioz says. "You get a skewed and warped view of the way the world works, and it's not because you're a bad person or you're corrupt, it's because you've been placed in a very narrow and very wealthy world."

While this is not a phenomenon solely of Citizens United's making, it has become a much more urgent issue in the past five years as people feel their voices – and their votes – are being drowned out.

At a Senate hearing last year, supporters delivered petitions with 3 million signatures calling for a constitutional amendment to undo the effects of the ruling, and 16 states have passed resolutions demonstrating the ability to ratify such an amendment.

The groundswell of support has spread beyond conventional clean governance groups to labor, environmental and other advocacy groups – an effect Rep. John Sarbanes, D-Md., calls the "soundcheck on the microphone."

"If you're standing in front of many audiences these days, if you don't start by saying, '… I know you feel locked out,' most of the rest of what you want to say to people they're not going to hear," he says.

Sarbanes is the lead sponsor of the House's Government By the People Act, which would put a small-donor matching program in place for federal elections. Candidates would pledge to take no donations over $1,000 and give up traditional PAC money, and in exchange receive matching funds for donations under $200, provided at least in part by voluntary contributions from taxpayers.

He says conservative estimates found about 80 percent of successful 2014 candidates would have raised more money though small-donor matching, if the program had been in place.

"I could say to [my constituents] and mean it, 'If you donate $25 to my campaign, you're actually going to have an impact,'" Sarbanes says. "And if you get 15 or 20 or 30 of your friends to come do the same thing, I have incentive now to spend some time with you, instead of calling some high donor on the phone or going to some K Street fundraiser, so that's real power."

Sarbanes will reintroduce his measure Wednesday afternoon in the House, where it already has 138 co-sponsors. A similar bill, the Fair Elections Now Act from Sen. Dick Durbin, D-Ill., also will be reintroduced in the Senate and has 19 co-sponsors.

As with any current legislation, the sponsors recognize the uphill battle in a Republican-controlled Congress. So far, all but one of the bills' co-sponsors are Democrats (along with left-leaning Sen. Bernie Sanders, I-Vt.). Funding a donation-matching program also poses another obstacle toward passage, as proponents have suggested closing the same tax loopholes that Democrats have targeted for years.

But Sarbanes says he's hopeful he'll be able to convince Republicans whose constituents support campaign finance reform, especially those like Rep. Dave Brat – a Virginia freshman who defeated Eric Cantor on a message that the former majority leader was too beholden to his Washington inner circle – or Sen. Ted Cruz, R-Texas, who emphasized that "D.C. isn't listening" in his 2013 filibuster.

"It may take a while for Republicans here to catch up in terms of getting behind specific reforms that will address this sentiment, but I think increasingly they're going to be feeling the heat from their own constituents," Sarbanes says. "If they know what's good for them politically, they're going to start adopting a lot of these narratives."

Print Citations

CMS: Levy, Gabrielle. "How Citizens United Has Changed Politics in 5 Years." In *The Reference Shelf: Campaign Trends and Election Law*, edited by Betsy Maury, 29-32. Ipswitch, MA: Salem Press, 2016.

MLA: Levy, Gabrielle. "How Citizens United Has Changed Politics in 5 Years." *The Reference Shelf: Campaign Trends and Election Law*. Ed. Betsy Maury. Ipswitch: Salem Press, 2016. 29-32. Print.

APA: Levy, G. (2016). How Citizens United has changed politics in 5 years. In Betsy Maury (Ed.), *The reference shelf: Campaign trends and election law* (pp. 29-32). Ipswitch, MA: Salem. (Original work published 2015)

The Many Sins of "Citizens United"

By Senator Sheldon Whitehouse
The Nation, September 24, 2015

Our politics is awash in cash. Super PACs supporting presidential candidates have banked more than $250 million through June 30—nearly 10 times more than at this point in the 2012 cycle. "Dark money" from anonymous donors is also surging (dark to us, of course; you can bet the candidates know). The political network of Charles and David Koch has said that it plans to spend as much as $900 million in the 2016 election cycle, raised mostly from undisclosed donors.

"For that kind of money, you could buy yourself a president," said Republican strategist Mark McKinnon. "Oh, right," he added. "That's the point."

This pollution of our democracy is the product of the Supreme Court's appalling 2010 decision in *Citizens United v. Federal Election Commission*. Despite decades of warnings by the elected branches of government about the dangers of corporate political corruption, and despite more than 100 years of settled law, the conservative majority made the fateful finding that "independent expenditures, including those made by corporations, do not give rise to corruption or the appearance of corruption." Not stopping there, the justices went on to find that "the appearance of influence or access, furthermore, will not cause the electorate to lose faith in our democracy."

The sins of *Citizens United* are many, but the first is that these "facts" are bonkers. Before looking at their merits, though, remember the well-established principle that the Supreme Court is constrained by the factual record presented to it and must interpret the law based on that record. Here, the case had no record on the fundamental question of corporate political corruption. That's sin two.

Sin three is that the absence of a record was no accident. *Citizens United* was initially a narrow case challenging whether the McCain-Feingold campaign-finance law prohibited the airing of an on-demand cable video critical of a candidate in the 30 days before the primary election. After the briefing and oral arguments were done, the Court issued new "questions presented," reframing the case as a broad challenge of the government's power to regulate corporate spending on elections. As Justice John Paul Stevens aptly explained in his dissent, "Five Justices were unhappy with the limited nature of the case before us, so they changed the case to give themselves an opportunity to change the law."

Sin four is that we know what an extensive legislative or trial-court record concerning corruption would have revealed: Political corruption by corporate interests is a very real threat. Only in the absence of such a record was it possible to make those bogus "findings of fact." And once they were established, the conservatives were able to get the ruling they wanted. To open the floodgates, the Court had to find that "independent expenditures, including those made by corporations, do not give rise to corruption or the appearance of corruption." Otherwise, the First Amendment premise for unlimited corporate political spending would fail. This all smells very rankly of "strategy." And that is the big sin, the one that unites them all: The majority's ruling on *Citizens United* revealed a deliberate strategy to change the law in favor of powerful corporate interests.

Now let's return to the assertion that "the appearance of influence or access, furthermore, will not cause the electorate to lose faith in our democracy." A 2012 poll found that approximately 70 percent of Americans believe Super-PAC spending will lead to corruption. According to the same survey, 75 percent of Republicans and 78 percent of Democrats agreed that there would be less corruption if there

> **The majority's ruling on 'Citizens United' revealed a deliberate strategy to change the law in favor of corporate interests.**

were limits on how much could be given to Super PACs. A June 2015 *New York Times/ CBS News* poll found that more than 80 percent of Americans believe money plays too great a role in campaigns, while two-thirds say that the wealthy have a greater chance of influencing the electoral process than other Americans. As Justice Stevens warned in his dissent, "A democracy cannot function effectively when its constituent members believe laws are being bought and sold."

With *Citizens United*, the Supreme Court didn't simply confirm its well-documented preference for ruling in favor of corporate interests. The case also fits a pattern of support by conservative justices for Republican interests in election cases, whether it's the Rehnquist Court's *Vieth v. Jubelirer* decision, which declared a field day for gerrymandering, or the Roberts Court's *Shelby County v. Holder*, which gutted key voter protections and enabled conservative state legislatures to enact new barriers to minority voting.

So, too, did the Republican Party unduly benefit from *Citizens United*. Super PACs and other nonprofit organizations spent upward of $390 million in the 2012 presidential election supporting Republicans or attacking President Obama, compared with $164 million in spending by groups supporting Democrats. And so far in this election cycle, PACs and Super PACs supporting Republicans have raised 93 percent of all outside donations.

Not to worry, the *Citizens United* majority assured us, since a regime of prompt and effective disclosure would "provide shareholders and citizens with the information needed to hold corporations and elected officials accountable for their positions and supporters." In reality, of course, disclosure has completely broken down in the wake of the ruling. In the 2014 elections, the most expensive midterms in US history, the *Washington Post* reported that dark money made up at least 31 percent of all independent spending. And that doesn't count spending on so-called issue ads, which is also not reported.

The Supreme Court may someday grow sufficiently sickened by the "tsunami of slime" it has unleashed and correct itself. Until then, it will fall to Congress to restore a measure of integrity to our campaign-finance system.

The DISCLOSE Act, which I have introduced in each Congress since 2012, would require organizations spending money in elections—including tax-exempt 501(c)(4) groups—to promptly disclose donors who have given $10,000 or more during an election cycle. This is not a new idea. Many Republicans, including several in the Senate, used to support disclosure—until *Citizens United*. Suddenly, Republicans are fighting to keep voters in the dark and have repeatedly blocked passage of the bill.

Americans of all political stripes are disgusted by the influence of unlimited secret cash in our elections. With so many candidates vying for the support of powerful interests, the stage is set for a 2016 campaign that caters to the needs of a wealthy few. It's time for the rest of us to make our voices heard and demand a change.

Print Citations

CMS: Whitehouse, Sheldon. "The Many Sins of 'Citizens United'." In *The Reference Shelf: Campaign Trends and Election Law*, edited by Betsy Maury, 33-35. Ipswitch, MA: Salem Press, 2016.

MLA: Whitehouse, Sheldon. "The Many Sins of 'Citizens United'." *The Reference Shelf: Campaign Trends and Election Law*. Ed. Betsy Maury. Ipswitch: Salem Press, 2016. 33-35. Print.

APA: Whitehouse, S. (2016). The many sins of "Citizens United." In Betsy Maury (Ed.), *The reference shelf: Campaign trends and election law* (pp. 33-35). Ipswitch, MA: Salem. (Original work published 2015)

The First Postmodern Political Machine

By Walter Russell Mead
The American Interest, **August 21, 2015**

How do the Clintons, dogged by scandal and suspicion at every turn, not just stay afloat in American political life, but thrive?

The contrast between the apparent inevitability that surrounded Hillary Clinton's procession toward the Democratic presidential nomination for so long and the air of scandal and suspicion that seems to trail behind her wherever she goes is striking. And it points to something important: Hillary Clinton isn't a candidate borne aloft on a wave of popular enthusiasm. She is no JFK, no Ronald Reagan. She is no George Wallace or William Jennings Bryan. The marching bands processing before her have to be paid; she can't fill vast halls with cheering throngs like Bernie Sanders or, heaven help us, Donald Trump. But she soldiers gamely on, determined to struggle through the exhausting and degrading routine of the eternal campaign.

One has to ask what propels her toward the nomination with such force. Yes, it is partly her inner drive. Love her or loathe her, Hillary Clinton brings a focus to her political and professional engagements that is admirable and pure. If shaking another hand, kissing another baby, chomping down another pork chop at yet another state fair will bring her closer to the nomination, Secretary Clinton will be there, wearing her game face and giving the job all she has. And, to be fair, if it means reading another policy brief, mastering the intricacies of another important budget question, wrapping her head around another complex set of foreign policy problems, she will be there too.

But determination and grit aren't the only forces behind her. To understand the Clinton candidacy and the odd mix of acceptance and resistance it conjures up in the party, one has to understand that she represents something that is at once very old and very new in American politics. She is a machine politician, but the machine behind her is a new kind of American political machine: a postmodern one.

The old kind of political machine, like the one Rahm Emmanuel rides in Chicago, is based on geography and office. Loyalists get contracts, favors and jobs. In return, they give money to the organization and they turn out to vote.

Chicago isn't the last of the old time machines; American cities have been run more or less in this way for 200 years, give or take. Some, like Detroit's dysfunctional kleptocracy, jumped the shark long ago; others, as in Los Angeles, thrive on the energy from new immigrants.

But the Clintons have invented something new. The Clinton Machine doesn't depend on holding local offices or controlling a particular city or state; it floats untethered from geography. Bill Clinton isn't the Mayor of anything, and he's constitutionally ineligible for another term in the White House, but few people in the United States have more influence than he does.

That isn't typical for post-Presidents. Some, notably Jimmy Carter and Herbert Hoover, continue to advocate for the issues and viewpoints they brought to their office. Many, like Gerald Ford, make speeches, play golf, and do charity fundraisers. But not since Theodore Roosevelt, who remained a major political force and was widely believed to have cinched the Republican presidential nomination for 1920 before he died, has an ex-President had the power and visibility Bill Clinton does.

Bill Clinton is charming and smart and most Americans prefer him to his successors, but that's not why he's a force in the land. He's a force in the land because he continues to operate a political machine that underwrites his wife's ambitions and his own continuing power. He is a new kind of ex-President; he and his wife share a new understanding of how power works in a new age.

The Clinton political machine, like all machines, ultimately runs on money. Somebody has to pay the apparatchiks and loyal technicians who keep the wheels turning. In traditional machines, the money came out of the rough and tumble of local politics: You stroke City Hall, and City Hall strokes you. Private contractors who depend on city contracts, public sector unions, law firms, and Wall Street banks who manage city pension funds and peddle the city's bonds: There is an army of special interests whose businesses do well when the Mayor is a friend. But the Clintons don't do it that way anymore; they figured out something better.

The Clintons stand where money, influence, and celebrity form a nexus. When Hillary Clinton was running the State Department and Bill Clinton was shaking down contributors to the Foundation, the donors knew, or thought they knew, what they were getting. Now that Hillary is running for President, the donors have an even better idea of what good things might come to them—or what problems and complications could develop if they cut the Clintons off.

I don't say that the Clintons are breaking the law, at least as far as the basic principles of the machine go. As Tammany Hall's George Washington Plunkett once said, there is such a thing as "honest graft." In the old fashioned political machine, that meant that you only take money from the group you had already decided on legitimate grounds would get the contract. The new machine offers even more opportunities for honest graft than the old kind. The machine gathers the cash that provides perches and incomes to Clinton loyalists; the loyalists keep the publicity machine pumping, keep the networks of contacts and patronage refreshed throughout the vast Clinton network, and staff what amounts to a permanent campaign. This is what party machines used to do: provide incomes for the army of operatives who would jump into action to make sure the machine stayed in office.

But the cash doesn't come from a system of payoffs that go all the way from the cop on the beat up to the Board of Aldermen and the Mayor. The cash comes from donations and speaking fees. When the husband of the Secretary of State or potential next President calls about a special charity project, most people, even if they happen to be CEOs of major companies or senior government officials, take the call. More than that, there will be times when government and corporate officials will reach out and make the call themselves, rather than waiting passively to hear that the Clinton machine has an ask.

The donor proposition is rock solid. Any fashionable cause that can gain applause at Davos and in the world of gentry liberalism here at home (empowering women in development, climate change, entrepreneurship and the poor, disaster relief, medical research, and and so on) gets office space and a PR package at the Foundation. Sometimes some real good gets done, though one doesn't read much about how the Clinton Foundation's rigorous financial controls, inspired programmatic vision, tight management, and relentless concentration on keeping costs low make it one of the leaders in philanthropy for getting the job done cheaply and effectively. What donors buy, or think they are buying, is influence and face time with two of the most powerful people in the world and their political machine; what they get on the side includes good PR, some invites and connections, one's picture with a Clinton or a courageous and charismatic human rights figure from the developing world, and a tax deduction for a charitable contribution. For big donations, you get more; Clintons, if we can believe Donald Trump, will come to your wedding if the invite comes with enough "warmth."

> **Many find something deeply repellent in the ways that the new machine facilitates the integration of global and American politics and lobbying.**

Whether the Clintons understood this from the beginning, or whether they just pursued opportunities without understanding how it would all add up, they've discovered a new way to yoke money and power onto a self-sustaining machine. There seem to be four pillars for this new kind of edifice.

First, there are the unintended consequences of the dysfunctional campaign finance "reforms" over the past thirty years that gutted traditional party organizations while empowering billionaires. Both the Democratic and Republican parties are, institutionally speaking, mere shadows of their former selves. Today, every politician is a freelance operator, accumulating bundlers and backers. Those contacts are power, and power is at least partly heritable. Being part of a political dynasty matters more when parties matter less. Look at Jeb Bush, who, according to the AP, has received about half of his financial backing from people who supported his father and brother.

Expect to see more family firms like the Bushes and the Clintons going into politics. Daddy's rolodex is a useful thing to have.

Second, there is the synergy created by the intersection of the Power Couple and the Twenty-second Amendment, which limited Presidents to two terms. Term-limited Presidents have a hard time convincing donors that further gifts will result in future benefits. This is a problem the Clintons do not have.

Hillary Clinton is the first person who can convince power brokers that she's ready to make the transition from FLOTUS to POTUS. In former times, women were not considered serious political leaders in the United States; some wives followed their husbands into politics, but the husband, unless dead, remained at the head of the firm. Nobody thought that Lurleen Wallace was the most important politician in the Alabama Governor's mansion. But in the 21st century, women can be wives and formidable officeholders as well. Nobody doubts that Hillary will be wearing the pantsuit if the Clintons go back to the White House.

In an age when access to money hinges on celebrity and familiarity, having two star politicians in the same family can make a big difference. The Twenty-second Amendment, adopted after Franklin D. Roosevelt smashed the third term taboo dating back to the time of George Washington, limits Presidents to two terms. But when you have a Power Couple like the Clintons, that gives you four terms in which you can dominate national life. What the Clintons have figured out is that a successful Power Couple can stay at the top of national life for decades—two terms for the first member, an interregnum of unspecified length followed, hopefully, but two terms for the second member, by which time the torch may have passed to a new generation. The Twenty-second Amendment was written to prevent the centralization of political power that would come if a powerful and popular President used his (or her) time in office to use patronage and power to build a machine that would keep the President in office indefinitely. The Clintons have found a workaround, and as a result they have changed the way political power works in the United States.

Third, the Foundation vehicle allows the Clintons to attract enormous sums of money from foreign as well as domestic donors. Unlike ordinary politicians, the Clintons can take money from foreign individuals, states and firms without breaking US laws. They can even sidestep much if not all of the odium that comes from running an American campaign with foreign money. Raising money to fight breast cancer in Botswana is a much more creditable activity than taking political contributions from an African mining company with a dubious reputation. Moreover, one can actually fight breast cancer in Botswana, or at least make moves in that direction, in ways that strengthen the network at home. The network of feminist political activists and operatives includes many people one can credibly hire to administer such a project. This is honest graft at work: one hires someone who is a reasonably qualified administrator for the program, but who is also plugged into the network of activists and operatives needed to keep the permanent campaign up and running. One can also spread the money around: the Clinton Foundation can make grants to other like minded non-profits, providing good jobs to loyal supporters.

Patronage in the service of doing good, that can effectively and legally use foreign donations in ways that build a powerful domestic political force: this might not be up there with the discovery of fire or the wheel as an invention that changes history, but it is not an insignificant contribution to the art of American governance. At a time when globalization and the explosion of non-American wealth has changed the dynamics of wealth and power everywhere, the Clintons have built a machine that facilitates the integration of global power into American politics.

Fourth, the Clintons have captured the power of networks. Like Facebook, the Clinton network is powerful because almost everyone is part of it. Since 1992, when the Clintons stormed out of Arkansas to take the White House, they have been at the center of world power and fame. Everybody who is anybody knows them or knows of them. They can introduce anybody to anybody; they can put together the most star-studded guest list for any purpose. The power of celebrity gives them the ability to publicize and glamorize almost anything; there are powerful reasons to be part of the network that includes virtually everyone in the media, in government, in finance, in business or academia that anyone wants to know or do business with.

Opposition is the price of power, and from the "Bimbo eruptions" through Whitewater on up to Servergate, the Clintons have weathered their share of storms. As public awareness of their new political business model sinks in, expect the criticism to rise. This is partly because there is something genuinely innovative and therefore debatable in the way the Clintons acquire and hold power, and partly because Americans have a long history of disliking the institutions and intermediaries who make our system work. There was nothing the Founding Fathers hated more than political parties, but the kind of republic they wanted to build simply could not function without them. All right thinking Americans united in the 19th century to deplore the malign influence of corrupt big city political machines, but it is hard to think how else the tens of millions of immigrants streaming into those cities from all over the world could have learned to govern themselves and begin the process of integration into American life. Everybody hates lobbies and lobbyists, but it is hard to think of any other system that would allow the worlds of government and business to interact in ways that are in fact necessary for the smooth working of the economy on which all of us depend.

The postmodern political machine that the Clintons have built will stoke outrage for much the same reasons. Many find something deeply repellent in the ways that the new machine facilitates the integration of global and American politics and lobbying. Many will denounce the self-interested mingling of charity and political power-broking; others will gasp at the depth and degree of conflict of interest that a system like this inevitably entails. All these problems are real, and the Clintons, whatever their virtues, have never been at their best when it comes to disentangling the public good and their political interests. But the integrated global economy of the 21st century does need new forms of political organization that were lacking in earlier times. In an era when traditional political party institutions have been so dramatically undermined, the United States still needs organizations who keep its political life on something like an even keel. (The alternative to Clintonian machine politics might just be successive rounds of disorganized Trumpian populism. Would that really be an improvement?)

The most searching questions about the Clinton machine may not have to do with its structure or its propensity for institutionalizing and channeling power, but about the purposes to which all this power is put. In part because of its deep roots in

20th-century liberal Democratic politics, the Clinton machine is deeply entangled with interest groups and lobbies who want to perpetuate blue model governance even as the economic realities that empower the machine are no longer consistent with blue model methods. Bill Clinton's presidency advertised itself as a quest for a new kind of politics ("The era of big government is over"); Secretary Clinton seems more attuned to the ideas that, more than twenty years ago, her husband said it was time to leave behind.

It is much too early to know if Secretary Clinton will get the nomination, much less win the general election. If anything, her position looks weaker today than it did six months ago. Even the power of a great political machine cannot (yet?) deliver electoral victory on a national scale. Barack Obama (who seems increasingly interested in setting up a rival postmodern machine when his own presidency comes to an end) can tell us about that. In the old days, machine politicians had a hard time winning national campaigns; people out in the less corrupted (or, if you prefer, less sophisticated) flyover states aren't always happy about big city politicians with big city connections. The future of the machine is also open to question. If Secretary Clinton fails to win the election and a third try doesn't seem either likely or feasible, the machine loses one of its most valuable assets: the connection to future political power. Will the donations continue to flow in that case, or will the machine gradually lose coherence and strength? Can Chelsea Clinton carry the machine into a new era, and does she want to? Will the partnership, often under stress, between Hillary and Bill be strong enough to fuel the machine if the return to the White House fails to occur?

The Clintons have built something new and important, if not necessarily durable or good. They have changed, at least for a time, the way power works in the United States and even in the world. They have built a new kind of institution for a different time. Politicians and power brokers all over the world are paying attention; expect many more efforts to create postmodern political machines in a time when the key institutions of governance and organization are increasingly out of date and out of tune.

Print Citations

CMS: Mead, Walter Russell. "The First Postmodern Political Machine." In *The Reference Shelf: Campaign Trends and Election Law*, edited by Betsy Maury, 36-41. Ipswitch, MA: Salem Press, 2016.

MLA: Mead, Walter Russell. "The First Postmodern Political Machine." *The Reference Shelf: Campaign Trends and Election Law*. Ed. Betsy Maury. Ipswitch: Salem Press, 2016. 36-41. Print.

APA: Mead, W.R. (2016). The first postmodern political machine. In Betsy Maury (Ed.), *The reference shelf: Campaign trends and election law* (pp. 36-41). Ipswitch, MA: Salem. (Original work published 2015)

2
Campaign Trends: Populism and the Anti-Establishment— Class, Race, and Gender

Thos Robinson / Getty Images for MoveOn.org Political Action

Members of MoveOn.org Political Action stand outside the studios of *Good Morning America* to broadcast messages of love, dignity, and equality in New York City on Wednesday, March 16, 2016.

Political Outsiders: Class, Race, and Gender in the 2016 Election

The state of the union is a matter of perspective. An individual's access to the benefits of US citizenship and the degree to which an individual is personally affected by the nation's social, economic, and cultural challenges depends on a person's position within economic and social hierarchies, and it is because these hierarchies still exist that race, gender, and class are still critical issues. Many Americans, often for deeply divergent reasons, are concerned about the state of America and the nation's future. Many middle-class and working-class white men and women believe that America is a worse place to live now than it was in the past and have rallied behind the idea of returning America to a more ideal past state. For others, including those in groups that have been historically marginalized, the ideal is not to harken back to an earlier time, but to move forward more aggressively towards a more egalitarian future.

Who Is the Real Populist?

Income inequality is not a new issue, but has come to have a renewed significance in the wake of the 2008–09 financial crisis and a subsequent increase in popular awareness about the unequal distribution of wealth. The "99 percent" and "Occupy Wall Street" movements demonstrated the scope of popular concern and helped to fuel what analysts called a resurgence of populism, defined generally as the position that the "regular people," rather than special interests or a social elite, should control the nation. The media and candidates on both sides embraced the idea that Americans are "angrier" with their government than in the past,[1] and that dissatisfaction is the reason behind unexpected levels of support for "outsider" candidates like Donald Trump and Bernie Sanders.

Bernie Sanders proposed some of the most progressive policies in Democratic Party history, thus representing a more uncompromisingly socialist facet of the liberal electorate. Though Hillary Clinton supports many of the same policies as Sanders, such as a federal minimum wage increase, an expansion of free public education, and increased taxes on the wealthy, Clinton's proposals have been more moderate. Clinton is also typically seen as a representative of the political establishment and thus viewed with skepticism by those who feel the government has failed to address the needs of the disenfranchised. In addition, the belief that Clinton tends to "flip-flop" on important issues created the impression, among Sanders' supporters, that Clinton would not be as effective a champion for America's marginalized social classes.

On the other side of the spectrum, Republican candidate Donald Trump capitalized on the needs of middle and working class white Americans who believe that America has been headed in the wrong direction and needs to "return" to an as yet unclear past "greatness."[2] Michael Kazin, author of *The Populist Persuasion*, believes Trump appeals to conservatives who feel *both* frustration with the political establishment *and* are disproportionately (in comparison to the average person) fearful of outside influence, whether in the form of immigrants, terrorism, globalization, or the dilution of American culture by prioritizing minority rights.[3]

Since the beginning of Trump's campaign, politicians and journalists have argued about whether Trump can legitimately be called a "populist." In June, President Obama refuted Trump's populist credentials on the basis that Trump does not demonstrate any concern for the working class. An analysis of Trump's economic proposals, for instance, indicates that his tax proposals will primarily benefit the wealthiest 10 percent of Americans. For instance, Trump's repeated promise to eliminate the "estate tax" will provide no benefit for most Americans as the estate tax is only applicable to individuals with an estate in excess of $5.43 million.[4] Writing in *New York* magazine, journalist Jonathan Chait argued that Trump *is* a populist in that his campaign is based on the idea that existing political powers are either evil or corrupt and that an uprising is needed to return political power to the citizenry.[5]

Race in the 2016 Race

A June Pew Research report indicated that 43 percent of African Americans believe the United States will *never* make the necessary changes to achieve equal rights. In contrast, 38 percent of white Americans believe that the nation has already made the necessary changes to achieve racial equality, while only 8 percent of African Americans agreed. On specific issues, a similar racial divide can be seen. For instance, while 84 percent of African Americans believed that African Americans were treated less fairly by police, only 50 percent of white respondents agreed. In issue after issue, the Pew study demonstrates the ongoing, some say deepening, racial divide in America. This divide has inspired a new civil rights movement, organized in contemporary fashion through social media movements like *#BlackLivesMatter*, and has helped to bring institutional racism among police and in the justice system as a whole to the forefront of the civil rights debate.[6] Across racial lines, 63 percent of voters agree that the treatment of racial and ethnic minorities is a "very important" issue.[7]

Numerous journalists and political analysts have accused Donald Trump of racism. Trump has personally made racially insensitive remarks about Mexican Americans and Muslims around the world during the election campaign. Trump has also been subject to numerous racial controversies in his pre-political career, including two US Justice Department suits against Trump's New York real estate company for racial discrimination against African-American tenants. A 1991 book by a former president of Trump Plaza Hotel and Casino contains startling accusations of Trump personally disparaging African-American employees and expressing the belief that African Americans are "lazy" by nature.[8] Trump refutes all claims that he is racist and claims that all such allegations have been concocted, taken out of context, or exaggerated to discredit him, while some critics allege that Trump's public statements contain *clear* and irrefutable evidence of racial bias. Trump has been criticized for refusing to acknowledge the legitimacy of the *#BlackLivesMatter* movement, while frequently touting his support for police and so has effectively alienated a large proportion of African-American voters. In an August speech in Michigan, meant to reach out to African-American voters, Trump reductively described African-American culture in the statement, "You're living in poverty, your schools are no good, you have no jobs, 58% of your youth is unemployed—what the hell do you have to lose?"[9] Critics responded with the assertion that claiming *all* African American schools are "no good" or that *all* African Americans are "living in poverty," were, in themselves, examples of racist generalizations.

Whether or not Trump's failure to market himself to minority voters is a product of racism, he has become historically unpopular with minority voters. In Pennsylvania and Ohio, for instance, polls indicated that 0 percent of African Americans would support Trump, an unprecedented low for a Republican candidate in either state.[10] A June poll from *Washington Post-ABC News* indicated that more than 88 percent of all voters of color reported "unfavorable" views of Trump.[11] Some have also criticized Trump for failing to refute controversial endorsements by white supremacist groups and by encouraging the support of racist voters. A Reuters poll found that Trump's supporters are more than twice as likely as the average Republican to hold negative, racially biased views of African Americans and to believe that increasing diversity has been bad for the nation.[12]

The Politics of Gender

Numerous studies indicate that a significant gender gap remains in America, with women typically earning less than 75 percent of what men earn in the same position. Some economists have argued that the remaining "gender gap" actually reflects personal choices and priorities, with women preferring lower paying fields and prioritizing family over professional advancement, and thus argue that the gender gap is not reflecting gender bias. Critics refute this position with research indicating continued widespread bias in hiring and advancement of women in key industries and with the assertion that no individual, whether male or female, should be forced to choose between career or family. Both Sanders and Clinton agreed with this position, and promised to support federal family leave legislation if elected. Public opinion on the issue is divided along political and gender lines, with Republicans and men more likely to believe gender equality is no longer an issue, while Democrats and women believe more work is needed. A 2015 Pew study, for instance, found that 65 percent of women, but only 48 percent of men, believe that gender discrimination is still an issue in the United States.[13]

There has been relatively little attention paid to the historic importance of the 2016 election: The first time in history that a major party has nominated a woman for president. Writing in *Time* magazine, Philip Elliott and Sam Frizell theorize that public familiarity with Clinton, given her four decades in politics, coupled with the fact that the minority ceiling has already been broken by President Obama, the fact that women are no longer new to presidential politics, have collectively diluted the impact of Clinton's nomination. According to a CNN poll, while 8 in 10 believe that America is prepared to elect a woman president, only 31 percent list it as an important priority.[14] Clinton's support among women is also complex. A *USA Today* poll of female voters found that 37 percent said her election would make them "uneasy," compared to 34 percent who were excited by the prospect of her presidency.[15]

While some dislike Clinton because of her "hawkishness" as secretary of state, or because they believe Clinton is politically or economically corrupt, or has a tendency to "flip-flop" on crucial issues, Clinton's political failures do not fully explain the vehemence directed towards her. *Slate* columnist Michelle Goldberg believes that misogyny plays a role in the antipathy towards Clinton, noting the popularity (reflected in sales) of merchandise featuring sexist slurs sold by vendors at Trump rallies and through web stores. Such items include shirts that read "Trump That Bitch" and "Life's A Bitch: Don't Vote For One."[16] Misogyny has also been noted in statements by Clinton's opponents, such as Republican Ted Cruz' suggestion that the voters should "spank" Clinton for being untruthful, like Cruz would his five-year old daughter for lying. *Time* magazine columnist Laura Bates argues that Clinton has been subject to misogynistic attacks throughout her career, with opponents criticizing her wardrobe, hair, and appearance, far more than critics highlight the same superficial qualities in male politicians. Bates argues that the use of sexist slurs and misogynistic language is an important issue because such characterizations reinforce stereotypes that have been used to marginalize women in leadership roles for centuries.[17]

Micah L. Issitt

Works Used:

"2016 Campaign: Strong Interest, Widespread Dissatisfaction." *Pew Research*. Pew Research Center. Jul 7 2016. Web. 16 Aug 2016.

Bates, Laura. 'Spanking' Hillary Clinton Is Grotesque Misogyny." *Time*. Time Inc. Feb 8 2016. Web. 19 Aug 2016.

"Beyond Distrust: How Americans View Their Government." *Pew Research*. Pew Research Center. Nov 23 2015. Web. 16 Aug 2016.

Blake, Aaron. "Is 2016 the Anger Election? Not Quite." *The Washington Post*. Jan 26 2016. Web. 16 Aug 2016.

Bump, Philip. "Donald Trump Is Getting ZERO Percent of the Black Vote in Polls in Pennsylvania and Ohio." *The Washington Post*. Nash Holdings. Jul 13 2016. Web. 16 Aug 2016.

Chait, Jonathan. "Sorry, Obama: Donald Trump Is a Populist, and You're Not." *New York*. New York Media LLC. Jun 30 2016. Web. 17 Aug 2016.

Chotiner, Isaac. "Is Donald Trump a Populist? Or, Is He Just Popular?" *Slate*. Slate Monthly Group. Feb 24 2016. Web. 16 Aug 2016.

Elliott, Philip and Sam Frizell. "Why It's Easy to Forget Hillary Clinton Is Making History." *Time*. Jun 6 2016. Web. 17 Aug 2016.

"Exclusive: Trump Supporters More Likely to View Blacks Negatively – Reuters/ Ipsos Poll." *Reuters*. Reuters. Jun 28 2016. Web. 17 Aug 2016.

Goldberg, Michelle. "The Hillary Haters." *Slate*. The Slate Group. Jul 24 2016. Web. 20 Aug 2016.

LoBianco, Tom and Ashley Killough. "Trump Pitches Black Voters: 'What the Hell Do You Have to Lose?'." *CNN*. Cable News Network. Aug 19 2016. Web. 18 Aug 2016.

Maloy, Simon. "Trump's Economic Speech: Lots of Goodies for the Rich, With a Hearty Dose of Gaffes." *Salon*. Salon Media Group, Ltd. Aug 9 2016. Web. 16 Aug 2016.

McCarthy, Justin. "In U.S., 65% Dissatisfied with How Gov't System Works." *Gallup*. Gallup Inc. Jan 22 2014. Web.

"O'Connor, Lydia and Daniel Marans. "Here Are 13 Examples of Donald Trump Being Racist." *Huffington Post*. Huffington Post. Feb 29 2016. Web. 17 Aug 2016.

"On Views of Race and Inequality, Blacks and Whites Are Worlds Apart." *Pew Research*. Jun 27 2016. Web. 16 Aug 2016.

Page, Susan. "For Clinton, Sisterhood Is Powerful – and Trump Helps." *USA Today*.

Sanchez, Gabriel and Alan L. Abramowitz. "Hillary Clinton's Lead in the Polls May Be Larger Than it Seems. Here's Why." *The Washington Post*. Nash Holdings. Jun 20 2016. Web. Aug 17 2016.

Williams, Vanessa and Scott Clement. "Three in Four Voters of Color 'Strongly' Dislike Trump." *The Washington Post*. Nash Holdings. Jun 20 2016. Web. 17 Aug 2016.

"Women and Leadership." *Pew Research*. Pew Research Center. Jan 14 2015. Web. 19 Aug 2016.

Notes

1. Blake, "Is 2016 the Anger Election? Not Quite."
2. "2016 Campaign: Strong Interest, Widespread Dissatisfaction," *Pew Research*.
3. Chotiner, "Is Donald Trump a Populist?"
4. Maloy, "Trump's Economic Speech: Lots of Goodies for the Rich, With a Hearty Dose of Gaffes."
5. Chait, "Sorry, Obama: Donald Trump Is a Populist, and You're Not."
6. "On Views of Race and Inequality, Blacks and Whites Are Worlds Apart," Pew Research.
7. "2016 Campaign," *Pew Research*.
8. O'Connor and Marans, "Here Are 13 Examples of Donald Trump Being Racist."
9. LoBianco and Killough, "Trump Pitches Black Voters: 'What the Hell Do You Have to Lose?'."
10. Bump, "Donald Trump is Getting ZERO Percent of the Black Vote in Polls in Pennsylvania and Ohio."
11. Williams and Clement, "Three in Four Voters of Color 'Strongly' Dislike Trump."

12. "Exculsive: Trump Supporters More Likely to View Blacks Negatively – Reuters/Ipsos Poll," *Reuters*.

13. "Women and Leadership," *Pew Research*.

14. Elliott and Frizell, "Why It's Easy to Forget Hillary Clinton Is Making History."

15. Page, "For Clinton, Sisterhood Is Powerful – and Trump Helps."

16. Goldberg, "The Hillary Haters."

17. Bates, 'Spanking' Hillary Clinton Is Grotesque Misogyny."

The Woman Card: How Feminism and Antifeminism Created Hillary Clinton and Donald Trump

By Jill Lepore
The New Yorker, June 27, 2016

"IT MEANS FREEDOM FOR WOMEN TO VOTE AGAINST THE PARTY THIS DONKEY REPRESENTS" read the sign on a donkey named Woodrow who, wearing a bow, was paraded through Denver by the National Woman's Party during its campaign against the Democratic incumbent, President Wilson, in 1916. This year, the hundredth anniversary of the Woman's Party arrived, unnoticed, on June 5th. Two days later, Hillary Clinton became the first woman to claim the Presidential nomination of a major party: the Democratic Party.

If elected, Clinton will become the first female President in the nation's history. She will also join John Quincy Adams, James Monroe, Martin Van Buren, and James Buchanan as the only Presidents to have served both in the Senate and as Secretary of State. If she loses the election to Donald Trump, he will be the first man elected President who has never served the public either in government or in the military. Trump wants to make America great again; Clinton wants to make history. That history is less about the last glass ceiling than about a party realignment as important as the Nixon-era Southern Strategy, if less well known. Call it the Female Strategy.

For the past century, the edges of the parties have been defined by a debate about the political role and constitutional rights of women. This debate is usually reduced to cant, as if the battle between the parties were a battle between the sexes. Republicans and Democrats are "just like men and women," Trent Lott liked to say: Democrats might be from Venus, but the GOP is "the party of Mars." Democrats have talked about a Republican "war on women"; Trump says, of Clinton, "The only card she has is the woman card." She polls better among women; he polls better among men. The immediacy and starkness of the contrast between the candidates obscures the historical realignment hinted at in their own biographies: she used to be a Republican and he used to be a Democrat. This election isn't a battle between the sexes. But it is a battle between the parties, each hoping to win the votes of women without losing the votes of men. It's also marked by the sweeping changes to American politics caused by women's entry into public life. Long before women could vote, they carried into the parties a political style they had perfected first as abolitionists and then as prohibitionists: the moral crusade. No election has been the same since.

For a very long time, the parties had no idea what to do with women. At the nation's founding, women made an argument for female citizenship based on their role as mothers: in a republic, the civic duty of women is to raise sons who will be virtuous citizens. Federalists doffed their top hats, and no more. In the eighteen-twenties and thirties, Jacksonian democracy involved a lot of brawls: women were not allowed. When the social reformer Fanny Wright spoke at a political meeting in 1836, she was called a "female man." Instead, women entered public affairs by way of an evangelical religious revival that emphasized their moral superiority, becoming temperance reformers and abolitionists: they wrote petitions. "The right of petitioning is the only political right that women have," Angelina Grimké pointed out in 1837.

The Whig Party was the first to make use of women in public, if ridiculously: in 1840, Tennessee women marched wearing sashes that read "Whig Husbands or None." Because neither the Whig nor the Democratic Party was able to address the question of slavery, a crop of new parties sprang up. Fuelled by antislavery arguments, and adopting the style of moral suasion favored by female reformers, these parties tended to be welcoming to women, and even to arguments for women's rights.

The Republican Party was born in 1854, in Ripon, Wisconsin, when fifty-four citizens founded a party to oppose the Kansas-Nebraska Act, which threatened to create two new slave states. Three of those citizens were women. Women wrote Republican campaign literature, and made speeches on behalf of the Party. Its first Presidential nominee, in 1856, was John Frémont, but more than one Republican observed that his wife, Jessie Benton Frémont, "would have been the better candidate." One of the Party's most popular and best-paid speakers was Anna Dickinson, who became the first woman to speak in the Hall of the House of Representatives.

The women's-rights movement was founded in 1848. "It started right here in New York, a place called Seneca Falls," Clinton said in her victory speech on June 7th, after effectively clinching the Democratic nomination. Advocates of women's rights were closely aligned with the Republican Party, and typically fought to end slavery and to earn for both black men and all women political equality with white men. In 1859, Elizabeth Cady Stanton wrote to Susan B. Anthony, "When I pass the gate of the celestials and good Peter asks me where I wish to sit, I will say, 'Anywhere so that I am neither a negro nor a woman. Confer on me, great angel, the glory of White manhood, so that henceforth I may feel unlimited freedom.'"

After Lincoln signed the Emancipation Proclamation, Stanton and Anthony gathered four hundred thousand signatures on petitions demanding the Thirteenth Amendment. They then began fighting for the Fourteenth Amendment, which they expected to guarantee the rights and privileges of citizenship for all Americans. Instead, they were told that "this is the Negro's hour," and that the amendment would include the word "male," so as to specifically exclude women. "Do you believe the African race is composed entirely of males?" Stanton asked Wendell Phillips. And then she warned, "If that word 'male' be inserted, it will take us a century at least to get it out."

The insertion of the word "male" into the Fourteenth Amendment had consequences that have lasted well into this year's Presidential election. At the time, not everyone bought the argument that it was necessary to disenfranchise women in order to secure ratification. "Can any one tell us why the great advocates of Human Equality . . . forget that when they were a weak party and needed all the womanly strength of the nation to help them on, they always united the words 'without regard to sex, race, or color'?" one frustrated female supporter of the Republican Party asked. She could have found an answer in an observation made by Charles Sumner: "We know how the Negro will vote, but are not so sure of the women."

This election, many female voters, especially younger ones, resent being told that they should support Hillary Clinton just because she's a woman. It turns out that women don't form a political constituency any more than men do; like men, women tend to vote with their families and their communities. But, in 1865, how women would vote was impossible to know. Would black women vote the way black men voted? Would white women vote like black women? The parties, led by white men, decided they'd just as soon not find out.

Women tried to gain the right to vote by simply seizing it, a plan that was known as the New Departure. Beginning in 1868, black and white women went to the polls all over the country and got arrested. Sojourner Truth tried to vote in Battle Creek, Michigan. Five black women were arrested for voting in South Carolina in 1870, months before Victoria Woodhull became the first woman to run for President. She announced that women already had the right to vote, under the privileges-and-immunities clause of the Constitution, and, in 1871, she made this argument before the House Judiciary Committee. Anthony was arrested for voting in 1872—not for Woodhull but for the straight Republican ticket—and, in the end, the Supreme Court ruled against Woodhull's interpretation of the Constitution. Thus ended the New Departure.

Prevented from entering the electorate, women who wanted to influence public affairs were left to plead with men. For decades, these women had very little choice: whatever fight they fought, they had only the weapons of the nineteenth-century religious revival: the sermon, the appeal, the conversion, the crusade. The full measure of the influence of the female campaign on the American political style has yet to be taken. But that influence was felt first, and longest, in the Republican Party.

At the Republican nominating convention in 1872, the Party split into two, but neither faction added a suffrage plank to its platform. "We recognize the equality of all men before the law," the Liberal Republicans declared, specifically discounting women. Stanton called the position taken by the regular Republicans—"the honest demand of any class of citizens for additional rights should be treated with respectful consideration"—not a plank but a splinter. Still, a splinter was more than suffragists ever got from the Democratic Party. In 1880, Anthony wrote a speech to deliver at the Democratic National Convention. It began, "To secure to twenty millions of women the rights of citizenship is to base your party on the eternal principles of justice." Instead, her statement was read by a male clerk, while Anthony looked on, furious, after which, as the *Times* reported, "No action whatever was taken in regard to it, and Miss Anthony vexed the Convention no more."

Close elections seemed to be good for the cause because, in a tight race, both parties courted suffragists' support, but women soon discovered that this was fruitless: if they allied with Republicans, Democrats campaigned against Republicans by campaigning against suffrage. This led to a certain fondness for third parties—the Equal Rights Party, the Prohibition Party, the Home Protection Party. J. Ellen Foster, an Iowa lawyer who had helped establish the Woman's Christian Temperance Union, spoke at a Republican rally and cautioned that a third party rewards women's support with nothing more than flattery: "It gives to women seats in conventions and places their names on meaningless committees and tickets impossible of success." In 1892, Foster founded the Women's National Republican Association, telling the delegates at the Party's Convention that year, "We are here to help you. And we have come to stay."

In the second decade of the twentieth century, anticipating the ratification of the Nineteenth Amendment, the parties scrambled to secure the loyalty of voters who would double the size of the electorate, no less concerned than Sumner had been about how women would vote. "With a suddenness and force that have left observers gasping women have injected themselves into the national campaign this year in a manner never before dreamed of in American politics," the *New York Herald* reported in 1912. When Theodore Roosevelt founded the Progressive Party, it adopted a suffrage plank, and he aggressively courted women. He considered appointing Jane Addams to his cabinet. At the Progressive Party's Convention, Addams gave the second nominating speech. Then she grabbed a "Votes for Woman" flag and marched it across the platform and up and down the auditorium. Roosevelt had tried to win the Republican nomination by bribing black delegates, who were then shut out of the Progressive Party's Convention. When Addams got back to Chicago, she found a telegram from a black newspaper editor: "Woman suffrage will be stained with Negro Blood unless women refuse all alliance with Roosevelt."

Alice Paul, a feminist with a Ph.D. from the University of Pennsylvania who'd been arrested for fighting for suffrage in England, decided that American women ought to form their own party. "The name Woman's Party is open to a quite natural misunderstanding," Charlotte Perkins Gilman admitted, introducing the National Woman's Party in 1916. It wasn't a party, per se; it was a group of women whose strategy was to protest the existing parties, on the theory that no party could be trusted to advance the interests of women.

Terrified by the very idea of a party of women, the D.N.C. formed a "Women's Division" in 1917, the R.N.C. in 1918. The G.O.P. pursued a policy of "complete amalgamation," its chairman pledging "to check any tendency toward the formation of a separate women's party." White women worked for both parties; black women worked only for the G.O.P., to fight the Democratic Party, which had become the party of Southern whites. "The race is doomed unless Negro Women take an active part in local, state and national politics," the National League of Republican Colored Women said.

After 1920, Carrie Chapman Catt, the longtime head of the National American Woman Suffrage Association, turned it into the League of Women Voters, providing voter education and other aids to good government. Meanwhile, she told women to join the parties: "The only way to get things in this country is to find them on the inside of the political party." Inside those parties, women fought for equal representation. The Women's Division of the D.N.C. implemented a rule mandating an equal number of male and female delegates, in 1920. In 1923, the Republican National Committee introduced rule changes—billed as "seats for women"—that added bonus delegates for states that had voted Republican in the previous election. But the Democrats' fifty-fifty rule was observed only in the breach, and, as both Catherine E. Rymph and Melanie Gustafson have pointed out in their rich histories of women in the Republican Party, the real purpose of adding the new G.O.P. seats was to reduce the influence of black Southern delegates.

The League of Women Voters was nonpartisan, but the National Woman's Party remained antipartisan. It focused on securing passage of an Equal Rights Amendment, drafted by Paul, who had lately earned a law degree, and first introduced into Congress in 1923. Yet, for all the work of the Woman's Party, the G.O.P. was the party of women or, rather, of white women, for most of the twentieth century. In the late nineteen-twenties and thirties, black men and women left the Republican Party, along with smaller numbers of white women, eventually forming a New Deal coalition of liberals, minorities, labor unionists, and, from the South, poor whites. F.D.R. appointed Molly Williams Dewson the director of the D.N.C.'s Women's Division, which grew to eighty thousand members.

In 1937, determined to counter the efforts of the lady known as "More Women" Dewson, the R.N.C. appointed Marion Martin its assistant chairman; during her tenure, she founded a national federation of women's clubs whose membership grew to four hundred thousand. Martin, thirty-seven and unmarried, had a degree in economics and had served a combined four terms in the Maine legislature. She led a moral crusade against the New Deal. In 1940, she also got the R.N.C. to pass its own fifty-fifty rule and to endorse the Equal Rights Amendment, formally, in its platform. This went only so far. In 1946, Martin argued that party women needed more power. "We need it not because we are feminists but because there are a great many non-partisan women's organizations that do wield an influence in this country," she said. Five days later, she was forced to resign.

Hillary Rodham was born in Chicago in 1947. In 1960, when Richard Nixon ran against J.F.K., she checked voter lists for the G.O.P. By then, the majority of Republican Party workers were female. During the Cold War, the G.O.P. boasted about "the women who work on the home front, ringing the doorbells, filling out registration cards, and generally doing the housework of government." As the historian Paula Baker has pointed out, party work is just like other forms of labor; women work harder, are paid less, are rarely promoted, and tend to enter a field when men begin to view it as demeaning. The elephant was the right symbol for the Party, one senator said, because it has "a vacuum cleaner in front and a rug beater behind."

Betty Farrington, one of Martin's successors, turned the women's federation into a powerhouse of zealous crusaders. After Truman defeated Dewey, in 1948, Farrington wanted the G.O.P. to find its strongman:

How thankful we would have been if a leader had appeared to show us the path to the promised land of our hope. The world needs such a man today. He is certain to come sooner or later. But we cannot sit idly by in the hope of his coming. Besides his advent depends partly on us. The mere fact that a leader is needed does not guarantee his appearance. People must be ready for him, and we, as Republican women, in our clubs, prepare for him.

That man, many Republican voters today appear to believe, is Donald J. Trump, born in New York in 1946.

Political parties marry interests to constituencies. They are not defined by whether they attract women, particularly. Nor are they defined by their positions on equal rights for women and men. But no plausible history of American politics can ignore, first, the influence of a political style perfected, over a century, by citizens who, denied the franchise, were forced to plead, and, second, the effects of the doubling of the size of the electorate.

The Republican Party that is expected to nominate Trump was built by housewives and transformed by their political style, which men then made their own. The moral crusade can be found among nineteenth-century Democrats—William Jennings Bryan, say—but in the twentieth century it became the hallmark of the conservative wing of the Republican Party; it is the style, for instance, of Ted Cruz. This began in 1950, when the Republican Women's Club of Ohio County, West Virginia, invited as its principal speaker for Lincoln Day Senator Joseph McCarthy. It was during this speech that McCarthy said he had a list of subversives working at the State Department. "The great difference between our Western Christian world and the atheistic Communist world is not political—it is moral," McCarthy said. His rhetoric was that of the nineteenth-century women's crusade. The great crusader Barry Goldwater said in 1955, "If it were not for the National Federation of Republican Women, there would not be a Republican Party." That year, Republican women established Kitchen Cabinets, appointing a female equivalent to every member of Eisenhower's cabinet; their job was to share "political recipes on G.O.P. accomplishments with the housewives of the nation," by sending monthly bulletins on "What's Cooking in Washington." One member of the Kitchen Cabinet was Phyllis Schlafly.

In 1963, Schlafly nominated Goldwater to speak at a celebration marking the twenty-fifth anniversary of the National Federation of Republican Women. In a straw poll taken after Goldwater delivered his speech, 262 out of 293 Federation delegates chose him. Meanwhile, Margaret Chase Smith was drafted into the race, a liberal alternative. As the historian Ellen Fitzpatrick recounts in a terrific new book, *The Highest Glass Ceiling*, Smith was the first woman elected on her own to the Senate and the first woman to serve in both houses of Congress. Asked why she agreed to run against Goldwater, she once said, "There was nowhere to go but the Presidency." She was the first and boldest member of the Senate to oppose McCarthy, in a speech she made from the floor, known as the Declaration of Conscience: "I don't want to see the Republican Party ride to political victory on the Four Horsemen of Calumny—Fear, Ignorance, Bigotry, and Smear." At the Convention in 1964, she refused to endorse Goldwater, and denied him her delegates.

Young Trump had little interest in politics. He liked the movies. In 1964, he graduated from military school, where he'd been known as a ladies' man, and thought about going to the University of Southern California, to study film. Hillary Rodham was a "Goldwater Girl." But Smith was her hero. She decided to run for president of her high-school class, against a field of boys, and lost, "which did not surprise me," she wrote in her memoir, "but still hurt, especially because one of my opponents told me I was 'really stupid if I thought a girl could be elected president.'"

It's right about here that the G.O.P. began to lose Hillary Rodham. In 1965, as a freshman at Wellesley, she was president of the Young Republicans; she brought with her to college Goldwater's *The Conscience of a Conservative*. But Goldwater's defeat led to a struggle for the future of the Party, and that struggle turned on Schlafly. In 1966, Elly Peterson, a Michigan state party chairman and supporter of George Romney, tried to keep Schlafly from becoming the president of the National Federation. "The nut fringe is beautifully organized," Peterson complained. At a three-thousand-woman Federation convention in 1967, Schlafly was narrowly defeated. Three months later, she launched her monthly newsletter. Rejecting the nascent women's-liberation movement, she nevertheless blamed sexism for the G.O.P.'s failure to fully embrace its most strenuous conservatives:

> **Trump wants to make America great again; Clinton wants to make history. That history is less about the last glass ceiling than about a party realignment as important as the Nixon-era Southern Strategy, if less well known. Call it the Female Strategy.**

The Republican Party is carried on the shoulders of the women who do the work in the precincts, ringing doorbells, distributing literature, and doing all the tiresome, repetitious campaign tasks. Many men in the Party frankly want to keep the women doing the menial work, while the selection of candidates and the policy decisions are taken care of by the men in the smoke-filled rooms.

In the summer of 1968, Trump graduated from Wharton, where, he later said, he spent most of his time reading the listings of foreclosures on federally financed housing projects. That September, in Atlantic City, feminists staged a protest at the Miss America pageant, the sort of pageant that Trump would one day buy, run, and cherish. They carried signs reading "Welcome to the Cattle Auction."

Rodham, a twenty-year-old Capitol Hill intern, attended the Republican National Convention in Miami as a supporter of the antiwar candidate, Nelson Rockefeller. For the first time since 1940, the G.O.P. dropped from its platform its endorsement of equal rights. Rodham went home to see her family, and, hiding the fact from her parents, drove downtown to watch the riots outside the Democratic National Convention. One month too young to vote, she'd supported the antiwar Democrat, Eugene McCarthy, before the Convention, but later said she would probably have voted for the Party's nominee, Hubert Humphrey.

In 1969, Rodham, senior class president at Wellesley, became the first student invited to deliver a commencement address, a speech that was featured in *Life*. In 1970, a leader of her generation, a student at Yale Law School, and wearing a black armband mourning the students killed at Kent State, she spoke about her opposition to the Vietnam War at a convention of the League of Women Voters, on the occasion of its fiftieth anniversary. She had become a feminist, and a Democrat.

What followed is more familiar. Between 1964 and 1980, Schlafly's arm of the Party steadily gained control of the G.O.P., which began courting evangelical Christians, including white male Southern Democrats alienated by their party's civil-rights agenda. In the wake of *Roe v. Wade*, and especially after the end of the Cold War, the Republican Party's new crusaders turned their attention from Communism to abortion. The Democratic Party became the party of women, partly by default. For a long time, it could have gone another way.

In 1971, Hillary Rodham met Bill Clinton, Donald Trump took over the family business, and Gloria Steinem, Tanya Melich, Bella Abzug, and Shirley Chisholm helped found the National Women's Political Caucus, which, like the National Woman's Party, sought to force both parties to better represent women and to gain passage of the Equal Rights Amendment. At the 1972 G.O.P. Convention, in Miami, Republican feminists demanded that the Party restore its E.R.A. plan to the platform. They won, but at a cost. After the Convention, Schlafly founded STOP ERA.

The Democratic Party, meanwhile, was forging a new coalition. "A new hat, or rather a bonnet, was tossed into the Democratic Presidential race today," Walter Cronkite said on *CBS News*, when Chisholm, the first black woman to be elected to Congress, announced her bid. She went all the way to the Convention. Chisholm said, "You can go to that Convention and you can yell, 'Woman power! Here I come!' You can yell, 'Black power! Here I come!' The only thing those hard-nosed boys are going to understand at that Convention: 'How many delegates you got?'" She got a hundred and fifty-two.

By 1973, Trump was making donations to the Democratic Party. "The simple fact is that contributing money to politicians is very standard and accepted for a New York City developer," he explains in *The Art of the Deal*. He also appeared, for the first time, in a story in the *Times*, with the headline "MAJOR LANDLORD ACCUSED OF ANTIBLACK BIAS IN CITY." The Department of Justice had charged Trump and his father with violating the 1968 Fair Housing Act. "We never have discriminated," Trump told the *Times*, "and we never would."

In 1974, Rodham moved to Washington, D.C., where she worked for the special counsel preparing for the possible impeachment of Richard Nixon. The next year, she married Bill Clinton, though she didn't take his name. The G.O.P., weakened by Watergate, and thinking to stanch the flow of departing women, elected as party chair Mary Louise Smith, an ardent feminist. In 1975, some thirty G.O.P. feminists formed the Republican Women's Task Force to support the E.R.A., reproductive rights, affirmative action, federally funded child care, and the extension of the Equal Pay Act.

The shift came in 1976. Rodham went to the Democratic Convention, at Madison Square Garden. Schlafly went to the Republican Convention, in Kansas City*, where, as the political scientist Jo Freeman has argued, feminists won the battle but lost the war. For the nomination, Ford, a supporter of the E.R.A., defeated Reagan, an opponent, but the platform committee defeated the E.R.A. by a single vote.

In 1980, Republican feminists knew they'd lost when Reagan won the nomination; even so moderate a Republican as George Romney called supporters of the E.R.A. "moral perverts," and the platform committee urged a constitutional ban on abortion. Tanya Melich, a Republican feminist, began talking about a "Republican War against Women," a charge Democrats happily made their own. Mary Crisp, a longtime R.N.C. co-chair, was forced out, and declared of the party of Lincoln and of Anthony, "We are reversing our position and are about to bury the rights of over a hundred million American women under a heap of platitudes."

Buried they remain. Until 1980, during any Presidential election for which reliable data exist and in which there had been a gender gap, the gap had run one way: more women than men voted for the Republican candidate. That changed when Reagan became the G.O.P. nominee; more women than men supported Carter, by eight percentage points. Since then, the gender gap has never favored a G.O.P. Presidential candidate. The Democratic Party began billing itself as the party of women. By 1987, Trump had become a Republican.

In the Reagan era, Republican strategists believed that, in trading women for men, they'd got the better end of the deal. As the Republican consultant Susan Bryant pointed out, Democrats "do so badly among men that the fact that we don't do quite as well among women becomes irrelevant." And that's more or less where it lies.

With the end of the E.R.A., whose chance at ratification expired in 1982, both parties abandoned a political settlement necessary to the stability of the republic. The entrance of women into politics on terms that are, fundamentally and constitutionally, unequal to men's has produced a politics of interminable division, infused with misplaced and dreadful moralism. Republicans can't win women; when they win, they win without them, by winning with men. Democrats need to win both the black vote and the female vote. Trump and Clinton aren't likely to break that pattern. Trump, with his tent-revival meetings, is crusading not only against Clinton and against Obama but against immigrants, against Muslims, and, in the end, against every group of voters that has fled the Republican Party, as he rides with his Four Horsemen: Fear, Ignorance, Bigotry, and Smear.

"This is a movement of the American people," Trump wrote in an e-mail to supporters. "And the American people NEVER lose." It took a very long time, and required the work of the Republican Party, to change the meaning of "the American

*An earlier version misstated the site of the 1976 Republican Convention.

people" to include everyone. It hasn't taken very long at all for Trump to change it back. The next move is Clinton's, and her party's.

Print Citations

CMS: Lepore, Jill. "The Woman Card: How Feminism and Antifeminism Created Hillary Clinton and Donald Trump." In *The Reference Shelf: Campaign Trends and Election Law*, edited by Betsy Maury, 51-60. Ipswitch, MA: Salem Press, 2016.

MLA: Lepore, Jill. "The Woman Card: How Feminism and Antifeminism Created Hillary Clinton and Donald Trump."*The Reference Shelf: Campaign Trends and Election Law*. Ed. Betsy Maury. Ipswitch: Salem Press, 2016. 51-60. Print.

APA: Lepore, J. (2016). The woman card: How feminism and antifeminism created Hillary Clinton and Donald Trump. In Betsy Maury (Ed.), *The reference shelf: Campaign trends and election law* (pp. 51-60). Ipswitch, MA: Salem. (Original work published 2016)

Working-Class Heroes: The 2016 Election Shows That, When Talking About Class, Americans and Their Candidates Are Both Out of Practice

By Jelani Cobb

The New Yorker April 25, 2016

During the 2008 Vice-Presidential debate between Joe Biden and Sarah Palin, in St. Louis, Biden offered a memorable brief on behalf of struggling communities like the one in Pennsylvania where he spent his childhood. Biden, whose common-man bona fides were seen as an antidote to Barack Obama's Ivy League credentials and relative aloofness, spoke evocatively of the pain felt by a portion of America that is more usually described in the gauzy, romantic tones of American greatness. "Look, the people in my neighborhood, they get it," Biden said. "They know they've been getting the short end of the stick. So walk with me in my neighborhood, go back to my old neighborhood, in Claymont, an old steel town, or go up to Scranton with me. These people know the middle class has gotten the short end. The wealthy have done very well. Corporate America has been rewarded. It's time we change it."

In hindsight, what's notable about Biden's statement is not how it presaged the populist concerns of this year's Presidential election but the fact that he referred to his neighbors—steelworkers, denizens of factory towns—as middle class, not as working class. In fact, the phrase "working class" came up twice during the debate—but it was Palin who said it, not Biden. Things didn't change much rhetorically in the 2012 election. Obama and Mitt Romney, in the course of three Presidential debates, invoked the "middle class" forty-three times but never mentioned the proletariat.

For decades, both American culture and American politics have elided the differences between salaried workers and those who are paid hourly, between college-educated professionals and those whose purchasing power is connected to membership in a labor union. Some ninety per cent of Americans, including most millionaires, routinely identify as middle class. For many years, this glossing over of the distinctions between the classes served a broad set of interests, particularly during the Cold War, when any reference to class carried a whiff of socialist sympathies. Americans considered themselves part of a larger whole, and social animosities were mostly siphoned off in the direction of racial resentment. But, this year, Americans are once again debating class.

We are clearly out of practice. The current language of "income inequality" is a low-carb version of the Old Left's "class exploitation." The new phrase lacks rhetorical zing; it's hard to envision workers on a picket line singing rousing anthems about "income inequality." The term lacks a verb, too, so it's possible to think of the condition under discussion as a random social outcome, rather than as the product of deliberate actions taken by specific people. Bernie Sanders has tended to frame his position as a defense of an imperilled middle class, but he has also called out the "greedy billionaires" and "Wall Street"—a synecdoche for exploitation in general.

Donald Trump's populist appeals are all the more remarkable given that the modern Republican Party has been the largest beneficiary of this collapsing of class interests. Ever since Ronald Reagan's Presidency, progressives have pondered why working-class and poor whites vote Republican, against their own interests. The fact that the charge is being led on the right by a billionaire real-estate developer, however, suggests that the new recognition of class is not without its contradictions. It's also worth noting that Romney, the man leading the attempt to quell this populist uprising, on behalf of the Party's alarmed establishment, is a multimillionaire who lost the previous election, in part, because he dismissed forty-seven per cent of Americans as "freeloaders."

Strikingly, the emerging dialogue on class is informed by the ways in which we have typically talked about race. In 1976, the majority of welfare recipients in the United States were not black. But when, during the Presidential campaign that year, Reagan made his famous comments about the "welfare queen," they were widely taken to mean that the problem wasn't poor people in general but, rather, certain blacks in inner cities, who were purportedly cheating the system (and whose votes the Republican Party had already jettisoned). Today, in the battle over, say, public-sector unions, it's hard not to hear an echo of those complaints about social parasitism, though when Governor Scott Walker, of Wisconsin, campaigned to strip most public-sector unions of their collective-bargaining rights he did so in the language of Madison progressivism: "We can no longer live in a society where the public employees are the haves and taxpayers who foot the bills are the have-nots."

> **For many years, this glossing over of the distinctions between the classes served a broad set of interests, particularly during the Cold War, when any reference to class carried a whiff of socialist sympathies.**

There are other hints that the old stereotypes about inner-city blacks are beginning to be deployed against working-class whites. Heightened mortality rates among middle-aged working-class whites and the concomitant spike in opioid addiction have, on the whole, generated sympathetic examinations of social displacement, in which addiction is seen as a public-health concern symptomatic of the changing economy, as opposed to a sign of moral failure. But, last month, in *National Review*, Kevin Williamson wrote:

The truth about these dysfunctional, downscale communities is that they deserve to die. Economically, they are negative assets. Morally, they are indefensible. Forget all your cheap theatrical Bruce Springsteen crap. Forget your sanctimony about struggling Rust Belt factory towns. . . . The white American underclass is in thrall to a vicious, selfish culture whose main products are misery and used heroin needles. Donald Trump's speeches make them feel good. So does OxyContin.

These are the communities that Biden spoke of in 2008. Yet, according to Williamson, the apt metaphor isn't getting the short end of the stick but dropping the ball. In 2010, Charles Murray published *Coming Apart*, a lamentation on the decline among poor whites of religiosity, of the work ethic, and of family values. It received just a fraction of the attention paid to his 1994 book, *The Bell Curve*, which argued that a supposed intellectual inferiority factored into the plight of poor blacks. But in 2016 there is a new market for the ideas in *Coming Apart*. The fact that we are examining class may be novel, but it is almost certain that what we'll hear said about poverty won't be.

Print Citations

CMS: Cobb, Jelani. "Working-Class Heroes: The 2016 Election Shows That, When Talking About Class, Americans and Their Candidates Are Both Out of Practice." In *The Reference Shelf: Campaign Trends and Election Law*, edited by Betsy Maury, 61-63. Ipswitch, MA: Salem Press, 2016.

MLA: Cobb, Jelani. "Working-Class Heroes: The 2016 Election Shows That, When Talking About Class, Americans and Their Candidates Are Both Out of Practice." *The Reference Shelf: Campaign Trends and Election Law*. Ed. Betsy Maury. Ipswitch: Salem Press, 2016. 61-63. Print.

APA: Cobb, J. (2016). Working-class heroes: The 2016 election shows that, when talking about class, Americans and their candidates are both out of practice. In Betsy Maury (Ed.), *The reference shelf: Campaign trends and election law* (pp. 61-63). Ipswitch, MA: Salem. (Original work published 2016)

Outsiders' Chance

The Economist, **January 30, 2016**

When Jeb Bush announced he was running for president seven months ago the tutting newspaper commentaries almost wrote themselves. With his famous name and war chest of over $100m, whistled up from Bush family benefactors in a matter of months, the former Florida governor was almost as strong a favourite for the Republican ticket as Hillary Clinton, who had made her inaugural campaign speech two days earlier, was for the Democratic one. Bush against Clinton? The prospect made American democracy seem stale and dynastic, rigged on behalf of a tiny political elite, whose members alone had the name recognition and deep pockets required to win its overpriced elections.

But now the primary process is about to get serious. In Iowa on February 1st perhaps 250,000 voters will brave icy roads to pick their champion in small groups, or caucuses. And the tutting has given way to real fear. On the Republican side, Mr Bush—or "Jeb!" as his campaign has cruelly styled him—is all but irrelevant. The son and brother of past presidents is clever and has a solid record of cutting taxes and privatising services. But Republican voters have dismissed him as dull and out-of-touch, an emblem of the political class they despise. The Republican front-runner, Donald Trump, is a celebrity builder with no previous political experience. He has raised little money, was once a registered Democrat and still refers derisively to his party as "the Republicans", as if it is some unpromising acquisition he has been arm-twisted into buying.

Mr Trump is quick-witted, charismatic and, during years as a reality television star, has built an outrageous public persona around his gargantuan ego. "I'm intelligent," he likes to say. "Some people would say I'm very, very, very intelligent." Uncertainty over whether this is self-parody or undiluted egomania is part of the act. Mr Trump is to public service what professional wrestling, which he loves, is to sport: entertaining and ludicrously implausible, a suspension of disbelief for escapists, a crude deception for the gullible.

The digs he makes at his rivals, often in the form of tweets offering "advice", can be amusing. A former propagator of conspiracy theories about Barack Obama's place of birth, Mr Trump is now dishing out the same treatment to his closest challenger, Ted Cruz. A first-term senator from Texas, Mr Cruz was born in Canada, but to an American mother, which puts his eligibility to be president beyond serious doubt. "Ted—free legal advice on how to pre-empt the Dems on citizen issue. Go to court now & seek declaratory judgment—you will win!" Mr Trump tweeted to his

From the print edition: Briefing

nearly 6m followers. Yet his front-runner status is based less on Mr Trump's wit than on his gift for understanding and pandering to people's fears.

The billionaire says that America has been beggared and wrecked by immigrant rapists, venal bankers and idiot politicians, is imperilled by Muslim maniacs, and mocked by the rest of the world. He rages against the Chinese, whom he accuses of inventing global warming to destroy American industry. Announcing his run at Trump Tower, his Manhattan skyscraper, he lamented: "We got $18 trillion in debt... we need money. We're dying. We're dying. We need money... Sadly, the American dream is dead."

Trumped-Up Charges

Trumped-Up Charges has a plan to "make America great again", a Reaganite phrase he has purloined. He wants to deport 11m illegal immigrants and their offspring, impose a 45% tariff on Chinese imports, kill the relatives of terrorist suspects and bar Muslims from entering America. To stanch the influx of "rapists" (never mind that for the past six years there has been a net outflow of people from America to Mexico), he would build a "beautiful wall" along the southern border. This is his signature policy and the subject of a much-anticipated call-and-response moment at the rallies he—descending from the sky in his monogrammed helicopter—has held all over America. "What are we gonna build?" he asks. "A wall!" the crowds holler back. "Who's gonna pay?" "Mexico!"

The notion of Mr Trump, who is backed by around 35% of Republican voters, as a presidential nominee is alarming. Yet Mr Cruz, who has 20% and is running close behind in Iowa, is hardly a reassuring alternative. The self-made son of a Cuban immigrant, he came to national attention in 2013 when he tried to shut down the federal government in a vainglorious bid to defund Barack Obama's health-care reform, an effort he compared to the resistance against Adolf Hitler. It was an example of the sort of cynical self-promotion for which Mr Cruz is loathed by his colleagues in the Senate.

He aims to unite the most fiscally conservative part of the Republican coalition with the most socially conservative, evangelical Christians. Offering himself as a no-compromise right-winger and scourge of the party's elite, Mr Cruz has done well in televised debates, raised more money than most of his ten surviving rivals—including $20m in the last three months of 2015—and covered the ground assiduously in pious Iowa. Hence his new preacherly style.

"In the days that follow," Mr Cruz recently declaimed while touring the state's ultra-devout north-west, "we will send the regulators that descend on farmers like locusts back to Washington!" Raising his nasal voice, he then beseeched his small audience of corn farmers and their wives to pray, "for just a minute every day", that God would make him president. If He does, Mr Cruz promises to scrap the Internal Revenue Service, institute a 10% flat-tax on income and urge the Federal Reserve to readopt the gold standard.

Without divine intervention, it is hard to imagine Americans electing either of the Republican front-runners to be president. The lesson the party drew from Mitt

Romney's failure to dislodge Mr Obama in 2012 was that, in an increasingly diverse society, the Grand Old Party needed to widen its appeal. Mr Cruz's target audience, white Christians, represent less than half the population. The obvious solution was to woo Hispanics, one of America's fastest-growing electoral groups, who hold some conservative views, though only 27% of them voted for Mr Romney.

That was why, in 2013, a handful of Republican senators, including Marco Rubio, who is running third in the primary contest, joined a bipartisan, and ultimately fruitless, effort to legalise the status of millions of illegal immigrants. "It's really hard to get people to listen to you…if they think you want to deport their grandmother," declared Mr Rubio, a son of poor Cuban immigrants, at the time. It is even harder when you call them rapists. Mr Trump is easily the most disliked candidate of either party; 60% of voters disapprove of him.

There is a consolation for the Republicans. The Democrats could nominate someone even less electable. In Mrs Clinton's path stands Bernie Sanders, a 74-year-old "democratic socialist", who says American capitalism is rigged against the 99% and vows to dismantle banks and build Medicare into a universal health-care system. His claim that this would save $10 trillion over a decade has elicited scepticism. An independent senator from Vermont, Mr Sanders was until recently neither a member nor even an admirer of the Democratic Party, which he has called "ideologically bankrupt". Yet polls suggest he has the support of 37% of its primary voters and could win in Iowa and at the New Hampshire primary on February 9th.

From William Jennings Bryan and Huey Long to Ross Perot and Pat Buchanan, populists are as much a part of the American political tradition as tirades against Washington. They have typically thrived at a time of anxiety. Bryan and Long were creatures of depressed economies; Mr Perot went to war with free-trade, which many Americans feared, just as the two big parties decided to embrace it; Mr Buchanan stoked the same nativist fires that have given Mr Trump's candidacy much of its heat. This time the unease seems to be mainly economic, and it is widespread.

America has recovered well from the great recession of 2008-09—its unemployment rate is low, at 5%—yet wage growth remains anaemic. Real median household income in 2014 was almost $4,000 below its peak in 2007. That has shaken the national self-esteem; so have unsuccessful wars in Iraq and Afghanistan, and their messy aftermath, including the rise of Islamic State. Asked "Are America's best days behind us?", in a recent survey, 49% of respondents said that they were. Black Americans, for whom that is clearly not true, are almost the only hopeful group.

The squeeze has been hardest for people feeling pre-existing pressures: blue-collar workers, hurt by globalisation, and millennials facing rising college debts and competition for jobs. Last year's college-leavers are, on average, $35,000 in the red, more than twice the figure of two decades ago. One or both groups are at the forefront of Europe's many populist insurgencies: including, on the left, Syriza in Greece and the socialist leadership of Britain's Labour Party; and on the right the French National Front and the UK Independence Party. America is no different.

Mr Trump's biggest fans are the most pessimistic Americans, working-class whites. "The country's spiralling downwards, people are not getting pay rises, we're not the superpower we think we are," lamented Todd Winslow, an office-equipment supplier, at a Trump rally in Claremont, New Hampshire. By articulating such fears, Mr Trump has validated them. That is why his supporters love him, whether or not they believe his promises. "He tells us what we all think but are afraid to say," Mr Winslow declared. Others in the crowd liked Mr Trump's success in business, his tough-guy style and the fact that he was not a politician. These qualities were evident in the diatribe that followed.

Ad-libbing as usual, Mr Trump boasted of his "big beautiful brain", suggested dumping Bowe Bergdahl, an American prisoner-of-war released in a hostage swap with the Taliban, from the air over Afghanistan, and, after inviting questions from the crowd, showed familiarity with none of the issues raised. Asked whether he supported equal pay for men and women, he said: "I love equal pay, I mean I have many women, I was very, very far advanced on women…We're going to come up with the right answer."

Bern Brightly

Mr Sanders's crowds are similarly fervent, but younger. They are often dominated by bearded, beaded and disgruntled 18- to 29-year-olds, to whom Mr Sanders promises free education in public universities and relief on college debts. The sheer improbability of his assault on American power—he is old, cranky and wears crumpled suits—is to this group part of his appeal. If the humour of Mr Trump's campaign is WrestleMania burlesque, Mr Sanders's is college rag. "Feel the Bern" is its unofficial slogan. Yet that gentler tone reflects a big difference between America's red and blue insurgencies, which is likely to determine how far they go and how much damage they do their respective parties.

Mr Sanders's supporters want to undo the accommodation with business that the Democrats reached under Bill Clinton. But they do not hate their party: most strongly approve of Mr Obama, who is much closer politically to Mrs Clinton than he is to the Bern. That she is not doing better is largely down to her shortcomings as a candidate. Her well-funded campaign is being run by veterans of Mr Obama's brilliant grass-roots operations and aims to emulate it in seeding and revving up networks of autonomous volunteers; but Mrs Clinton, a continuity candidate when the mood is for change, is not doing much revving. Mr Sanders's campaign, which in 2015 netted over 2.5m donations, resembles the president's more closely.

A scandal concerning Mrs Clinton's foolish use of a private e-mail account while secretary of state has been damaging. It has highlighted her longstanding reputation for being untrustworthy; in a general election, that could hurt her badly. So could the independent run mulled by Michael Bloomberg, a moneybags former-mayor of New York. A free trader who worries about the environment, he would probably take more votes from the left than from the right.

Yet Mrs Clinton, who is at 52% in the polls, is lucky in her opponent. Had Elizabeth Warren, a senator from Massachusetts and a milder version of Mr Sanders, decided to run, she might now be in Jeb! territory. She is lucky in her party's residual discipline. And she is lucky that a series of southern states, where black voters, who tend to like her, matter more, will vote shortly after Iowa and New Hampshire. This will present her with an early opportunity to douse whatever fires Mr Sanders may have started.

For the Republican establishment, none of that good fortune applies. Mr Trump and Mr Cruz are more formidable and the Republican voters who like them more mutinous than their Democratic counterparts. In their shadows, a clutch of more electable candidates, of whom Mr Rubio along with two serving governors, John Kasich of Ohio and Chris Christie of New Jersey, are probably the last serious contenders, have meanwhile struggled to distinguish themselves.

Mr Bush's spluttering campaign has exacerbated the problem. Its fund-raising drew resources from other mainstreamers; Mr Rubio raised a paltry $6m in the third quarter of 2015, a third of the amount raised by Ben Carson, a former neurosurgeon and momentary front-runner. Now it is hurting them even more, with Mr Bush desperately splurging on attack ads against his establishment rivals, especially Mr Rubio. The result is that the Republicans' erstwhile centre ground—the "somewhat conservative" vote that constitutes about 40% of the total and usually decides the party's nomination—is hopelessly split.

The early results may fix that problem. Whichever of the three surviving mainstreamers does best in Iowa and New Hampshire, a "somewhat conservative" state, could swiftly consolidate the establishment's share of the vote and take on the frontrunners. Mr Rubio, who is clever, fresh-faced, Spanish-speaking and almost the only Republican candidate to beat Mrs Clinton in head-to-head polling, has long looked most suitable for that role.

He is expected to top the establishment roster in Iowa. Mr Kasich, who has a good governing record, and Mr Christie, an articulate bruiser, have worked harder in New Hampshire and could beat Mr Rubio in that state. But it would have to be by a decent margin to impress the conservative donors and media eagerly waiting to anoint the next establishment champion. Mr Kasich seems too much of a stick-in-the-mud for this election, Mr Christie too moderate for many Republicans. And Mr Rubio—if he can only survive the early states—would probably do better in later-voting, more moderate states, especially his native Florida. In a protracted contest, that could prove decisive

A three-horse race could even mean that no candidate wins a majority of delegates, which might also argue for Mr Rubio over his mainstream rivals. The candidates would then try to woo each other's delegates at the party's convention in July, something that last happened in 1948. And across the Republican coalition Mr Rubio is a popular second choice.

Yet it is also possible that no candidate of the establishment will do well enough in the early states to rise above the others. Its vote would then remain split. In that case, Mr Trump, if his supporters turn out, or Mr Cruz, whom the early schedule favours, by moving from evangelical Iowa to the southern Bible-belt, could wrap up the nomination while the mainstreamers are stuck squabbling among themselves.

It is bad luck for Republican leaders. But they have earned it, for having long encouraged the sort of polarising invective that Mr Trump and Mr Cruz spout. Mr

Obama's health-care reform is socialist; climate science is a liberal fraud; Democrats are not just wrong but anti-American: such are mainstream Republican verities. Even before Mr Trump doubled down on it, this sort of rabble-rousing had damaged the party, because its leaders never acted commensurately with their rhetoric, making them seem weak or insincere.

An Uninviting Establishment

Mistrusted by voters, the establishment candidates have found it increasingly hard to offer a positive alternative to Mr Trump's miserabilism. To some degree, all have emulated it. Invited to condemn Mr Trump's promised ban on Muslims, at a televised debate on January 14th, Mr Rubio instead praised his rival for having "tapped into some of that anger that's out there". Yet if the Republican pitch is about anger, not optimism, Mr Trump should win, because he is best at that. This has probably already made it harder for the party to win a general election; before Mr Rubio could woo many Hispanics, he would have some explaining to do. Naturally, his capitulation to Mr Trump hasn't won him any favour with the front-runner, either. After Mr Rubio, who is of average height, was recently pictured wearing Cuban heels, Mr Trump commented: "I don't know, they're big heels. They're big heels. I mean those heels were really up there... I just hope it works out fine for him."

It still might. But if Mr Trump or Mr Cruz takes Iowa and New Hampshire, the establishment will start to fear the worst. Some Republican grandees are already seeking to build bridges with Mr Trump—including Bob Dole, a former presidential candidate, in a recent article in the *New York Times*—on the basis that even a narcissistic bully is less awful than Mr Cruz. That is a startling admission of weakness, before any vote has been cast. Yet the leadership's usual means of influence—money and endorsements—have proved strikingly ineffective in this strange contest.

Mr Trump has spent less than any other leading candidate; his campaign has received more television news coverage than all his rivals combined. Neither of the front-runners has been endorsed by any serving Republican governor or senator. Their strength is from a different source. "We're Not Gonna Take It" is the shouty rock anthem that concludes Mr Trump's seething rallies. Americans, and the world, have a nail-biting few weeks ahead, wondering what that could mean.

Print Citations

CMS: "Outsiders' Chance." In *The Reference Shelf: Campaign Trends and Election Law*, edited by Betsy Maury, 64-69. Ipswitch, MA: Salem Press, 2016.

MLA: "Outsiders' Chance." *The Reference Shelf: Campaign Trends and Election Law*. Ed. Betsy Maury. Ipswitch: Salem Press, 2016. 64-69. Print.

APA: The Economist. (2016). Outsiders' chance. In Betsy Maury (Ed.), *The reference shelf: Campaign trends and election law* (pp. 64-69). Ipswitch, MA: Salem. (Original work published 2016)

Class, Trump, and the Election

By Victor David Hanson
National Review, May 31, 2016

If the "high IQs" of the establishment have let America down, where is a voter to turn?

Donald Trump seems to have offended almost every possible identity group. But the New York billionaire still also seems to appeal to the working classes (in part no doubt precisely because he has offended so many special-interest factions; in part because he was seen in the primaries as an outsider using his own money; in part because he seems a crude man of action who dislikes most of those of whom Middle America is tired). At this point, his best hope in November, to the extent such a hope exists, rests on turning 2016 into a referendum on class and a collective national interest that transcends race and gender— and on emphasizing the sad fact that America works now mostly for an elite, best epitomized by Clinton, Inc.

We should not underestimate the opportunities for approaching traditional issues from radically different perspectives. The National Rifle Association is running the most effective ads in its history, hitting elites who wish to curtail gun ownership on the part of those who are not afforded the security blankets of the wealthy. Why should not an inner-city resident wish to buy a legal weapon, when armed security guards patrol America's far safer gated communities? For most of the Clintons' adult lives, they have been accompanied by men and women with concealed weapons to ensure their safety— on the premise that firearms, not mace, not Tasers, not knives or clubs, alone would ultimately keep the two safe.

Fracking provides jobs and cheaper fuel; the elites of the Democratic party care about neither. Indeed, Barack Obama and Energy Secretary Steven Chu proclaimed their desire for spiraling gas and electricity prices. Boutique environmentalism is a losing issue for the Democrats. The very wealthy can afford to be more concerned for a three-inch smelt than for irrigation water that will ensure that there are jobs for tractor drivers and affordable food for the less-well-off. When Hillary Clinton talks about putting miners out of work, she's talking about people she has no desire to see unless she needs their votes.

Illegal immigration is another issue that offers class leverage. Middle-class Mexican-Americans cannot afford to put their kids in private schools when local districts are overwhelmed with non-English-speaking students. Trying to provide parity for 11 million or more illegal aliens naturally comes at the expense of fewer safety-net protections for minority citizens, just as driving down wages is good for the employer but hardly for the citizen who competes with illegal aliens for entry-level jobs. And what about lower-middle-class communities that are overwhelmed with foreign nationals whose backgrounds were never checked.

Outsourcing jobs affects predominantly the lower middle classes; no pundit, D.C. staffer, or New York lawyer is replaced by some cheaper English-speaker from the Punjab. Obamacare follows the same pattern. Elites who praise it to the skies either have the money or the Cadillac plans to navigate around it. I doubt that Rahm Emanuel and his brothers queue up at a surgery center, hoping to win five minutes with an ophthalmologist who now treats 70 patients a day to survive under Obamacare.

Donald Trump is unlikely to defeat Hillary Clinton unless he, an insider billionaire with little political knowledge, can appeal to the concerns of millions that cut across the Democratic firewalls of race and class. If a mom in Orange County thinks that Benghazi did make a difference and ISIS is a murderous Islamic terrorist enterprise, if an African-American youth believes that someone should try to hire him on a building site in preference to an illegal alien, and if a cosmetician believes that one violation of a federal law will land her in jail while many violations may land Hillary in the White House, then class trumps identity politics.

The entire establishments of both political parties are losing the illusion that they are clothed. The Clintons and their appendages famously became rich by monetizing their public positions through shakedowns of the international corporate set, under the patina of egalitarian progressivism. No one in the media

> **The entire establishments of both political parties are losing the illusion that they are clothed.**

for a decade has said a word about their criminal enterprise; commentators were more likely to donate to the Clinton Foundation as a sort of business investment or indemnity insurance. And how in the world does a middle-class ex-teacher and congressman with a 20-year tenure like Dennis Hastert end up with millions to pay hush money to the victims of his alleged pederastic assaults? How did a Harry Reid become a Nevada multimillionaire? How many middle-class workers' annual incomes does Hillary Clinton trump in a single 20-minute Wall Street speech, whose content is vacuous? Where, then, is Occupy Wall Street?

Why the NeverTrump movement has so far failed is in part a matter of class as well, defined not so much in terms of cash, as of influence, education, and lifestyle. In 2008 it was gauche to bring up the vicious racist Rev. Jeremiah Wright, whose trite cast-off slogan "audacity of hope" inspired the title of Barack Obama's campaign primer. In 2012, it would have apparently been rude for Mitt Romney to have fired back at Candy Crowley, "How dare you hijack a presidential debate!" Yes, Trump may be creepy, but the reluctance to challenge our present naked emperors is just as creepy. Is the so-called establishment going to warn us that Trump would be capable of running up $10 trillion in debt, socializing our medical system, unleashing the IRS and EPA on perceived enemies, and weakening friends and empowering enemies abroad, as he offers the world historically challenged pop riffs on Islam, Hiroshima, and global geography? For each take-down of NeverTrump, can we at least have commensurate analysis of how and why a monstrosity like the Clinton cash operation was allowed to thrive without audit; or how it is that the secretary of state and her minions snubbed the law and behaved in a fashion that would have put any other federal employees in jail; or how it is that 155 years after the start of the Civil War over 300 cities, counties, and states have declared federal law null and void in their jurisdictions— and with complete impunity?

Turn on an evening cable show and ask which interviewer is married to which anchor on another channel, or which of the pundits are former politicos, or how many in the White House worked for Big News or are married or related to someone who does. How many pundits were advisers to political candidates or related to someone who was? How does Ben Rhodes do an interview on *CBS News* or George Stephanopoulos interview Hillary Clinton or a writer expound on the primaries when he is also an adviser to a particular campaign? The problem is not just that all this is incestuous or unethical, but that it blinds a tiny elite to what millions of quite different Americans value and experience.

Charles Murray recently wrote in anger, addressing those who would vote for Trump because "Hillary is even worse": "I know that I am unlikely to persuade any of my fellow Establishmentarians to change their minds. But I cannot end without urging you to resist that sin to which people with high IQs (which most of you have) are unusually prone: Using your intellectual powers to convince yourself of something despite the evidence plainly before you. Just watch and listen to the man. Don't concoct elaborate rationalizations. Just watch and listen."

I wish that the high IQs of the establishment class had taken Murray's sage advice eight years ago and just listened to what Obama had said in denigration of the Pennsylvania working classes or the "typical white person" grandmother who raised him; or to his pseudo-macho references to guns and knives, and "get in their face"; or to the hokey promises to lower global temperatures and stop the seas from rising; and all the other *Vero possumus* tripe. Or that they had used their presumably formidable mental powers to review Obama's public record as a state legislator and a U.S. senator— which presaged everything from Obamacare and the unconstitutional undermining of federal law to the apology tours and the near-destruction of 70 years of bipartisan foreign policy. What was the IQ of the presidential historian who declared Obama the smartest man ever to be elevated to the White House?

Murray has a point that Trump's crudity and buffoonery should be taken seriously, but when he says establishmentarians have "high IQs," what exactly does he mean? Did a high IQ prevent an infatuated David Brooks (whom he quotes approvingly) from fathoming presidential success as if he were a sartorial seancer, from the crease of Senator Obama's pants leg? What was the IQ of the presidential historian who declared Obama the smartest man ever to be elevated to the White House? Or the *Newsweek* editor who envisioned an apotheosized Obama? Or the MSNBC host who motor-mouthed about the tingle in his leg at the sound of an Obama speech? Or, yes, the conservative policy analyst (and self-confessed "starry-eyed

Obama groupie") who wrote approvingly ("flat-out plain brilliant") of the Obama race speech in March 2008, in which Obama revealed to the world that his own grandmother— the sole steady working breadwinner of Obama's extended family, whose labors sent him to prep school— was a supposedly "typical white person" in her prejudices, while he further contextualized the abject racism and anti-Semitism of the Rev. Jeremiah Wright— a speech renounced by Obama himself when Wright later felt empowered to double down on his racism. Or perhaps the conservative wit who once wrote that Obama has a "first-class temperament and a first-class intellect," and that he is the rare politician who "writes his own books," which were "first rate"?

Establishmentarian high IQs? The point is not to castigate past poor judgment, but to offer New Testament reminders about hubris and the casting of first stones— and why hoi polloi are skeptical of their supposed intellectual betters.

So how did a blond comb-over real-estate dealer destroy an impressive and decent Republican field and find himself near dead even with Hillary Clinton— to the complete astonishment, and later fury, of the Washington establishment?

Simply because lots of people have become exhausted by political and media elites who have thought very highly of themselves— but on what grounds it has become increasingly impossible to figure out.

Print Citations

CMS: Hanson, Victor David. "Class, Trump, and the Election." In *The Reference Shelf: Campaign Trends and Election Law*, edited by Betsy Maury, 70-73. Ipswitch, MA: Salem Press, 2016.

MLA: Hanson, Victor David. "Class, Trump, and the Election." *The Reference Shelf: Campaign Trends and Election Law*. Ed. Betsy Maury. Ipswitch: Salem Press, 2016. 70-73. Print.

APA: Hanson, V.D. (2016). Class, Trump, and the election. In Betsy Maury (Ed.), *The reference shelf: Campaign trends and election law* (pp. 70-73). Ipswitch, MA: Salem. (Original work published 2016)

Race, Class, and the 2016 Election

By Keeanga-Yamahtta Taylor
Tikkun, March 8, 2016

The 2016 presidential election will be the first to unfold against the backdrop of the national Black Lives Matter movement. Even as the movement remains most active in local campaigns and continues to have a fractured national character, its imprint is all over the Democratic Party's primary process. This is, of course, of little consequence to the Republican Party, but matters greatly in the Democratic Party race where the two leading candidates for the party's nomination—for Secretary of State Hillary Clinton and Vermont Senator Bernie Sanders—attempt to position themselves as heirs to Barack Obama's historically high Black voter turnout in 2008 and 2012.

From the earliest moments of the 2016 campaign season, Democratic Party candidates have been racing to keep up with the movement. For example, Clinton reluctantly declared in a public setting "black lives matter," in December of 2014 as Black protests erupted nationally after the non-indictment of Darren Wilson and Daniel Pantaleo, the officer who choked Eric Garner to death.

Those protests boiled over into the spring, fueled by the brutal murder of Walter Scott in South Carolina by officer Michael Slaeger that was captured on video. Indeed, the frustrations with perceptions of police lawlessness erupted into open rebellion in Baltimore, Maryland, in April when young Freddie Gray died of injuries sustained while in police custody. The struggle in Baltimore not only applied pressure on sitting politicians to reign in the police, but it also pressured those candidates vying for the Democratic Party's nomination for president.

Clinton used the anxious atmosphere in the aftermath of Baltimore to speak more broadly about police violence in American cities. She said "Walter Scott shot in the back in Charleston, South Carolina, unarmed, in debt, terrified of spending any more time in jail for child support payments he couldn't afford. Tamir Rice shot in a park in Cleveland, Ohio, unarmed and just 12 years old. Eric Garner, choked to death after being stopped for selling cigarettes on the streets of our city. And now Freddie Gray, his spine nearly severed while in police custody… Not only as a mother and a grandmother, but as a citizen, a human being, my heart breaks for these young men and their families… We have to come to terms with some hard truths about race and justice in America."

Finally, Clinton declared, "it's time we end the era of mass incarceration… We have allowed our criminal justice system to get out of balance. And these recent tragedies should galvanize us to come together as a nation to find our balance again."

Bernie Sanders, who jumped in the race after Clinton, understood that in order to have a chance at the Party's nomination, he would have to cut into Clinton's considerable support among Blacks and Latinos. Sanders later traveled to the West Baltimore neighborhood where Freddie Gray was picked up by police and remarked, "Anyone who took the walk that we took around this neighborhood would not think you are in a wealthy nation," Sanders said. "You would think you are in a third world country."

The Black Lives Matter movement has pulled Black suffering and oppression from the margins of US society right into the center of American politics in the midst of a presidential election year.

A section of movement activists initiated protests directed at Democratic Party candidates hoping to motivate a greater focus on racism, poverty and injustice in their political programs. #BlackLivesMatters activists, including founder Patrisse Cullors, stormed high profile events of Bernie Sanders and Clinton, enduring insults as a result, but the heat generated by the protests certainly forced Clinton and Sanders to adjust or even create "racial justice" platforms to stay relevant to the developing Black movement.

The immediate results were multiple meetings between well-known activists in the movement and the campaigns of Clinton and Sanders. The focus on racial politics has been a crucial aspect of the broader Democratic Party agenda to keep Black voters engaged in the political process this year especially.

In 2008 and 2012, African Americans voted in historically high numbers for Barack Obama and were decisive in his winning the presidency. There is concern that the absence of Obama on the ticket will depress Black voter turnout, jeopardizing the Democrats' goal of retaining the White House and potentially competing for several Congressional seats as well, as the Party also hopes to reclaim the Congress.

With the primary season in full swing, the focus on Black voters has intensified especially as Clinton and Sanders split the first two contests in Iowa and New Hampshire with almost no Black votes at stake. But Clinton's prowess among Black voters was on display as she decisively swept Southern states on the strength of African American support.

There had been some hope within Sanders' campaign that several high profile Black activists, writers, and entertainers' support could cut into Clinton's lead among African American voters. This was especially true when articles began to appear documenting Hillary Clinton's support for law-and-order and anti-social welfare policies during her husband, Bill Clinton's, tenure in the 1990s.

But none of it appeared to have any impact on Black support for Clinton. The raging question in the days and weeks since has been on the meaning of Black electoral support for the Clinton campaign. In some ways, it is not very difficult to understand. There are three primary reasons for Clinton's dominance among Black voters that begins with her close relationship with the Black political establishment. The political wing of the Congressional Black Caucus (CBC) came out early in support of Clinton for president. The CBC, of course, had been a close and reliable ally of Bill Clinton in the 1990s—backing even his most regressive policies like the 1994 Crime Bill in order to maintain political access to the Clinton White House. The CBC has become even more conservative and politically cautious accepting donations from Walmart and the Koch brothers in fundraising ventures. Nevertheless, their championing of Clinton while admonishing Sanders has been influential among a significant layer of Black voters.

The CBC's support has been important but so has Clinton's own ability to clearly articulate her vision of a Black agenda. In a high profile speech made in central Harlem in New York City, Clinton pledged that ending "systemic racism" would be the "centerpiece" of her presidential administration. She also unveiled a vague, but actual, multi-billion dollar plan that she described as key to "revitalizing economically" urban and rural Black enclaves. The focus on Black voters is a sharp departure from Obama who could not or would not commit to a specific plan to address Black poverty and inequality. In the

> **The Black Lives Matter movement has pulled Black suffering and oppression from the margins of US society right into the center of American politics in the midst of a presidential election year.**

run-up to the 2012 Presidential election, Obama reminded voters that he was not the president of Black America. Clinton, however, is in need of a robust Black voter turnout and has had to actively solicit the Black vote to compensate for the lack of excitement in the coming election. There is no reason to believe that Clinton will actually follow through on any of her promises, given the dysfunction of the US Congress and that much of her program does not actually address the racial discrimination that is the key to Black inequality and oppression in the US. Instead, Clinton is focused on job training and other "opportunity" centered programs that do not really address the changing political economy of metropolitan areas across the country where Blacks are concentrated. Nevertheless, Clinton has clearly tried to articulate an agenda to appeal to Black voters.

Sanders has a campaign platform that should appeal widely to Black voters, including his opposition to the death penalty, his support for a $15 minimum wage, universal healthcare, and free public college tuition. Sanders, who hails from the lily white state of Vermont and whose tenure in the Senate has been as an Independent, has not had to build political relationships with the CBC or other Black political operatives. Thus, he is not very well known among Black voters. In South Carolina exit polls, familiarity with the candidate and experience was rated significantly higher than "electability" in the November election. Even still, Sanders did well among Black voters under thirty which indicates that if Sanders had more time, and had not endured a virtual media blackout until the Iowa caucuses he may have won even more Black voters to his campaign. Despite Sanders growing appeal among some Black voters, it is difficult to build the reputation and connections to Black political and civic organizations that are key to turning voters out in a matter of weeks and months compared to the twenty-five year history of the Clinton political machine.

Finally, the horror show of the Republican Party primary is compelling reason enough for some to vote for what is considered the sure bet of Hillary Clinton against whomever emerges as the Republican nominee. In most election cycles there are withering arguments to defeat the Republican nominee as the greater evil, but this year the pressure is even more intense. This is not the typical racism and xenophobia of most Republican Party contests, but the rise of Donald Trump as a leading figure among Republicans has generated legitimate concern. Trump appears to adhere to his own rules, ignoring the racial codes and innuendo that have been the norm in American politics since the end of the Civil Rights era of the 1960s. Trump calls for the deportation of undocumented immigrants, the torture of Muslims, and has played coy with his welcoming of white supremacists around the fringes of his campaign. Clinton and the Democratic Party will be relying on the fear of a Trump presidency to motivate Black voters in the fall election.

Given the epic crisis in legitimacy facing the Republican Party, the Democrats should have no problem in the general election. But the lingering fear remains that without a significant turnout of the Democratic Party base, including Black voters, the Democrats may not have as easy a time as polls indicate both Clinton and Sanders would have in a head-to-head contest against Trump. While the media has been breathlessly reporting on their perceptions of the deep wells of political support for Clinton in Black communities, especially in the South, what has been less reported on is the significant drop in the number of Democrats, including Black Democrats, voting in the primaries this year compared to 2008.

For example, across the South where Clinton dominated Sanders in the primary votes, Democratic voter turnout was, in some cases, dramatically lower than it had been in 2008. In Texas and Tennessee there were 50 percent and 40 percent fewer voters, respectively. In Arkansas, Alabama, and Georgia voter turnout was down between a quarter and a third. This dramatic decrease in voter turnout also includes the much sought after Black vote. South Carolina, which many mark as a turning point for Clinton's campaign, saw a 40 percent decrease in Black voter turnout.

For all of the discussion of the Clinton machine, politically she has not been able to generate the interest or enthusiasm of Obama in 2008. Unlike Obama, Clinton has been forced to curtail expectations raised by the Sanders campaign. Where Obama's campaign was able to activate new layers of Black voters on the promise of "hope" and "change," Hillary has looked to temper expectations by contrasting her candidacy to Sanders who she accuses of "over promising" things like universal healthcare and ending tuition at public universities. Many of those millenials activated by the promise of the Obama administration and then dejected by the sclerosis of his administration went on to join the Occupy struggle against economic inequality and later the Black Lives Matter movement. Clinton's main slogan "breaking down barriers" hardly ignites the same kind of passion and excitement witnessed in 2008—especially when some African Americans believe that Clinton and her husband were responsible for perpetuating many of those barriers when doing so seemed politically opportune in the 1990s.

One can imagine that there is a formidable amount of skepticism about reentering electoral politics with the same rigor that swept many up into the 2008 Obama campaign. If the election of an African American president, swept into office by the promises of fundamental change, could produce such small and, at times, imperceptible changes in the lives of ordinary Black people, then it would be hard to find excitement in a Clinton or Sanders campaign this time around. This may explain how even in Sanders' home state of Vermont, the under 30 vote in the primary was almost 40 percent lower than it had been in 2008. Sanders has tried to tap into hope, but for all of the enthusiasm he has garnered, the Obama experience has surely left an untold number of people disillusioned with the entire political process.

The feeling of exasperation with formal politics is not only fueled by the utter dysfunction of the US Congress—from the refusal of the Senate to even entertain any Obama nominee for the US Supreme Court to the annual ritual of House Republicans voting to overturn Obama's healthcare plan—but it is bolstered by the persistence of racism. If the Obama presidency was intended to usher in a new era of postracial relief, the Republican primaries, the rise of the Trump mob, and the ongoing epidemic of unchecked police violence and murder exposes the limits of electoral politics in changing the fundamental nature of American society.

This exasperation is not necessarily political apathy but it can represent an opportunity for the political left to continue to build the kind of activist alternative to the stasis of the Democratic Party. Sanders has certainly tapped into the sentiment that something more substantive than simply pulling the lever for this or that candidate in the coming election is the most important use of people's time. Instead, he has called for a political revolution by which he means the massive participation of the public in demonstrations and political action intended to get elected officials to act more in the interest of the public. This, of course, is a great idea, but the notion that such a "revolution" can happen under the leadership of the Democratic Party is deeply mistaken.

In the last five years, we have seen the insurgent Occupy movement and Black Lives Matter transform the politics and discussion of economic and racial inequality in the United States. Both movements worked to uncover the hypocrisy and hollowness of American democracy and both demonstrated direct action, pickets, and protest as the most effective means of social change in contrast to voting for millionaire politicians. The Occupy movement would go on to suffer police repression and physical attack but the issues uncovered have not gone away. Instead, as the anemic economic recovery sputters along, there has been a deepening of the disparity between the rich and the rest of us in the US. Black Lives Matter continues along with police murder and violence. The movement has done much to expose the injustice of American policing but it has also been confronted with the difficulty of transforming the systems of the criminal justice system that have their entire origins and history rooted in the oppression of Black and Brown people in the

United States. This is difficult to undo through demonstrations alone. The movement can, however, provide a home and a direction to the hundreds of thousands of voters who have expressed little interest in the pending contest for president but remain concerned about the state of the world. The last eighteen months of protest and movement building have shown to be vastly more effective in exposing the issues entangled with police violence than the empty promises of elected officials.

Print Citations

CMS: Taylor, Keeanga-Yamahtta. "Race, Class, and the 2016 Election." In *The Reference Shelf: Campaign Trends and Election Law*, edited by Betsy Maury, 74-79. Ipswitch, MA: Salem Press, 2016.

MLA: Taylor, Keeanga-Yamahtta. "Race, Class, and the 2016 Election." *The Reference Shelf: Campaign Trends and Election Law*. Ed. Betsy Maury. Ipswitch: Salem Press, 2016. 74-79. Print.

APA: Taylor, K.Y. (2016). Race, class, and the 2016 election. In Betsy Maury (Ed.), *The reference shelf: Campaign trends and election law* (pp. 74-79). Ipswitch, MA: Salem. (Original work published 2016)

The Great Republican Revolt

By David Frum
The Atlantic, January/February 2016

The angriest and most pessimistic people in America aren't the hipster protesters who flitted in and out of Occupy Wall Street. They aren't the hashtavists of #BlackLivesMatter. They aren't the remnants of the American labor movement or the savvy young dreamers who confront politicians with their American accents and un-American legal status.

The angriest and most pessimistic people in America are the people we used to call Middle Americans. Middle-class and middle-aged; not rich and not poor; people who are irked when asked to press 1 for English, and who wonder how white male became an accusation rather than a description.

You can measure their pessimism in polls that ask about their expectations for their lives—and for those of their children. On both counts, whites without a college degree express the bleakest view. You can see the effects of their despair in the new statistics describing horrifying rates of suicide and substance-abuse fatality among this same group, in middle age.

White Middle Americans express heavy mistrust of every institution in American society: not only government, but corporations, unions, even the political party they typically vote for—the Republican Party of Romney, Ryan, and McConnell, which they despise as a sad crew of weaklings and sellouts. They are pissed off. And when Donald Trump came along, they were the people who told the pollsters, "That's my guy."

They aren't necessarily superconservative. They often don't think in ideological terms at all. But they do strongly feel that life in this country used to be better for people like them—and they want that older country back.

You hear from people like them in many other democratic countries too. Across Europe, populist parties are delivering a message that combines defense of the welfare state with skepticism about immigration; that denounces the corruption of parliamentary democracy and also the risks of global capitalism. Some of these parties have a leftish flavor, like Italy's Five Star Movement. Some are rooted to the right of center, like the U.K. Independence Party. Some descend from neofascists, like France's National Front. Others trace their DNA to Communist parties, like Slovakia's governing Direction–Social Democracy.

These populists seek to defend what the French call "acquired rights"—health care, pensions, and other programs that benefit older people—against bankers and technocrats who endlessly demand austerity; against migrants who make new claims and challenge accustomed ways; against a globalized market that depresses wages and benefits. In the United States, they lean Republican because they fear the Democrats want to take from them and redistribute to Americans who are newer, poorer, and in their view less deserving—to "spread the wealth around," in candidate Barack Obama's words to "Joe the Plumber" back in 2008. Yet they have come to fear more and more strongly that their party does not have their best interests at heart.

Against all evidence, GOP donors interpreted the Tea Party as a movement in favor of the agenda of the *Wall Street Journal* editorial page.

A majority of Republicans worry that corporations and the wealthy exert too much power. Their party leaders work to ensure that these same groups can exert even more. Mainstream Republicans were quite at ease with tax increases on households earning more than $250,000 in the aftermath of the Great Recession and the subsequent stimulus. Their congressional representatives had the opposite priorities. In 2008, many Republican primary voters had agreed with former Arkansas Governor Mike Huckabee, who wanted "their next president to remind them of the guy they work with, not the guy who laid them off." But those Republicans did not count for much once the primaries ended, and normal politics resumed between the multicultural Democrats and a plutocratic GOP.

This year, they are counting for more. Their rebellion against the power of organized money has upended American politics in ways that may reverberate for a long time. To understand what may come next, we must first review the recent past.

Not so long ago, many observers worried that Americans had lost interest in politics. In his famous book *Bowling Alone*, published in 2000, the social scientist Robert Putnam bemoaned the collapse in American political participation during the second half of the 20th century. Putnam suggested that this trend would continue as the World War II generation gave way to disengaged Gen Xers.

But even as Putnam's book went into paperback, that notion was falling behind the times. In the 1996 presidential election, voter turnout had tumbled to the lowest level since the 1920s, less than 52 percent. Turnout rose slightly in November 2000. Then, suddenly: overdrive. In the presidential elections of 2004 and 2008, voter turnout spiked to levels not seen since before the voting age was lowered to 18, and in 2012 it dipped only a little. Voters were excited by a hailstorm of divisive events: the dot-com bust, the Bush-versus-Gore recount, the 9/11 terrorist attacks, the Iraq War, the financial crisis, the bailouts and stimulus, and the Affordable Care Act.

Putnam was right that Americans were turning away from traditional sources of information. But that was because they were turning to new ones: first cable news channels and partisan political documentaries; then blogs and news aggregators like the *Drudge Report* and *The Huffington Post*; after that, and most decisively, social media.

Politics was becoming more central to Americans' identities in the 21st century than it ever was in the 20th. Would you be upset if your child married a supporter of a different party from your own? In 1960, only 5 percent of Americans said yes. In 2010, a third of Democrats and half of Republicans did. Political identity has become so central because it has come to overlap with so many other aspects of identity: race, religion, lifestyle. In 1960, I wouldn't have learned much about your politics if you told me that you hunted. Today, that hobby strongly suggests Republican loyalty. Unmarried? In 1960, that indicated little. Today, it predicts that you're a Democrat, especially if you're also a woman.

Meanwhile, the dividing line that used to be the most crucial of them all—class—has increasingly become a division within the parties, not between them. Since 1984, nearly every Democratic presidential-primary race has ended as a contest between a "wine track" candidate who appealed to professionals (Gary Hart, Michael Dukakis, Paul Tsongas, Bill Bradley, and Barack Obama) and a "beer track" candidate who mobilized the remains of the old industrial working class (Walter Mondale, Dick Gephardt, Bill Clinton, Al Gore, and Hillary Clinton). The Republicans have their equivalent in the battles between "Wall Street" and "Main Street" candidates. Until this decade, however, both parties—and especially the historically more cohesive Republicans—managed to keep sufficient class peace to preserve party unity.

Not anymore, at least not for the Republicans.

The Great Recession ended in the summer of 2009. Since then, the U.S. economy has been growing, but most incomes have not grown comparably. In 2014, real median household income remained almost $4,000 below the pre-recession level, and well below the level in 1999. The country has recovered from the worst economic disaster since the Great Depression. Most of its people have not. Many Republicans haven't shared in the recovery and continued upward flight of their more affluent fellow partisans.

It was these pessimistic Republicans who powered the Tea Party movement of 2009 and 2010. They were not, as a rule, libertarians looking for an ultraminimal government. The closest study we have of the beliefs of Tea Party supporters, led by Theda Skocpol, a Harvard political scientist, found that "Tea Partiers judge entitlement programs not in terms of abstract free-market orthodoxy, but according to the perceived deservingness of recipients. The distinction between 'workers' and 'people who don't work' is fundamental to Tea Party ideology."

It's uncertain whether any Tea Partier ever really carried a placard that read KEEP YOUR GOVERNMENT HANDS OFF MY MEDICARE. But if so, that person wasn't spouting gibberish. The Obama administration had laid hands on Medicare. It hoped to squeeze $500 billion out of the program from 2010 to 2020 to finance health insurance for the uninsured. You didn't have to look up the figures to have a sense that many of the uninsured were noncitizens (20 percent), or that even more were foreign-born (27 percent). In the Tea Party's angry town-hall meetings, this issue resonated perhaps more loudly than any other—the ultimate example of redistribution from a deserving "us" to an undeserving "them."

Yet even as the Republican Main Street protested Obamacare, it rejected the hardening ideological orthodoxy of Republican donors and elected officials. A substantial minority of Republicans—almost 30 percent—said they would welcome "heavy" taxes on the wealthy, according to Gallup. Within the party that made Paul Ryan's entitlement-slashing budget plan a centerpiece of policy, only 21 percent favored cuts in Medicare and only 17 percent wanted to see spending on Social Security reduced, according to Pew. Less than a third of ordinary Republicans supported a pathway to citizenship for illegal immigrants (again according to Pew); a majority, by contrast, favored stepped-up deportation.

As a class, big Republican donors could not see any of this, or would not. So neither did the politicians who depend upon them. Against all evidence, both groups interpreted the Tea Party as a mass movement in favor of the agenda of the *Wall Street Journal* editorial page. One of the more dangerous pleasures of great wealth is that you never have to hear anyone tell you that you are completely wrong.

It was Mitt Romney who got the first post–Tea Party presidential nomination, and he ran on a platform of Conservatism Classic: tax cuts, budget cuts, deregulation, free trade—all lightly seasoned with some concessions to the base regarding stricter immigration enforcement. The rank and file did not like it. But they could not stop it. The base kept elevating "not Romneys" into first place, and each rapidly failed or fizzled; Romney, supported by a cumulative total of $139 million in primary funds by March 2012, trundled on.

Romney ultimately lost the presidential election, of course, to the surprise and dismay of a party elite confident of victory until the very end. One might have expected this shock to force a rethink. The Republicans had now lost four out of the past six presidential elections. Another election had been won only in the Electoral College, despite the loss of the popular vote. Even their best showing, 50.7 percent of the vote in 2004, represented the closest escape of any incumbent president who won reelection since the first recorded popular vote.

> **By mid-2015, a majority of self-identified Republicans disapproved of their party's congressional leadership—an intensity of disapproval never seen by the Republican majority of the 1990s nor by Democrats during their time in the majority after the 2006 midterm elections.**

And yet, within hours of Romney's defeat, Republican donors, talkers, and officials converged on the maximally self-exculpating explanation. The problem had not been the plan to phase out Medicare for people younger than 55. Or the lack of ideas about how to raise wages. Or the commitment to ending health-insurance coverage for millions of working-age Americans. Or the anthems to wealth creation and entrepreneurship in a country increasingly skeptical of both. No, the problem was the one element of Romney's message they had never liked anyway: immigration enforcement.

Maybe it was not a good idea for Jeb Bush's allies to describe his fund-raising strategy as "shock and awe."

Owners of capital assets, employers of low-skill laborers, and highly compensated professionals tend to benefit economically from the arrival of immigrants. They are better positioned to enjoy the attractive cultural and social results of migration (more-interesting food!) and to protect themselves against the burdensome impacts (surges in non-English-proficient pupils in public schools). A pro-immigration policy shift was one more assertion of class interest in a party program already brimful of them.

Nobody expressed the party elites' consensus view more assuredly than Charles Krauthammer. "Ignore the trimmers," he wrote in his first postelection column. "There's no need for radical change. The other party thinks it owns the demographic future—counter that in one stroke by fixing the Latino problem. Do not, however, abandon the party's philosophical anchor … No reinvention when none is needed."

"We've gotta get rid of the immigration issue altogether," Sean Hannity told his radio audience the day after the election. "It's simple for me to fix it. I think you control the border first, you create a pathway for those people that are here, you don't say, 'You gotta go home.' And that is a position that I've evolved on."

A co-owner of Fox News—Krauthammer and Hannity's TV network—agreed: "Must have sweeping, generous immigration reform," tweeted Rupert Murdoch on November 7, 2012. "It would be inhumane to send those people back, to send 12 million people out of this country," the casino mogul and Republican donor Sheldon Adelson told *The Wall Street Journal* in December of that year. "We've got to find a way, find a route, for those people to get legal citizenship." The Republican National Committee made it all official in a March 2013 postelection report signed by party eminences. The report generally avoided policy recommendations, with a notable exception: "We must embrace and champion comprehensive immigration reform." To advance the cause, Paul Singer, one of the most open-pocketed GOP donors, made a six-figure contribution to the National Immigration Forum that spring.

If all of this sounds like a prescription for a Jeb Bush candidacy for president … well, perhaps that was not an entirely unintended consequence.

Almost as soon as the new Congress convened in 2013, Senate Republicans worked to strike a deal over immigration issues. A bipartisan "Gang of Eight," including Florida's ambitious young Marco Rubio, agreed on a plan that would create a path to citizenship for millions of illegal immigrants and substantially increase legal-immigration limits for both high- and low-skilled workers. Otherwise, the party yielded on nothing and doubled down on everything. No U-turns. No compromises.

The new strategy soon proved a total and utter failure. George W. Bush's tax cuts for high earners expired in 2013, and Republicans could not renew them. The drive to cut the deficit ended in budget sequestration, whose harshest effect fell on the military. The Gang of Eight deal never came to a vote in the House. All the while, Republicans' approval ratings slipped and slid. Instead of holding on to their base and adding Hispanics, Republicans alienated their base in return for no gains at all. By mid-2015, a majority of self-identified Republicans disapproved of their party's congressional leadership—an intensity of disapproval never seen by the Republican majority of the 1990s nor by Democrats during their time in the majority after the 2006 midterm elections.

In fact, disapproval had flared into an outright revolt of the Republican base in the summer of 2014. House Majority Leader Eric Cantor, the No. 2 man in the Republican caucus, had emerged as a leader of the new line on immigration. Up for reelection in Virginia's Seventh District, Cantor was challenged that year by a conservative Christian professor of economics, Dave Brat. During Obama's first term, Tea Party insurgents had toppled incumbents and defeated party favorites in primaries from Delaware to Nevada. Those challenges had ended badly in the general election, for the most part: Tea Party Republicans lost at least five Senate seats that might plausibly have been won. Party leaders believed the lesson had been learned and expected their voters to be more tractable in future elections.

Cantor's loss to Brat jolted House leaders. Immigration reform slipped off their agenda. Marco Rubio repudiated his own deal. But Republican elites outside Congress did not get the message. They rationalized Cantor's defeat as a freak event, the sad consequence of a nationally minded politician's neglect of his district. They continued to fill the coffers of Jeb Bush and, to a lesser extent, Rubio and Scott Walker, all reliable purveyors of Conservatism Classic. Last February, three of the party's most important moneymen—the fast-food executive Andrew Puzder, the health-care investor Mike Fernandez, and the national finance chair of Mitt Romney's 2012 campaign, Spencer Zwick—publicly urged the GOP to push ahead toward more-open immigration. "America should be a destination for hardworking immigrants from all over the world," said Puzder, an advocate of importing more low-skilled laborers to meet the needs of his high-turnover industry. Zwick said that any presidential candidate who wanted to be taken seriously had better "be in a similar place" to Jeb Bush on the immigration issue.

Maybe it was not a good idea for Jeb Bush's allies to describe his fund-raising strategy as "shock and awe." Perhaps the Iraq War reference stirred painful memories, even among Republicans. Still, Bush's fund-raising genuinely inspired awe. In his financial disclosure for the second quarter of 2015, Bush reported raising $11.4 million for his formal campaign and another $103 million for his super PAC. These funds were provided by a relatively small number of very wealthy people. Of Bush's presidential-campaign dollars, only 3 percent arrived in amounts of $200 or less. Almost 82 percent arrived in the maximum increment of $2,700. Nearly 80 percent of Bush's super-PAC take arrived in increments of $25,000 or more; about a quarter of the haul was made up of donations of $1 million or more.

Yet seldom in the history of fund-raising has so much bought so little, so fleetingly. Between December 2014 and September 2015, Jeb Bush plunged from first place in the Republican field to fifth. Between late September and mid-October, he purchased 60 percent of all political spots aired in New Hampshire. That ad barrage pushed his poll numbers in the state from about 9 percent to about 8 percent.

As the governor of Florida, Bush had cut taxes and balanced budgets. He'd challenged unions and championed charter schools. At the same time, Bush passionately supported immigration liberalization. The central event in his life history was his reinvention as an honorary Latino American when he married a Mexican woman, Columba Garnica de Gallo. He spoke Spanish at home. He converted to Catholicism. He sought his fortune with a Cuban American business partner. In his most quotable phrase, he described illegal immigration as an "act of love."

Bush's update of Conservatism Classic had made him a hit with the party's big donors. He had won accolades from Karl Rove ("the deepest thinker on our side") and Arthur Brooks, the president of the American Enterprise Institute ("a top-drawer intellect"). Yet within five weeks of his formal declaration of candidacy on June 15, Bush's campaign had been brutally rejected by the GOP rank and file.

From Jupiter Island, Florida, to Greenwich, Connecticut; from Dallas's Highland Park to Sea Island, Georgia; from Fifth Avenue in Manhattan to California's Newport Beach, the baffled question resounded: What went wrong?

Big-dollar Republican favorites have run into trouble before, of course. Rudy Giuliani imploded in 2007–08; Mitt Romney's 2012 nomination was knocked off course as Republicans worked their way through a series of alternative front-runners: Rick Perry, Herman Cain, Newt Gingrich, and finally Rick Santorum. But Giuliani lost ground to two rivals equally acceptable to the donor elite, or nearly so: Mitt Romney and John McCain. In 2011–12, the longest any of the "not Romneys" remained in first place was six weeks. In both cycles, resistance to the party favorite was concentrated among social and religious conservatives.

The mutiny of the 2016 election cycle has been different. By the fall of 2015, a majority of Republicans favored candidates who had never been elected to anything: Donald Trump, Ben Carson, and Carly Fiorina. Fiorina's campaign was perhaps not so unusual. A former CEO, she appealed to the same business-minded Republicans who might have voted for Romney in 2012. Carson appealed to the same religious conservatives that candidates like Mike Huckabee and Santorum had appealed to in prior presidential cycles. What was new and astonishing was the Trump boom. He jettisoned party orthodoxy on issues ranging from entitlement spending to foreign policy. He scoffed at trade agreements. He said rude things about Sheldon Adelson and the Koch brothers. He reviled the campaign contributions of big donors—himself included!—as open and blatant favor-buying. Trump's surge was a decisive repudiation by millions of Republican voters of the collective wisdom of their party elite.

Trump's grim pessimism didn't resonate with those who'd ridden the S&P 500 giddily upward. But it found an audience all the same.

When Trump first erupted into the Republican race in June, he did so with a message of grim pessimism. "We got $18 trillion in debt. We got nothing but problems ... We're dying. We're dying. We need money ... We have losers. We have people that don't have it. We have people that are morally corrupt. We have people that are selling this country down the drain ... The American dream is dead."

That message did not resonate with those who'd ridden the S&P 500 from less than 900 in 2009 to more than 2,000 in 2015. But it found an audience all the same. Half of Trump's supporters within the GOP had stopped their education at or before high-school graduation, according to the polling firm YouGov. Only 19 percent had a college or postcollege degree. Thirty-eight percent earned less than $50,000. Only 11 percent earned more than $100,000.

Trump Republicans were not ideologically militant. Just 13 percent said they were very conservative; 19 percent described themselves as moderate. Nor were they highly religious by Republican standards.

What set them apart from other Republicans was their economic insecurity and the intensity of their economic nationalism. Sixty-three percent of Trump supporters wished to end birthright citizenship for the children of illegal immigrants born on U.S. soil—a dozen points higher than the norm for all Republicans. More than other Republicans, Trump supporters distrusted Barack Obama as alien and dangerous: Only 21 percent acknowledged that the president was born in the United States, according to an August survey by the Democratic-oriented polling firm PPP. Sixty-six percent believed the president was a Muslim.

Trump promised to protect these voters' pensions from their own party's austerity. "We've got Social Security that's going to be destroyed if somebody like me doesn't bring money into the country. All these other people want to cut the hell out of it. I'm not going to cut it at all; I'm going to bring money in, and we're going to save it."

He promised to protect their children from being drawn into another war in the Middle East, this time in Syria. "If we're going to have World War III," he told *The Washington Post* in October, "it's not going to be over Syria." As for the politicians threatening to shoot down the Russian jets flying missions in Syria, "I won't even call them hawks. I call them the fools."

He promised a campaign independent of the influences of money that had swayed so many Republican races of the past. "I will tell you that our system is broken. I gave to many people. Before this, before two months ago, I was a businessman. I give to everybody. When they call, I give. And you know what? When I need something from them, two years later, three years later, I call them. They are there for me. And that's a broken system."

He promised above all to protect their wages from being undercut by Republican immigration policy.

It cannot last, can it? "The casino does not always win," Stuart Stevens, Mitt Romney's lead strategist during the 2012 campaign, quipped to me in September. "But that's the way to bet." The casino won in 2012, and will very likely win again in 2016.

And yet already, Trump has destroyed one elite-favored presidential candidacy, Scott Walker's, and crippled two others, Jeb Bush's and Chris Christie's. He has thrown into disarray the party's post-2012 comeback strategy, and pulled into the center of national discussion issues and constituencies long relegated to the margins.

Something has changed in American politics since the Great Recession. The old slogans ring hollow. The insurgent candidates are less absurd, the orthodox candidates more vulnerable. The GOP donor elite planned a dynastic restoration in 2016. Instead, it triggered an internal class war.

The contest for the presidency turns on external events as much as—or more than—internal party politics. George W. Bush's team believed that the last-minute revelation of a 1976 drunk-driving arrest cost him the popular vote in the 2000 election. Jimmy Carter blamed his 1980 defeat on the debacle of the attempted rescue of American hostages in Iran. So anything can happen. But that does not mean anything will happen. Barring shocks, presidential elections turn on the fundamentals of economics, demography, and ideology.

The puzzle for the monied leaders of the Republican Party is: What now? And what next after that? None of the options facing the GOP elite is entirely congenial. But there appear to be four paths the elite could follow, for this campaign season and beyond. They lead the party in very different directions.

Option 1: Double Down

The premise of the past few thousand words is that the Republican donor elite failed to impose its preferred candidate on an unwilling base in 2015 for big and important reasons. But maybe that premise is wrong. Maybe Jeb Bush has just been a bad candidate with a radioactive last name. Maybe the same message and platform would have worked fine if espoused by a fresher and livelier candidate. Such is the theory of Marco Rubio's campaign. Or—even if the donor message and platform have troubles—maybe $100 million in negative ads can scorch any potential alternative, enabling the donor-backed candidate to win by default.

And if not Rubio, maybe the core donor message could still work if joined to a true outsider candidacy: Ben Carson's, for example. Carson is often regarded as a protest candidate, but as *The Weekly Standard*'s Fred Barnes enthused back in January 2015: "One thing not in doubt is Carson's conservatism. He's the real deal, an economic, social, and foreign policy conservative." Carson may say wacky things, but he does not say heterodox things.

Yet even if the Republican donor elite can keep control of the party while doubling down, it's doubtful that the tactic can ultimately win presidential elections. The "change nothing but immigration" advice was a self-flattering fantasy from the start. Immigration is not the main reason Republican presidential candidates lose so badly among Latino and Asian American voters, and never was: Latino voters are more likely to list education and health care as issues that are extremely important to them. A majority of Asian Americans are non-Christian and susceptible to exclusion by sectarian religious themes.

So …

Option 2: Tactical Concession

Perhaps some concession to the disgruntled base is needed. That's the theory of the Cruz campaign and—after a course correction—also of the Christie campaign. Instead of 2013's "Conservatism Classic Plus Immigration Liberalization," Cruz and Christie are urging "Conservatism Classic Plus Immigration Enforcement." True, Cruz's carefully selected words on immigration leave open the possibility of guest-worker programs or other pro-employer reforms after a burst of border enforcement. But Cruz and Christie have seen the reaction to Donald Trump's message, and appear to appreciate the need to at least seem to do something to redress the grievances of the Republican base.

Much of the donor elite could likely be convinced that while Jeb Bush's idea of immigration reform would be good to have, it isn't a must-have. Just as the party elite reached a pact on abortion with social conservatives in the 1980s, it could concede the immigration issue to its Main Street base in the 2010s.

The party elites' "change nothing but immigration" advice after Romney's defeat was a self-flattering fantasy from the start.

Yet a narrow focus on immigration populism alone seems insufficient to raise Republican hopes. Trump shrewdly joins his immigration populism to trade populism. On the Democratic side, Bernie Sanders's opposition to open borders is logically connected to his hopes for a Democratic Socialist future: His admired Denmark upholds high labor standards along with some of the world's toughest immigration rules. Severed from a larger agenda, however—as Mitt Romney tried to sever the issue in 2012—immigration populism looks at best like pandering, and at worst like identity politics for white voters. In a society that is and always has been multiethnic and polyglot, any national party must compete more broadly than that.

Which brings us to …

Option 3: True Reform

Admittedly, this may be the most uncongenial thought of them all, but party elites could try to open more ideological space for the economic interests of the middle class. Make peace with universal health-insurance coverage: Mend Obamacare rather than end it. Cut taxes less at the top, and use the money to deliver more benefits to working families in the middle. Devise immigration policy to support wages, not undercut them. Worry more about regulations that artificially transfer wealth upward, and less about regulations that constrain financial speculation. Take seriously issues such as the length of commutes, nursing-home costs, and the anti-competitive practices that inflate college tuition. Remember that Republican voters care more about aligning government with their values of work and family than they care about cutting the size of government as an end in itself. Recognize that the gimmick of mobilizing the base with culture-war outrages stopped working at least a decade ago.

Such a party would cut health-care costs by squeezing providers, not young beneficiaries. It would boost productivity by investing in hard infrastructure—bridges, airports, water-treatment plants. It would restore Dwight Eisenhower to the Republican pantheon alongside Ronald Reagan and emphasize the center in center-right.

To imagine the change is to see how convulsive it would be—and how unlikely. True, center-right conservative parties backed by broad multiethnic coalitions of the middle class have gained and exercised power in other English-speaking countries, even as Republicans lost the presidency in 2008 and 2012. But the most-influential voices in American conservatism reject the experience of their foreign counterparts as weak, unprincipled, and unnecessary. In parliamentary democracy, winning or losing is starkly binary: A party either is in power or is the opposition. In the American system, that binary is much blurrier. Republicans can, of course, exert some control over government as long as they hold any one of the House, Senate, or presidency.

Which brings us finally to …

Option 4: Change the Rules of the Game

"The filibuster used to be bad. Now it's good." So Fred Thompson, the late actor and former Republican senator, jokingly told an audience on a *National Review* cruise shortly after Barack Obama won the presidency for the first time. How partisans feel about process issues is notoriously related to what process would benefit them at any given moment. Liberals loved the interventionist Supreme Court in the 1960s and '70s, hated it in the 1990s and 2000s—and may rotate their opinion again if a President Hillary Clinton can tilt a majority of the Supreme Court their way. It's an old story that may find a new twist if and when Republicans acknowledge that the presidency may be attainable only after they make policy changes that are unacceptable to the party elite.

There are metrics, after all, by which the post-2009 GOP appears to be a supremely successful political party. Recently, Rory Cooper, of the communications firm Purple Strategies, tallied a net gain to the Republicans of 69 seats in the House of Representatives, 13 seats in the Senate, 900-plus seats in state legislatures, and 12 governorships since Obama took office. With that kind of grip on state government, in particular, Republicans are well positioned to write election and voting rules that sustain their hold on the national legislature. The president may be able to grant formerly illegal immigrants the right to work, but he cannot grant them the right to vote. In this light, instead of revising Republican policies to stop future Barack Obamas and Hillary Clintons, maybe it's necessary to revise only the party rules to stop future Donald Trumps from confronting party elites with their own unpopularity.

The inaugural issue of *The Weekly Standard*, the conservative magazine launched in 1995, depicted then–Speaker of the House Newt Gingrich swinging into action, a submachine gun blazing in his left hand, under the headline "Permanent Offense." But that was then. Maybe the more natural condition of conservative parties is permanent defense—and where better to wage a long, grinding defensive campaign than in Congress and the statehouses? Maybe the presidency itself should be regarded as one of those things that is good to have but not a must-have, especially if obtaining it requires uncomfortable change.

What happens to an elite whose followers withdraw their assent? Does it self-examine? Or does it take refuge in denial? Does it change? Or does it try to prevent change? Does it challenge itself to build a new political majority? Or does it seize the opportunities the American political system offers to compact and purposeful minorities? When its old answers fail, will it think anew? Or will it simply repeat louder the dogmas that enthralled supporters in the past? Americans love the crush of competition, the hard-fought struggle, the long-slogging race. But much more than the pundit's "Who will win?," it is these deeper questions from the election of 2016 that will shape the future of American politics.

Print Citations

CMS: Frum, David. "The Great Republican Revolt." In *The Reference Shelf: Campaign Trends and Election Law*, edited by Betsy Maury, 80-91. Ipswitch, MA: Salem Press, 2016.

MLA: Frum, David. "The Great Republican Revolt." *The Reference Shelf: Campaign Trends and Election Law*. Ed. Betsy Maury. Ipswitch: Salem Press, 2016. 80-91. Print.

APA: Frum, D. (2016). The great Republican revolt. In Betsy Maury (Ed.), *The reference shelf: Campaign trends and election law* (pp. 80-91). Ipswitch, MA: Salem. (Original work published 2016)

Trump's America

By Charles Murray

The Wall Street Journal, **February 12, 2016**

If you are dismayed by Trumpism, don't kid yourself that it will fade away if Donald Trump fails to win the Republican nomination. Trumpism is an expression of the legitimate anger that many Americans feel about the course that the country has taken, and its appearance was predictable. It is the endgame of a process that has been going on for a half-century: America's divestment of its historic national identity.

For the eminent political scientist Samuel Huntington, writing in his last book, *Who Are We?* (2004), two components of that national identity stand out. One is our Anglo-Protestant heritage, which has inevitably faded in an America that is now home to many cultural and religious traditions. The other is the very idea of America, something unique to us. As the historian Richard Hofstadter once said, "It has been our fate as a nation not to have ideologies but to be one."

What does this ideology—Huntington called it the "American creed"—consist of? Its three core values may be summarized as egalitarianism, liberty and individualism. From these flow other familiar aspects of the national creed that observers have long identified: equality before the law, equality of opportunity, freedom of speech and association, self-reliance, limited government, free-market economics, decentralized and devolved political authority.

As recently as 1960, the creed was our national consensus. Running that year for the Democratic nomination, candidates like John F. Kennedy, Lyndon B. Johnson and Hubert Humphrey genuinely embraced the creed, differing from Republicans only in how its elements should be realized.

Today, the creed has lost its authority and its substance. What happened? Many of the dynamics of the reversal can be found in developments across the whole of American society: in the emergence of a new upper class and a new lower class, and in the plight of the working class caught in between.

In my 2012 book *Coming Apart*, I discussed these new classes at length. The new upper class consists of the people who shape the country's economy, politics and culture. The new lower class consists of people who have dropped out of some of the most basic institutions of American civic culture, especially work and marriage. Both of these new classes have repudiated the American creed in practice, whatever lip service they may still pay to it. Trumpism is the voice of a beleaguered working class telling us that it too is falling away.

Historically, one of the most widely acknowledged aspects of American exceptionalism was our lack of class consciousness. Even Marx and Engels recognized it. This was egalitarianism American style. Yes, America had rich people and poor people, but that didn't mean that the rich were better than anyone else.

Successful Americans stubbornly refused to accept the mantle of an upper class, typically presenting themselves to their fellow countrymen as regular guys. And they usually were, in the sense that most of them had grown up in modest circumstances, or even in poverty, and carried the habits and standards of their youths into their successful later lives.

America also retained a high degree of social and cultural heterogeneity in its communities. Tocqueville wrote of America in the 1830s as a place where "the more opulent citizens take great care not to stand aloof from the people." That continued well into the 20th century, even in America's elite neighborhoods. In the 1960 census, the median income along Philadelphia's Main Line was just $90,000 in today's dollars. In Boston's Brookline, it was $75,000; on New York's Upper East Side, just $60,000. At a typical dinner party in those neighborhoods, many guests would have had no more than a high-school diploma.

In the years since, the new upper class has evolved a distinctive culture. For a half-century, America's elite universities have drawn the most talented people from all over the country, socialized them and often married them off to each other. Brains have become radically more valuable in the marketplace. In 2016, a dinner party in those same elite neighborhoods consists almost wholly of people with college degrees, even advanced degrees. They are much more uniformly affluent. The current median family incomes for the Main Line, Brookline and the Upper East Side are about $150,000, $151,000 and $203,000, respectively.

And the conversation at that dinner party is likely to be completely unlike the conversations at get-togethers in mainstream America. The members of the new upper class are seldom attracted to the films, TV shows and music that are most popular in mainstream America. They have a distinctive culture in the food they eat, the way they take care of their health, their child-rearing practices, the vacations they take, the books they read, the websites they visit and their taste in beer. You name it, the new upper class has its own way of doing it.

Another characteristic of the new upper class—and something new under the American sun—is their easy acceptance of being members of an upper class and their condescension toward ordinary Americans. Try using "redneck" in a conversation with your highly educated friends and see if it triggers any of the nervousness that accompanies other ethnic slurs. Refer to "flyover country" and consider the implications when no one asks, "What does that mean?" Or I can send you to chat with a friend in Washington, D.C., who bought a weekend place in West Virginia. He will tell you about the contempt for his new neighbors that he has encountered in the elite precincts of the nation's capital.

For its part, mainstream America is fully aware of this condescension and contempt and is understandably irritated by it. American egalitarianism is on its last legs.

While the new upper class was seceding from the mainstream, a new lower class was emerging from within the white working class, and it has played a key role in creating the environment in which Trumpism has flourished.

Work and marriage have been central to American civic culture since the founding, and this held true for the white working class into the 1960s. Almost all of the adult men were working or looking for work, and almost all of them were married.

Then things started to change. For white working-class men in their 30s and 40s—what should be the prime decades for working and raising a family—participation in the labor force dropped from 96% in 1968 to 79% in 2015. Over that same period, the portion of these men who were married dropped from 86% to 52%. (The numbers for nonwhite working-class males show declines as well, though not as steep and not as continuous.)

These are stunning changes, and they are visible across the country. In today's average white working-class neighborhood, about one out of five men in the prime of life isn't even looking for work; they are living off girlfriends, siblings or parents, on disability, or else subsisting on off-the-books or criminal income. Almost half aren't married, with all the collateral social problems that go with large numbers of unattached males.

> **But the central truth of Trumpism as a phenomenon is that the entire American working class has legitimate reasons to be angry at the ruling class.**

In these communities, about half the children are born to unmarried women, with all the problems that go with growing up without fathers, especially for boys. Drugs also have become a major problem, in small towns as well as in urban areas.

Consider how these trends have affected life in working-class communities for everyone, including those who are still playing by the old rules. They find themselves working and raising their families in neighborhoods where the old civic culture is gone—neighborhoods that are no longer friendly or pleasant or even safe.

These major changes in American class structure were taking place alongside another sea change: large-scale ideological defection from the principles of liberty and individualism, two of the pillars of the American creed. This came about in large measure because of the civil rights and feminist movements, both of which began as classic invocations of the creed, rightly demanding that America make good on its ideals for blacks and women.

But the success of both movements soon produced policies that directly contradicted the creed. Affirmative action demanded that people be treated as groups. Equality of outcome trumped equality before the law. Group-based policies continued to multiply, with ever more policies embracing ever more groups.

By the beginning of the 1980s, Democratic elites overwhelmingly subscribed to an ideology in open conflict with liberty and individualism as traditionally understood. This consolidated the Democratic Party's longtime popularity with ethnic minorities, single women and low-income women, but it alienated another key Democratic constituency: the white working class.

White working-class males were the archetypal "Reagan Democrats" in the early 1980s and are often described as the core of support for Mr. Trump. But the grievances of this group are often misunderstood. It is a mistake to suggest that they are lashing out irrationally against people who don't look like themselves. There are certainly elements of racism and xenophobia in Trumpism, as I myself have discovered on Twitter and Facebook after writing critically about Mr. Trump.

But the central truth of Trumpism as a phenomenon is that the entire American working class has legitimate reasons to be angry at the ruling class. During the past half-century of economic growth, virtually none of the rewards have gone to the working class. The economists can supply caveats and refinements to that statement, but the bottom line is stark: The real family income of people in the bottom half of the income distribution hasn't increased since the late 1960s.

During the same half-century, American corporations exported millions of manufacturing jobs, which were among the best-paying working-class jobs. They were and are predominantly men's jobs. In both 1968 and 2015, 70% of manufacturing jobs were held by males.

During the same half-century, the federal government allowed the immigration, legal and illegal, of tens of millions of competitors for the remaining working-class jobs. Apart from agriculture, many of those jobs involve the construction trades or crafts. They too were and are predominantly men's jobs: 77% in 1968 and 84% in 2015.

Economists still argue about the net effect of these events on the American job market. But for someone living in a town where the big company has shut the factory and moved the jobs to China, or for a roofer who has watched a contractor hire illegal immigrants because they are cheaper, anger and frustration are rational.

Add to this the fact that white working-class men are looked down upon by the elites and get little validation in their own communities for being good providers, fathers and spouses—and that life in their communities is falling apart. To top it off, the party they have voted for in recent decades, the Republicans, hasn't done a damn thing to help them. Who wouldn't be angry?

There is nothing conservative about how they want to fix things. They want a now indifferent government to act on their behalf, big time. If Bernie Sanders were passionate about immigration, the rest of his ideology would have a lot more in common with Trumpism than conservatism does.

As a political matter, it is not a problem that Mr. Sanders doesn't share the traditional American meanings of liberty and individualism. Neither does Mr. Trump. Neither, any longer, do many in the white working class. They have joined the other defectors from the American creed.

Who continues to embrace this creed in its entirety? Large portions of the middle class and upper middle class (especially those who run small businesses), many people in the corporate and financial worlds and much of the senior leadership of the Republican Party. They remain principled upholders of the ideals of egalitarianism, liberty and individualism.

And let's not forget moderate Democrats, the spiritual legatees of the New Deal.

They may advocate social democracy, but they are also unhappy about policies that treat Americans as members of groups and staunch in their support of freedom of speech, individual moral responsibility and the kind of egalitarianism that Tocqueville was talking about. They still exist in large numbers, though mostly in the political closet.

But these are fragments of the population, not the national consensus that bound the U.S. together for the first 175 years of the nation's existence. And just as support for the American creed has shrunk, so has its correspondence to daily life. Our vaunted liberty is now constrained by thousands of petty restrictions that touch almost anything we want to do, individualism is routinely ignored in favor of group rights, and we have acquired an arrogant upper class. Operationally as well as ideologically, the American creed is shattered.

Our national identity is not altogether lost. Americans still have a vivid, distinctive national character in the eyes of the world. Historically, America has done a far better job than any other country of socializing people of many different ethnicities into displaying our national character. We will still be identifiably American for some time to come.

There's irony in that. Much of the passion of Trumpism is directed against the threat to America's national identity from an influx of immigrants. But the immigrants I actually encounter, of all ethnicities, typically come across as classically American—cheerful, hardworking, optimistic, ambitious. Keeping our national character seems to be the least of our problems.

Still, even that character is ultimately rooted in the American creed. When faith in that secular religion is held only by fragments of the American people, we will soon be just another nation—a very powerful one, a very rich one, still called the United States of America. But we will have detached ourselves from the bedrock that has made us unique in the history of the world.

Print Citations

CMS: Murray, Charles. "Trump's America." In *The Reference Shelf: Campaign Trends and Election Law*, edited by Betsy Maury, 92-96. Ipswitch, MA: Salem Press, 2016.

MLA: Murray, Charles. "Trump's America." *The Reference Shelf: Campaign Trends and Election Law*. Ed. Betsy Maury. Ipswitch: Salem Press, 2016. 92-96. Print.

APA: Murray, C. (2016). Trump's America. In Betsy Maury (Ed.), *The reference shelf: Campaign trends and election law* (pp. 92-96). Ipswitch, MA: Salem. (Original work published 2016)

Identity Heft: Why the Politics of Race and Gender Are Dominating the 2016 Election

By Jeet Heer

The New Republic, November 18, 2015

Just a year or so ago, the phrase "identity politics" had a musty and arcane air to it, redolent as it was of early 1990s campus battles over issues of gender and racial representation. Yet very quickly and unexpectedly, identity politics has gained a new urgency—not just because of the renewal of campus activism at places like Yale and Mizzou, but even more importantly because national politics has become infused with issues of group definition. In a time when the economy is still struggling to escape the Great Recession and where Middle Eastern turmoil still dominates the headlines, it would be natural to assume that the next presidential election would be about the economics or foreign policy. Yet in both the Republican and Democratic debates, identity politics has increasingly shaped and colored all other topics.

Economics and foreign policy haven't gone away, but they are increasingly being talked about in terms of identity. The debate over accepting Syrian refugees has been a prime example, with Republicans citing not just purported security fears but also playing up the idea that America's supposed Judeo-Christian identity is under threat—as evidenced by Ted Cruz's suggestion that only Christian refugees be admitted. On the left, the strongest argument for accepting refugees is also rooted in a conception of identity—that as a pluralist nation with international moral obligations, the United States has a duty to accept these refugees. Identity is the inescapable prism through which American national politics is now viewed.

Donald Trump has made a hardline stance against undocumented immigrants the central topic of debate on the Republican side. Trump's advocacy of deporting all undocumented immigrants isn't just a matter of economics or even of the supposed criminality he attributes to Mexicans immigrants (who he famously described en masse as "rapists"). Rather, immigration for Trump is fundamentally a matter of national identity: A country that doesn't have absolute control of its borders is for him a non-entity. "We either have a country or we don't have a country," Trump insisted in the fourth GOP debate, hosted by Fox Business. "But we have no choice if we're going to run our country properly and if we're going to be a country."

This issue of national identity is firmly linked with race, which is why Trump hasn't hesitated to draw attention to Jeb Bush's Mexican-born wife or to suggest that Marco Rubio favors amnesty because he is the son of Cuban immigrants. A similar racial cast could be detected in Trump's suggestion that Ben Carson was unfit to be president because of his "pathological" temper—which, as Dara Lind rightly noted on vox.com, carried with it undertones of the "black savage" trope.

But Republican identity politics isn't confined to Trump's savaging of his rivals. It is also taking the form of candidates implicitly arguing that they can present a more congenial image of the party. A large part of the appeal of both Carson and Rubio is that they have inspiring life stories that are proof of the conservative ideal that individual drive and talent can overcome social barriers. Moreover, Carson as a black man and Rubio as a Latino can present a face of the Republican Party that makes it more welcoming to a multiracial America. Part of Carly Fiorina's pitch is also based on identity—on the idea that as a successful female executive, she both offers an alternative model to Hillary Clinton's brand of feminism and helps shield the GOP from "war on women" accusations.

On the Democratic side, the crucial issue isn't who counts as an American but who can best further feminism and civil rights. Much more than in 2008, Hillary Clinton is playing up her status as a path-breaker who would vault a major barrier if elected as the first female president. When challenged in the second Democratic debate by Bernie Sanders about her Wall Street funding, Clinton won avid applause by saying, "I have hundreds of thousands of donors, most of them small. And I'm very proud that for the first time a majority of my donors are women, 60 percent."

Sanders might have wanted to run an old-fashioned bread-and-butter social democratic campaign based on economic issues, but he has become, perhaps inevitably, entangled with issues of identity. As Sanders supporter Kathleen Geier noted in a shrewd article at Salon, there's a feminist divide in the Democratic camp. "There are serious feminist cases to be made for both candidates," Geier writes. "In fact, the feminist divide on the 2016 election reflects a classic feminist dilemma between liberal feminists and socialist feminists, and the politics of representation vs. the politics of redistribution." Unfortunately, this feminist divide often devolves into a battle of competing caricatures, with "Bernie Bros" accused of being know-it-all sexists and feminist Clinton supporters portrayed as (to use Geier's words) "dumb, shallow chicks who care only about dumb, shallow chick stuff."

Beyond the feminist divide, all the Democratic candidates have had to grapple with the challenges of the new civil rights movement and learn to say "black lives matter." The failure of Jim Webb to get on board with this message was one prominent sign that his old-school centrist Democratic politics no longer had a place in the national party.

Why are issues of identity dominating the 2016 campaign? Partly it's a sign of how transformative Barack Obama's presidency has been. As the first African-American president, he has shown that the White House doesn't have to be the preserve of white men. This has both opened politics to a wider array of candidates and also produced a deep anxiety among conservative Americans about the changing demographics of the country. The rise of Donald Trump, who first gained traction as a political figure because of his Birther questioning of Obama's citizenship, has been part and parcel of the continued right-wing backlash against Obama. Conversely, the enthusiasm generated by figures like Carson and Rubio is an attempt by the Republicans to show that they also have non-white politicians who can win in post-Obama America.

The nature of national politics has also changed since the pivotal election of 2000. During that election and the subsequent one, Karl Rove showed how a national party could win not by appealing to the center but by revving up the base, a lesson that the Democrats applied with great success in 2008 and 2012. Getting out the vote is now seen as more important than winning over swing voters, which creates a strong incentive for parties to energize core voters by appealing to issues that define

> **Economics and foreign policy haven't gone away, but they are increasingly being talked about in terms of identity.**

their identity (and make it impossible for them to vote for the other party). The logic of identity politics has been building for a long time in national politics, and in this election cycle we see that a polarized political landscape also means a heightening of identity politics.

National politics is merely the crest of the deeper social movements that flow through society. With the rise of groups like Black Lives Matter and the new feminist energy that pervades popular culture and the online world, it is natural that identity issues (and the backlash they provoke) would echo loudly in presidential politics.

There's a tendency among a certain class of pundits to act as if identity politics were a distraction from more fundamental matters like economics and foreign policy. What this line of thought ignores is the fact that economics and foreign policy are themselves saturated with questions of identity. Donald Trump is right in emphasizing the question of whether "we're going to be a country." Politics is inevitably about not just policy but people: who is included, who gets excluded, who has power, and does not.

Print Citations

CMS: Heer, Jeet. "Identity Heft: Why the Politics of Race and Gender Are Dominating the 2016 Election." In *The Reference Shelf: Campaign Trends and Election Law*, edited by Betsy Maury, 97-99. Ipswitch, MA: Salem Press, 2016.

MLA: Heer, Jeet. "Identity Heft: Why the Politics of Race and Gender Are Dominating the 2016 Election." *The Reference Shelf: Campaign Trends and Election Law*. Ed. Betsy Maury. Ipswitch: Salem Press, 2016. 97-99. Print.

APA: Heer, J. (2016). Identity heft: Why the politics of race and gender are dominating the 2016 election. In Betsy Maury (Ed.), *The reference shelf: Campaign trends and election law* (pp. 97-99). Ipswitch, MA: Salem. (Original work published 2015)

The Populists

By George Packer
The New Yorker, September 7, 2015

Thomas E. Watson, the populist from Georgia who had a long and increasingly demagogic career in American politics, wrote in 1910:

The scum of creation has been dumped on us. Some of our principal cities are more foreign than American. The most dangerous and corrupting hordes of the Old World have invaded us. The vice and crime which they have planted in our midst are sickening and terrifying. What brought these Goths and Vandals to our shores? The manufacturers are mainly to blame. They wanted cheap labor: and they didn't care a curse how much harm to our future might be the consequence of their heartless policy.

The objects of Watson's bile were the Italians, Poles, Jews, and other European immigrants then pouring into the United States. A century later, in the populist summer of 2015, some of their great-grandchildren have been cheering Donald Trump as he denounces the latest generation of immigrants, in remarkably similar terms.

American populism has a complicated history, and Watson embodied its paradoxes. He ended his career, as a U.S. senator, whipping up white-Protestant enmity against blacks, Catholics, and Jews; but at the outset, as a leader of the People's Party in the eighteen-nineties, he urged poor whites and blacks to join together and upend an economic order dominated by "the money power." Watson wound up as Trump, but he started out closer to Bernie Sanders, and his hostility to the one per cent of the Gilded Age would do Sanders proud. Some of Watson's early ideas—rural free delivery of mail, for example—eventually came to fruition.

> **Populism is a stance and a rhetoric more than an ideology or a set of positions. It speaks of a battle of good against evil, demanding simple answers to difficult problems.**

That's the volatile nature of populism: it can ignite reform or reaction, idealism or scapegoating. It flourishes in periods like Watson's, and like our own, when large numbers of citizens who see themselves as the backbone of America ("producers" then, "the middle class" now) feel that the game is rigged against them. They aren't the wretched of the earth—Sanders attracts educated urbanites, Trump small-town businessmen. They're people with a sense of violated ownership, holding a vision of an earlier, better America that has come under threat.

Populism is a stance and a rhetoric more than an ideology or a set of positions. It speaks of a battle of good against evil, demanding simple answers to difficult problems. (Trump: "Trade? We're gonna fix it. Health care? We're gonna fix it.") It's suspicious of the normal bargaining and compromise that constitute democratic governance. (On the stump, Sanders seldom touts his bipartisan successes as chairman of the Senate Veterans' Affairs Committee.) Populism can have a conspiratorial and apocalyptic bent—the belief that the country, or at least its decent majority, is facing imminent ruin at the hands of a particular group of malefactors (Mexicans, billionaires, Jews, politicians).

Above all, populism seeks and thrills to the authentic voice of the people. Followers of both Sanders and Trump prize their man's willingness to articulate what ordinary people feel but politicians fear to say. "I might not agree with Bernie on everything, but I believe he has values, and he's going to stick to those and he will not lie to us," a supporter named Liam Dewey told *ABC News*. The fact that Sanders has a tendency to drone on like a speaker at the Socialist Scholars Conference circa 1986—one who happens to have an audience of twenty-seven thousand—only enhances his bona fides. He's the improbable beneficiary of a deeply disenchanted public. As for Trump, his rhetoric is so crude and from-the-hip that his fans are continually reassured about its authenticity.

Responding to the same political moment, the phenomena of Trump and Sanders bear a superficial resemblance. Both men have no history of party loyalty, which only enhances their street cred—their authority comes from a direct bond with their supporters, free of institutional interference. They both rail against foreign-trade deals, decry the unofficial jobless rate, and express disdain for the political class and the dirty money it raises to stay in office. Last week, Trump even denounced the carried-interest tax loophole for investment managers (a favorite target of the left). "These hedge-fund guys are getting away with murder," he told CBS News. "These are guys that shift paper around and they get lucky."

But the difference between Sanders and Trump is large, and more fundamental than the difference between their personal styles or their places on the political spectrum. Sanders, who has spent most of his career as an outsider on the inside, believes ardently in politics. He views the political arena as a battle of opposing classes (even more than Elizabeth Warren, he really does seem to hate the rich), but believes that their conflicts can be managed through elections and legislation. What Sanders calls a political revolution is closer to a campaign of far-reaching but plausible reforms. He proposes a financial-transactions tax and the breakup of the biggest banks; he doesn't demand the nationalization of banking. His views might appall Wall Street, but they exist within the realm of rational persuasion.

Trump (whatever he really believes) is playing the game of anti-politics. From George Wallace to Ross Perot, anti-politics has been a constant in recent American history; candidates as diverse as Jimmy Carter, Ronald Reagan, and Barack Obama have won the Presidency by seeming to reject or rise above the unlovely business of politics and government. Trump takes it to a demagogic extreme. There's no dirtier word in the lexicon of his stump speech than "politician." He incites his audiences' contempt for the very notion of solving problems through political means. China, the Islamic State, immigrants, unemployment, Wall Street: just let him handle it—he'll build the wall, deport the eleven million, rewrite the Fourteenth Amendment, create the jobs, kill the terrorists. He offers no idea beyond himself, the leader who can reverse the country's decline by sheer force of personality. Speaking in Mobile, Alabama, recently, he paused to wonder whether representative government was even necessary. After ticking off his leads in various polls, Trump asked the crowd of thirty thousand, "Why do we need an election? We don't need an election." When Trump narrows his eyes and juts out his lip, he's a showman pretending to be a strongman.

There aren't many examples of the populist strongman in American history (Huey Long comes to mind). Our attachment to democracy, if not to its institutions and professionals, has been too firm for that. There are more examples of populists who, while failing to win national election, extend the parameters of discourse and ultimately bring about important reforms (think of Robert M. La Follette, Sr.). Though populists seldom get elected President, they can—like the young Tom Watson and the old—cleanse or foul the political air.

Print Citations

CMS: Packer, George. "The Populists." In *The Reference Shelf: Campaign Trends and Election Law*, edited by Betsy Maury, 100-02. Ipswitch, MA: Salem Press, 2016.

MLA: Packer, George. "The Populists." *The Reference Shelf: Campaign Trends and Election Law*. Ed. Betsy Maury. Ipswitch: Salem Press, 2016. 100-02. Print.

APA: Packer, G. (2016). The populists. In Betsy Maury (Ed.), *The reference shelf: Campaign trends and election law* (pp. 100-102). Ipswitch, MA: Salem. (Original work published 2015)

3
Campaign Issues: Immigration, Trade, the Economy

Bill Clark

Karla and Francisca Ortiz, of Las Vegas, speak on stage during the Democratic National Convention in Philadelphia on Monday, July 25, 2016. Karla is an American citizen, but her parents are undocumented and live in fear of deportation.

Identity and Economics: Immigration and Globalization in the 2016 Race

The 2016 presidential debate encompassed a wide variety of economic issues including the potentially deleterious effects of automation and globalization on the American workforce, typically prejudicial and misinformed beliefs about the effects of immigration on the economy, and a high level of dissatisfaction with income inequality in general and its role in fostering a deepening class divide in America.

Jobs in the Globalized World

Globalization is the integration of international cultures and economic systems. Economic globalization specifically involved international trade agreements and the process of corporations conducting business in foreign countries. Economic globalization has accelerated in the Digital Age, with companies increasingly outsourcing work to foreign countries to save on the cost of hiring US workers. Globalization has been a controversial issue over the last half century as many feel that corporate outsourcing and trade competition with nations like China have put American workers at a disadvantage, precipitating the decline of the US manufacturing industry.

An example of the globalization debate can be seen in the controversial Trans-Pacific Partnership (TPP), an economic proposal calling for the establishment of a free trade zone between twelve nations including the United States, Australia, Japan, New Zealand, Peru, and Singapore. For participating nations, the TPP would reduce the taxes and custom duties on exports and imports as well as create new rules for intellectual property. Proponents argue that the TPP will create as many as 10,000 jobs in the United States and will help member countries to compete with China's dominance of the manufacturing market. However, critics fear that the TPP would encourage corporations to outsource jobs, similar to the North American Free Trade Agreement (NAFTA), which some economists believe resulted in the loss of more than 600,000 US jobs, while having a consequent negative effect on the Mexican economy.[1] Trump and Sanders took a hard line against the TPP, arguing that it profited "big business" while disadvantaging workers, while Clinton, by contrast, initially supported the TPP, though she later changed her stance on the issue.

While TPP became a contentious campaign issue, the US public was not as passionate. A poll of 10,000 respondents by *Morning Consult* found that 26 percent of respondents favored the proposal, while 29 percent opposed it. The largest single group, 45 percent, had no opinion and more than 72 percent had heard little or nothing about the issue before participating in the survey.[2] A less specific *Wall Street Journal* poll on the effects of free trade, found that 51 percent supported free trade while 39 percent believed free trade agreements had been detrimental to the economy, and the remaining 10 percent had no opinion.[3] Some have argued that Trump and Sanders' opposition to the TPP, and globalization in general, is a short-sighted form of protectionism, the idea that nations should protect domestic industries from foreign competition by taxing imports. According to this view, globalization is a necessity of the modern world and nations must attempt to manage and benefit from globalizing commerce rather than attempting to avoid the process.

Raising the Minimum

One facet of the income inequality debate involves the proposal to raise the federal minimum wage to between $12 (supported by Clinton) and $15 (supported by Sanders). Trump and the GOP, true to historic precedent, oppose a federal minimum wage law. The minimum wage issue is contentious because of the widespread belief that a wage increase will lead to higher levels of unemployment as businesses are forced to downsize their workforce to remain profitable.[4]

Tim Worstall, writing in *Forbes*, argues that a $15 minimum wage could threaten 5.3 million US manufacturing jobs by encouraging companies to lay off workers or outsource jobs.[5] A majority of economists, however, support a minimum wage increase and argue that research indicates minimum wage increases have little or no impact on employment, but significantly increase the well-being of minimum wage workers.[6] Other critics assert that a higher minimum wage does little for "average Americans" and primarily benefits teenagers and service industry workers (the federal minimum wage for tipped workers has been unchanged at $2.31/hr since 1991). Reviews of Bureau of Labor Statistics data indicate, however, that only 20 percent of minimum wage workers are teenagers and that most are adult, full-time employees.[7]

Logic and economic models predict that minimum wage increases, set against a theoretically static model, lead to a reduction in profit or competitiveness thereby forcing companies to lay off employees or to raise the price of goods or services. Critics argue that a wage increase is necessary to force companies to share their profits with low-income workers. In 2015, income for the top 1 percent of American households climbed by 7.7 percent, more than twice the rate for the remaining 99 percent. Even more staggering is the revelation, from census data, that income for 99 percent of Americans is less than it was in 1998 when adjusted for inflation.[8] McDonald's corporation has become a focus of the minimum wage movement, with the lowest paid employees earning under $8/hr while the CEO earned more than $8.75 million per year.[9]

The Immigration Debate

In 2014, the US immigrant population reached 42.4 million, constituting 13.3 percent of the total population. In the 2010s, most immigrants arriving in the United States came from India (147,500) and China (131,800) followed by Mexico (130,000), Canada (41,200), and the Philippines (40,500). The number of illegal immigrants living in the United States has been estimated at just under 11 million, with 30 percent coming from Mexico.[10]

The United States has a complex history of immigration policy, at times welcoming immigrants in an effort to build the nation's workforce but always with a passionate anti-immigrant movement motivated by xenophobic (fear of outsiders), nativist, and racially-biased beliefs about the effects of immigration on American culture. The prime historical example is the Chinese Exclusion Act of 1882, a misguided legislative effort allegedly meant to protect the United States from foreign influence but essentially motivated by racism and political manipulation in which Chinese immigrants were blamed for tenuously linked national issues.[11] Arguments used in favor of Chinese exclusion are disturbingly similar to arguments from Donald Trump and supporters in favor of drastic changes to US immigration policy, including building a wall separating the United States and Mexico. The idea of a border wall was first considered in 1924 but gained renewed steam after 9/11 when half of Americans supported the idea, having been led to believe that the Mexican border left the nation vulnerable to terrorists, despite no evidence, of any kind, to validate this concern. However, thanks to press coverage and Trump's extreme proposals, public opinion has shifted, with 59 percent now opposing the idea. Along partisan lines, 84 percent of Trump supporters approved, while 83 percent of Clinton supporters opposed.[12]

The most realistic, fact-driven arguments against immigration are based on statistics indicating that immigrants (especially illegal immigrants) can have a transient, but significant, negative effect on job availability in the working class population, while placing an increased burden on social services.[13,14] However, a large majority of experts supported by vast amounts of data argue that immigration is predominantly beneficial and that immigrants provide billions in revenue for the government and help grow the US economy by increasing the number of workers and consumers.[15] In addition, remittances sent by immigrants to their native nations reduce poverty and crime rates in recipient communities and, in this way, US immigration has persistently served as a positive global economic force.[16]

Trump has also suggested a highly controversial temporary ban on immigration from some as-yet-unspecified countries with "links to terrorism." Widespread media coverage of terrorist attacks in the EU and of the difficulties experienced by Germany since the nation agreed to accept an unprecedented number of Syrian refugees, have helped to fuel support for Trump's proposal. Most recently, Trump announced that his immigration policy would include a new process of "extreme, extreme vetting" in which prospective immigrants would be tested on their adherence to "American" values such as LBGT rights, women's rights, and religious freedom.[17] While critics theorized that Trump's plan would be extremely difficult if not impossible to implement, numerous journalists also pointed out that many among Trump's supporters would likely fail an extreme, extreme vetting test. A recent Pew Research poll, for instance, showed that 52 percent of Trump supporters oppose LGBT marriage rights.[18] The Republican party, as a whole, also has a questionable record of supporting religious and ethnic minorities. A 2016 survey in North

Carolina, for instance, found that 40 percent of Republican voters believed the practice of Islam should be made illegal.

Whether or not one agrees with Trump's controversial policies on Muslim or Mexican immigration, the immigration debate can never realistically be reduced to economic pros and cons or to concerns over terrorism. Immigration policies are ideological, demonstrating the way that voters view their nation's identity and reflecting the degree to which Americans feel that the United States should be responsive to nations in need and participatory in global society.

Micah L. Issitt

Works Used

Boak, Josh. "Why It Matters: Income Inequality." *U.S. News*. U.S. News and World Report. Aug 18 2016. Web. 18 Aug 2016.

Bult, Laura. "McDonald's CEO Gets 368% Pay Raise." *Daily News*. New York Daily News. Apr 16 2016. Web. 17 Aug 2016.

"Campaign Exposes Fissures Over Issues, Values and How Life Has Changed in the U.S." *Pew Research*. Pew Research Center. Mar 31 2016. Web. 18 Aug 2016.

"Changing Attitudes on Gay Marriage." *Pew Research*. Pew Research Center. May 12 2016. Web. 24 Aug 2016.

"Chinese Immigration and the Chinese Exclusion Acts." *Office of the Historian*. U.S. Department of State. 2016. Web. 18 Aug 2016.

Davis, Bob. "The Thorny Economics of Illegal Immigration." *Wall Street Journal*. Dow Jones & Co. Feb 9 2016. Web. 17 Aug 2016.

"Donald Trump Calls for 'Extreme Vetting' of Immigrants to US." *BBC News*. BBC. Aug 16 2016. Web. 18 Aug 2016.

Drezner, Daniel W. "Does the 2016 Campaign Provide a Mandate Against TPP?" *Washington Post*. Nash Holdings. Jun 23 2016. Web. 19 Aug 2016.

Hanson, Gordon H. "Immigration, Productivity, and Competitiveness in American Industry." *AEI*. American Enterprise Institute. 2011. Pdf. 18 Aug 2016.

"Michael Froman: Where the TPP Stands." *Wall Street Journal*. Dow Jones & Company. Jun 19 2016. Web. 24 Aug 2016.

"Minimum Wage Mythbusters." *DOL*. United States Department of Labor. 2015. Web. 17 Aug 2016.

Patton, Leslie. "McDonald's $8.25 Man and $8.75 Million CEO Shows Pay Gap." *Bloomberg*. Bloomberg Business. Dec 11 2012. Web. 25 Aug 2016.

Peri, Giovanni. "The Economic Benefits of Immigration." *CLAS Berkeley*. Center for Latin American Studies. University of California, Berkeley. Fall 2013. Web. 18 Aug 2016.

Ratha, Dilip. "The Impact of Remittances on Economic Growth and Poverty Reduction." *MPI Policy Brief*. Migration Policy Institute. Sep 2013. Web. 18 Aug 2015.

Saad, Lydia. "Trump Leads Clinton on Top-Ranking Economic Issues." *Gallup*. Gallup. Jun 2 2016. Web. 24 Aug 2016.

Sherman, Erik. "San Francisco Restaurant Jobs Grow Then Fall After Minimum Wage Jump." *Forbes*. Forbes Inc. Jan 15 2016. Web. 17 Aug 2016.

Strachan, Maxwell. "U.S. Economy Lost Nearly 700,000 Jobs Because of NAFTA, EPI Says." May 12 2011. Web. 25 Aug 2016. *Huffington Post*.

Smith, Noah. "Finally, an Answer to the Minimum Wage Question." *Bloomberg*. Bloomberg LP. May 27 2015. Web. 17 Aug 2016.

"Weighing Pros and Cons of the Proposed Trans-Pacific Partnership." *Stanford Economics*. Stanford University School of Economics. Nov 12 2015. Web. 24 Aug 2016.

Worstall, Tim. "$15 Minimum Wage Threatens 5.3 Million US Manufacturing Jobs." *Forbes*. Forbes, Inc. Sep 2 2015. Web. 16 Aug 2016.

Zong, Jie and Jeanne Batalova. "Frequently Requested Statistics on Immigrants and Immigration in the United States." *MPI*. Migration Policy Institute. Apr 14 2016. Web. Aug 17 2016.

Notes

1. Strachan, "U.S. Economy Lost Nearly 700,000 Jobs Because of NAFTA, EPI Says."
2. Drezner, "Does the 2016 Campaign Provide a Mandate Against TPP?"
3. "Michael Froman: Where the TPP Stands," *Wall Street Journal*.
4. Smith, "Finally, an Answer to the Minimum Wage Question."
5. Worstall, "$15 Minimum Wage Threatens 5.3 Million US Manufacturing Jobs."
6. Minimum Wage Mythbusters," *Department of Labor*.
7. Sherman, "San Francisco Restaurant Jobs Grow Then Fall After Minimum Wage Jump."
8. Boak, "Why It Matters: Income Inequality."
9. Patton, "McDonald's $8.25 Man and $8.75 Million CEO Shows Pay Gap."
10. Zong and Batalova, "Frequently Requested Statistics on Immigrants and Immigration in the United States."
11. "Chinese Immigration and the Chinese Exclusion Acts," *Office of the Historian*.
12. "Campaign Exposes Fissures Over Issues, Values and How Life Has Changed in the U.S.," *Pew Research*.
13. Hanson, "Immigration, Productivity, and Competitiveness in American Industry."
14. Davis, "The Thorny Economics of Illegal Immigration."
15. Peri, "The Economic Benefits of Immigration."
16. Ratha, "The Impact of Remittances on Economic Growth and Poverty Reduction."
17. "Donald Trump Calls for 'Extreme Vetting' of Immigrants to US," *BBC News*.
18. "Changing Attitudes on Gay Marriage," *Pew Research*.

The Truth About Trade: What Critics Get Wrong About the Global Economy

By Douglas A. Irwin

Foreign Affairs, July/August 2016

Just because a U.S. presidential candidate bashes free trade on the campaign trail does not mean that he or she cannot embrace it once elected. After all, Barack Obama voted against the Central American Free Trade Agreement as a U.S. senator and disparaged the North American Free Trade Agreement (NAFTA) as a presidential candidate. In office, however, he came to champion the Trans-Pacific Partnership (TPP), a giant trade deal with 11 other Pacific Rim countries.

Yet in the current election cycle, the rhetorical attacks on U.S. trade policy have grown so fiery that it is difficult to imagine similar transformations. The Democratic candidate Bernie Sanders has railed against "disastrous" trade agreements, which he claims have cost jobs and hurt the middle class. The Republican Donald Trump complains that China, Japan, and Mexico are "killing" the United States on trade thanks to the bad deals struck by "stupid" negotiators. Even Hillary Clinton, the expected Democratic nominee, who favored the TPP as secretary of state, has been forced to join the chorus and now says she opposes that agreement.

Blaming other countries for the United States' economic woes is an age-old tradition in American politics; if truth is the first casualty of war, then support for free trade is often an early casualty of an election campaign. But the bipartisan bombardment has been so intense this time, and has been so unopposed, that it raises real questions about the future of U.S. global economic leadership.

The anti-trade rhetoric paints a grossly distorted picture of trade's role in the U.S. economy. Trade still benefits the United States enormously, and striking back at other countries by imposing new barriers or ripping up existing agreements would be self-destructive. The badmouthing of trade agreements has even jeopardized the ratification of the TPP in Congress. Backing out of that deal would signal a major U.S. retreat from Asia and mark a historic error.

Still, it would be a mistake to dismiss all of the anti-trade talk as ill-informed bombast. Today's electorate harbors legitimate, deep-seated frustrations about the state of the U.S. economy and labor markets in particular, and addressing these complaints will require changing government policies. The solution, however, lies not in turning away from trade promotion but in strengthening worker protections.

By and large, the United States has no major difficulties with respect to trade,

---

nor does it suffer from problems that could be solved by trade barriers. What it does face, however, is a much larger problem, one that lies at the root of anxieties over trade: the economic ladder that allowed previous generations of lower-skilled Americans to reach the middle class is broken.

Scapegoating Trade

Campaign attacks on trade leave an unfortunate impression on the American public and the world at large. In saying that some countries "win" and other countries "lose" as a result of trade, for example, Trump portrays it as a zero-sum game. That's an understandable perspective for a casino owner and businessman: gambling is the quintessential zero-sum game, and competition is a win-lose proposition for firms (if not for their customers). But it is dead wrong as a way to think about the role of trade in an economy. Trade is actually a two-way street—the exchange of exports for imports—that makes efficient use of a country's resources to increase its material welfare. The United States sells to other countries the goods and services that it produces relatively efficiently (from aircraft to soybeans to legal advice) and buys those goods and services that other countries produce relatively efficiently (from T-shirts to bananas to electronics assembly). In the aggregate, both sides benefit.

To make their case that trade isn't working for the United States, critics invoke long-discredited indicators, such as the country's negative balance of trade. "Our trade deficit with China is like having a business that continues to lose money every single year," Trump once said. "Who would do business like that?" In fact, a nation's trade balance is nothing like a firm's bottom line. Whereas a company cannot lose money indefinitely, a country—particularly one, such as the United States, with a reserve currency—can run a trade deficit indefinitely without compromising its well-being. Australia has run current account deficits even longer than the United States has, and its economy is flourishing.

One way to define a country's trade balance is the difference between its domestic savings and its domestic investment. The United States has run a deficit in its current account—the broadest measure of trade in goods and services—every year except one since 1981. Why? Because as a low-saving, high-consuming country, the United States has long been the recipient of capital inflows from abroad. Reducing the current account deficit would require foreigners to purchase fewer U.S assets. That, in turn, would require increasing domestic savings or, to put it in less popular terms, reducing consumption. One way to accomplish that would be to change the tax system—for example, by instituting a consumption tax. But discouraging spending and rewarding savings is not easy, and critics of the trade deficit do not fully appreciate the difficulty involved in reversing it. (And if a current account surplus were to appear, critics would no doubt complain, as they did in the 1960s, that the United States was investing too much abroad and not enough at home.)

Trade still benefits the United States enormously.

Critics also point to the trade deficit to suggest that the United States is losing more jobs as a result of imports than it gains due to exports. In fact, the trade deficit usually increases when the economy is growing and creating jobs and decreases when it is contracting and losing jobs. The U.S. current account deficit shrank from 5.8 percent of GDP in 2006 to 2.7 percent in 2009, but that didn't stop the economy from hemorrhaging jobs. And if there is any doubt that a current account surplus is no economic panacea, one need only look at Japan, which has endured three decades of economic stagnation despite running consistent current account surpluses.

And yet these basic fallacies—many of which Adam Smith debunked more than two centuries ago—have found a new life in contemporary American politics. In some ways, it is odd that anti-trade sentiment has blossomed in 2016, of all years. For one thing, although the post-recession recovery has been disappointing, it has hardly been awful: the U.S. economy has experienced seven years of slow but steady growth, and the unemployment rate has fallen to just five percent. For another thing, imports have not swamped the country and caused problems for domestic producers and their workers; over the past seven years, the current account deficit has remained roughly unchanged at about two to three percent of GDP, much lower than its level from 2000 to 2007. The pace of globalization, meanwhile, has slowed in recent years. The World Trade Organization (WTO) forecasts that the volume of world trade will grow by just 2.8 percent in 2016, the fifth consecutive year that it has grown by less than three percent, down significantly from previous decades.

What's more, despite what one might infer from the crowds at campaign rallies, Americans actually support foreign trade in general and even trade agreements such as the TPP in particular. After a decade of viewing trade with skepticism, since 2013, Americans have seen it positively. A February 2016 Gallup poll found that 58 percent of Americans consider foreign trade an opportunity for economic growth, and only 34 percent viewed it as a threat.

The View From the Bottom

So why has trade come under such strident attack now? The most important reason is that workers are still suffering from the aftermath of the Great Recession, which left many unemployed and indebted. Between 2007 and 2009, the United States lost nearly nine million jobs, pushing the unemployment rate up to ten percent. Seven years later, the economy is still recovering from this devastating blow. Many workers have left the labor force, reducing the employment-to-population ratio sharply. Real wages have remained flat. For many Americans, the recession isn't over.

For many Americans, the recession isn't over.

Thus, even as trade commands broad public support, a significant minority of the electorate—about a third, according to various polls—decidedly opposes it. These critics come from both sides of the political divide, but they tend to be lower-income, blue-collar workers, who are the most vulnerable to economic change. They believe that economic elites and the political establishment have looked out only for themselves over the past few decades. As they see it, the government bailed out banks during the financial crisis, but no one came to their aid.

For these workers, neither political party has taken their concerns seriously, and both parties have struck trade deals that the workers think have cost jobs. Labor unions that support the Democrats still feel betrayed by President Bill Clinton, who, over their strong objections, secured congressional passage of NAFTA in 1993 and normalized trade relations with China in 2000. Blue-collar Republican voters, for their part, supported the anti-NAFTA presidential campaigns of Pat Buchanan and Ross Perot in 1992. They felt betrayed by President George W. Bush, who pushed Congress to pass many bilateral trade agreements. Today, they back Trump.

Among this demographic, a narrative has taken hold that trade has cost Americans their jobs, squeezed the middle class, and kept wages low. The truth is more complicated. Although imports have put some people out of work, trade is far from the most important factor behind the loss of manufacturing jobs. The main culprit is technology. Automation and other technologies have enabled vast productivity and efficiency improvements, but they have also made many blue-collar jobs obsolete. One representative study, by the Center for Business and Economic Research at Ball State University, found that productivity growth accounted for more than 85 percent of the job loss in manufacturing between 2000 and 2010, a period when employment in that sector fell by 5.6 million. Just 13 percent of the overall job loss resulted from trade, although in two sectors, apparel and furniture, it accounted for 40 percent.

This finding is consistent with research by the economists David Autor, David Dorn, and Gordon Hanson, who have estimated that imports from China displaced as many as 982,000 workers in manufacturing from 2000 to 2007. These layoffs also depressed local labor markets in communities that produced goods facing Chinese competition, such as textiles, apparel, and furniture. The number of jobs lost is large, but it should be put in perspective: while Chinese imports may have cost nearly one million manufacturing jobs over almost a decade, the normal churn of U.S. labor markets results in roughly 1.7 million layoffs every month.

Research into the effect of Chinese imports on U.S. employment has been widely misinterpreted to imply that the United States has gotten a raw deal from trade with China. In fact, such studies do not evaluate the gains from trade, since they make no attempt to quantify the benefits to consumers from lower-priced goods. Rather, they serve as a reminder that a rapid increase in imports can harm communities that produce substitute goods—as happened in the U.S. automotive and steel sectors in the 1980s.

Furthermore, the shock of Chinese goods was a one-time event that occurred under special circumstances. Imports from China increased from 1.0 percent of U.S. GDP in 2000 to 2.6 percent in 2011, but for the past five years, the share has stayed roughly constant. There is no reason to believe it will rise further. China's once-rapid economic growth has slowed. Its working-age population has begun to shrink, and the migration of its rural workers to coastal urban manufacturing areas has largely run its course.

The influx of Chinese imports was also unusual in that much of it occurred from 2001 to 2007, when China's current account surplus soared, reaching ten percent of GDP in 2007. The country's export boom was partly facilitated by China's policy of preventing the appreciation of the yuan, which lowered the price of Chinese goods. Beginning around 2000, the Chinese central bank engaged in a large-scale, persistent, and one-way intervention in the foreign exchange market—buying dollars and selling yuan. As a result, its foreign exchange reserves rose from less than $300 million in 2000 to $3.25 trillion in 2011. Critics rightly groused that this effort constituted currency manipulation and violated International Monetary Fund rules. Yet such complaints are now moot: over the past year, China's foreign exchange reserves have fallen rapidly as its central bank has sought to prop up the value of the yuan. Punishing China for past bad behavior would accomplish nothing.

The Right—And Wrong—Solutions

The real problem is not trade but diminished domestic opportunity and social mobility. Although the United States boasts a highly skilled work force and a solid technological base, it is still the case that only one in three American adults has a college education. In past decades, the two-thirds of Americans with no postsecondary degree often found work in manufacturing, construction, or the armed forces. These parts of the economy stood ready to absorb large numbers of people with limited education, give them productive work, and help them build skills. Over time, however, these opportunities have disappeared. Technology has shrunk manufacturing as a source of large-scale employment: even though U.S. manufacturing output continues to grow, it does so with many fewer workers than in the past. Construction work has not recovered from the bursting of the housing bubble. And the military turns away 80 percent of applicants due to stringent fitness and intelligence requirements. There are no comparable sectors of the economy that can employ large numbers of high-school-educated workers.

The anti-trade rhetoric of the campaign has made it difficult for even pro-trade members of Congress to support new agreements.

This is a deep problem for American society. The unemployment rate for college-educated workers is 2.4 percent, but it is more than 7.4 percent for those without a high school diploma—and even higher when counting discouraged workers who have left the labor force but wish to work. These are the people who have been left behind in the twenty-first-century economy—again, not primarily because of trade but because of structural changes in the economy. Helping these workers and ensuring that the economy delivers benefits to everyone should rank as urgent priorities.

But here is where the focus on trade is a diversion. Since trade is not the underlying problem in terms of job loss, neither is protectionism a solution. While the gains from trade can seem abstract, the costs of trade restrictions are concrete. For example, the United States has some 135,000 workers employed in the apparel industry, but there are more than 45 million Americans who live below the poverty line, stretching every dollar they have. Can one really justify increasing the price of clothing for 45 million low-income Americans (and everyone else as well) in an effort to save the jobs of just some of the 135,000 low-wage workers in the apparel industry?

Like undoing trade agreements, imposing selective import duties to punish specific countries would also fail. If the United States were to slap 45 percent tariffs on imports from China, as Trump has proposed, U.S. companies would not start producing more apparel and footwear in the United States, nor would they start assembling consumer electronics domestically. Instead, production would shift from China to other low-wage developing countries in Asia, such as Vietnam. That's the lesson of past trade sanctions directed against China alone: in 2009, when the Obama administration imposed duties on automobile tires from China in an effort to save American jobs, other suppliers, principally Indonesia and Thailand, filled the void, resulting in little impact on U.S. production or jobs.

And if restrictions were levied against all foreign imports to prevent such trade diversion, those barriers would hit innocent bystanders: Canada, Japan, Mexico, the EU, and many others. Any number of these would use WTO procedures to retaliate against the United States, threatening the livelihoods of the millions of Americans with jobs that depend on exports of manufactured goods. Trade wars produce no winners. There are good reasons why the very mention of the 1930 Smoot-Hawley Tariff Act still conjures up memories of the Great Depression.

Ripping up NAFTA would do immense damage.

If protectionism is an ineffectual and counterproductive response to the economic problems of much of the work force, so, too, are existing programs designed to help workers displaced by trade. The standard package of Trade Adjustment Assistance, a federal program begun in the 1960s, consists of extended unemployment compensation and retraining programs. But because these benefits are limited to workers who lost their jobs due to trade, they miss the millions more who are unemployed on account of technological change. Furthermore, the program is fraught with bad incentives. Extended unemployment compensation pays workers for prolonged periods of joblessness, but their job prospects usually deteriorate the longer they stay out of the labor force, since they have lost experience in the interim.

And although the idea behind retraining is a good one—helping laid-off textile or steel workers become nurses or technicians—the actual program is a failure. A 2012 external review commissioned by the Department of Labor found that the government retraining programs were a net loss for society, to the tune of about $54,000 per participant. Half of that fell on the participants themselves, who, on average, earned $27,000 less over the four years of the study than similar workers who did not find jobs through the program, and half fell on the government, which footed the bill for the program. Sadly, these programs appear to do more harm than good.

A better way to help all low-income workers would be to expand the Earned Income Tax Credit. The EITC supplements the incomes of workers in all low-income households, not just those the Department of Labor designates as having been adversely affected by trade. What's more, the EITC is tied to employment, thereby rewarding work and keeping people in the labor market, where they can gain experience and build skills. A large enough EITC could ensure that every American was able to earn the equivalent of $15 or more per hour. And it could do so without any of the job loss that a minimum-wage hike can cause. Of all the potential assistance programs, the EITC also enjoys the most bipartisan support, having been endorsed by both the Obama administration and Paul Ryan, the Republican Speaker of the House. A higher EITC would not be a cure-all, but it would provide income security for those seeking to climb the ladder to the middle class.

The main complaint about expanding the EITC concerns the cost. Yet taxpayers are already bearing the burden of supporting workers who leave the labor force, many of whom start receiving disability payments. On disability, people are paid—permanently—to drop out of the labor force and not work. In lieu of this federal program, the cost of which has surged in recent years, it would be better to help people remain in the work force through the EITC, in the hope that they can eventually become taxpayers themselves.

The Future of Free Trade

Despite all the evidence of the benefits of trade, many of this year's crop of presidential candidates have still invoked it as a bogeyman. Sanders deplores past agreements but has yet to clarify whether he believes that better ones could have been negotiated or no such agreements should be reached at all. His vote against the U.S.-Australian free-trade agreement in 2004 suggests that he opposes all trade deals, even one with a country that has high labor standards and with which the United States runs a sizable balance of trade surplus. Trump professes to believe in free trade, but he insists that the United States has been outnegotiated by its trade partners, hence his threat to impose 45 percent tariffs on imports from China to get "a better deal"—whatever that means. He has attacked Japan's barriers against imports of U.S. agricultural goods, even though that is exactly the type of protectionism the TPP has tried to undo. Meanwhile, Clinton's position against the TPP has hardened as the campaign has gone on.

> **Despite all the evidence of the benefits of trade, many of this year's crop of presidential candidates have still invoked it as a bogeyman.**

The response from economists has tended to be either meek defenses of trade or outright silence, with some even criticizing parts of the TPP. It's time for supporters of free trade to engage in a full-throated championing of the many achievements of U.S. trade agreements. Indeed, because other countries' trade barriers tend to be higher than those of the United States, trade agreements open foreign markets to U.S. exports more than they open the U.S. market to foreign imports.

That was true of NAFTA, which remains a favored punching bag on the campaign trail. In fact, NAFTA has been a big economic and foreign policy success. Since the agreement entered into force in 1994, bilateral trade between the United States and Mexico has boomed. For all the fear about Mexican imports flooding the U.S. market, it is worth noting that about 40 percent of the value of imports from Mexico consists of content originally made in the United States—for example, auto parts produced in the United States but assembled in Mexico. It is precisely such trade in component parts that makes standard measures of bilateral trade balances so misleading.

NAFTA has also furthered the United States' long-term political, diplomatic, and economic interest in a flourishing, democratic Mexico, which not only reduces immigration pressures on border states but also increases Mexican demand for U.S. goods and services. Far from exploiting Third World labor, as critics have charged, NAFTA has promoted the growth of a middle class in Mexico that now includes nearly half of all households. And since 2009, more Mexicans have left the United States than have come in. In the two decades since NAFTA went into effect, Mexico has been transformed from a clientelistic one-party state with widespread anti-American sentiment into a functional multiparty democracy with a generally pro-American public. Although it has suffered from drug wars in recent years (a spillover effect from problems that are largely made in America), the overall story is one of rising prosperity thanks in part to NAFTA.

Ripping up NAFTA would do immense damage. In its foreign relations, the United States would prove itself to be an unreliable partner. And economically, getting rid of the agreement would disrupt production chains across North America, harming both Mexico and the United States. It would add to border tensions while shifting trade to Asia without bringing back any U.S. manufacturing jobs. The American public seems to understand this: in an October 2015 Gallup poll, only 18 percent of respondents agreed that leaving NAFTA or the Central American Free Trade Agreement would be very effective in helping the economy.

A more moderate option would be for the United States to take a pause and simply stop negotiating any more trade agreements, as Obama did during his first term. The problem with this approach, however, is that the rest of the world would continue to reach trade agreements without the United States, and so U.S. exporters would find themselves at a disadvantage compared with their foreign competitors. Glimpses of that future can already be seen. In 2012, the car manufacturer Audi chose southeastern Mexico over Tennessee for the site of a new plant because it could save thousands of dollars per car exported thanks to Mexico's many more free-trade agreements, including one with the EU. Australia has reached trade deals with China and Japan that give Australian farmers preferential access in those markets, cutting into U.S. beef exports.

If Washington opted out of the TPP, it would forgo an opportunity to shape the rules of international trade in the twenty-first century. The Uruguay Round, the last round of international trade negotiations completed by the General Agreement on Tariffs and Trade, ended in 1994, before the Internet had fully emerged. Now, the United States' high-tech firms and other exporters face foreign regulations that are not transparent and impede market access. Meanwhile, other countries are already moving ahead with their own trade agreements, increasingly taking market share from U.S. exporters in the dynamic Asia-Pacific region. Staying out of the TPP would not lead to the creation of good jobs in the United States. And despite populist claims to the contrary, the TPP's provisions for settling disputes between investors and governments and dealing with intellectual property rights are reasonable.

(In the early 1990s, similar fears about such provisions in the WTO were just as exaggerated and ultimately proved baseless.)

The United States should proceed with passage of the TPP and continue to negotiate other deals with its trading partners. So-called plurilateral trade agreements, that is, deals among relatively small numbers of like-minded countries, offer the only viable way to pick up more gains from reducing trade barriers. The current climate on Capitol Hill means that the era of small bilateral agreements, such as those pursued during the George W. Bush administration, has ended. And the collapse of the Doha Round at the WTO likely marks the end of giant multilateral trade negotiations.

Free trade has always been a hard sell. But the anti-trade rhetoric of the 2016 campaign has made it difficult for even pro-trade members of Congress to support new agreements. Past experience suggests that Washington will lead the charge for reducing trade barriers only when there is a major trade problem to be solved— namely, when U.S. exporters face severe discrimination in foreign markets. Such was the case when the United States helped form the General Agreement on Tariffs and Trade in 1947, when it started the Kennedy Round of trade negotiations in the 1960s, and when it initiated the Uruguay Round in the 1980s. Until the United States feels the pain of getting cut out of major foreign markets, its leadership on global trade may wane. That would represent just one casualty of the current campaign.

Print Citations

CMS: Irwin, Douglas A. "The Truth About Trade: What Critics Get Wrong About the Global Economy." In *The Reference Shelf: Campaign Trends and Election Law*, edited by Betsy Maury, 110-18. Ipswitch, MA: Salem Press, 2016.

MLA: Irwin, Douglas A. "The Truth About Trade: What Critics Get Wrong About the Global Economy." *The Reference Shelf: Campaign Trends and Election Law*. Ed. Betsy Maury. Ipswitch: Salem Press, 2016. 110-18. Print.

APA: Irwin, D.A. (2016). The truth about trade: What critics get wrong about the global economy. In Betsy Maury (Ed.),*The reference shelf: Campaign trends and election law*(pp. 110-118). Ipswitch, MA: Salem. (Original work published 2016)

Immigration and the 2016 Election

By Victor Agbafe
Harvard Political Review, January 18, 2016

Most people who have been following the political climate over the past few decades will notice how increasingly polarized it has become. One of the markers of this division is the partisan divide over immigration, which has been and will continue to play a huge role in the upcoming presidential election cycle. And one of the reasons that Republicans and Democrats are so split on the issue may be their links to specific demographic groups in the American electorate that are changing their own views.

In the Republican Party, the immigration rhetoric has taken a further turn to the right due to the increase in exurban working class voters in its ranks. According to a Pew Research Center poll conducted this spring, more than 60 percent of GOP voters believe that immigrants today are more of a burden than a benefit on our society, and Tea Partiers are even more opposed towards lenient immigration policy than other Republicans. This general viewpoint is one not only espoused by immigration hardliners in the presidential campaign like Donald Trump but even by competitors like Jeb Bush, who has defended his use of the term "anchor babies" earlier this year by describing it as part of a "birth tourism … frankly more related to Asian people."

Bush and Trump's positions are consistent with those of many voters in the GOP base. A 2010 study by University of Maryland, College Park professor James Gimpel in the Center for Immigrant Studies explains that over the past 30 years Republicans have been strong in counties with a low portion of immigrants coming in but with a higher portion of native-born Americans. Simultaneously, since the 1970s a growing proportion of white, working-class voters have turned away from the Democratic party, dropping by about 20 percent between 1974 and 2004, according to a study at the University of Arizona. For the segments of rural, exurban and socially conservative voters that form the bedrock of the modern GOP's electoral coalition, this anti-immigrant rhetoric is a central policy component for winning the primary.

On the other side of the aisle, immigration plays a very different role. Many liberals in recent years have begun to advocate for policies like a pathway to citizenship for undocumented immigrants as well as opportunities for undocumented students to receive in-state tuition and drivers' licenses. As a result, several of the party's presidential candidates, including establishment favorite Hillary Clinton, are jockeying to demonstrate the immigration policy most favorable to immigrants. In fact, Hillary Clinton at a campaign event in May said, "We can't wait any longer for a path to full and equal citizenship."

This position would make sense, as a study cited in the *Washington Examiner* found that in 2012, 62 percent of naturalized immigrants identified as Democrats. To win the Democratic primary and to help mobilize the same coalition of voters that twice propelled President Obama to electoral victory, whichever Democrat wins the primary will need to capitalize on this advantage. A 2013 study by Philip E. Wolgin and Ann Garcia at the left-leaning Center for American Progress shows that immigrant support will be crucial especially be crucial for Democratic candidates in swing states like Colorado, Virginia, Florida, and North Carolina, which have seen a considerable influx of immigrants over the past decade.

To see the recent effects of immigrants on voting patterns, consider the changes in Broward and San Bernardino counties in Florida and California, respectively. In 1980, 11.1 percent of Broward County residents were immigrants, while today the county is is 31.2 percent immigrant; it was 55.9 percent Republican in 1980 and is 32.4 percent today. San Bernardino was 7.7 percent immigrant in 1980 and 21.4 immigrant percent at the present—it was 59.7 percent Republican back then, and is currently 46.2 percent.

> For the segments of rural, exurban and socially conservative voters that form the bedrock of the modern GOP's electoral coalition, this anti-immigrant rhetoric is a central policy component for winning the primary.

This change represents a much larger shift in urban populations nationwide that have consequential political effects. In 1980 the foreign-born population in the nation's 100 largest cities was 12 percent of those cities' populations. Today, that figure is about 30 percent. Over this same period, Republican support in these cities has dropped to about a range from 30 to 35 percent. Therefore, it makes sense as to why the Democratic Party and its many leaders have shifted solidly to the left in many of their stances on the issue of immigration: immigrants have tended to trend solidly left in their voting patterns in recent decades.

Overall, when one seeks to analyze the increasingly polarized bent of the bases of the Democratic and Republican parties and their respective candidates one should analyze the parties drift on divisive political issues like immigration. While there are Democrats like Jim Webb and Republicans like John Kasich who seem skeptical of the direction their parties take on immigration, individuals like these are increasingly the minority. This may be because candidates from both parties look toward their bases to determine the issues that could garner support in primaries and general elections. These electoral divisions further divide the parties on very divisive social issues. French sociologist Auguste Comte once said "demography is destiny," and this has never been truer: for the immigration issue, demographics have shaped politicians' positions.

Print Citations

CMS: Agbafe, Victor. "Immigration and the 2016 Election." In *The Reference Shelf: Campaign Trends and Election Law*, edited by Betsy Maury, 119-20. Ipswitch, MA: Salem Press, 2016.

MLA: Agbafe, Victor. "Immigration and the 2016 Election."*The Reference Shelf: Campaign Trends and Election Law*. Ed. Betsy Maury. Ipswitch: Salem Press, 2016. 119-20. Print.

APA: Agbafe, V. (2016). Immigration and the 2016 election. In Betsy Maury (Ed.), *The reference shelf: Campaign trends and election law* (pp. 119-120). Ipswitch, MA: Salem. (Original work published 2016)

Even Conservatives Say Trump's Immigration Plan Is Dystopian

By Issie Lapowsky
Wired, May 5, 2016

Donald Trump's plan to kick 11 million undocumented immigrants out of the United States over the course of two years sounds impractical. How impractical?

Well, for starters, it would eviscerate the economy and reduce the country's GDP by hundreds of billions of dollars. So: pretty impractical!

That's the conclusion of a report released today by the center-right think tank American Action Forum, which quantified just how much labor and productivity would be lost if Trump's plans became reality. The group's conclusions are terrifying—and they're supposed to be. This week, Trump became the presumptive Republican nominee, leaving #NeverTrump moderate GOPers with the unenviable task of convincing their more conservative colleagues that a Trump presidency would be a disaster for their own pro-business agenda.

Relying on data rather than morality, the AAF paints a picture of a dystopian future under President Trump in which deported immigrants would leave a gaping hole in the American economy—a hole that not even the sum total of unemployed lawful US residents would be able to fill.

> Relying on data rather than morality, the AAF paints a picture of a dystopian future under President Trump in which deported immigrants would leave a gaping hole in the American economy—a hole that not even the sum total of unemployed lawful US residents would be able to fill.

In 2012, roughly 6.8 million workers in the US were undocumented, according to some estimates. The report breaks that figure down by industry and compares the results to Bureau of Labor Statistics data to arrive at a best guess of how many jobs those industries would have to fill with lawful residents to fill the gap. Even if every single unemployed lawful resident filled the jobs left by undocumented immigrants, the report found, the economy would still lose a net total of 4 million workers. That loss of labor equals a productivity decrease of $381.5 billion. Industries like agriculture and construction would be hit hardest, but even the tech industry would stand to lose nearly $21 billion.

Then there's the massive amount of money the federal government would have to spend to actually arrest and transport 11.3 million people out of the country in two years. The report estimates the forced deportations would require roughly 85,000 new apprehension workers; about 48,000 more immigration detention personnel; 31,000 new federal immigration attorneys; and about 1,250 more immigration courts. That's in addition to more than 300,000 new detention beds; about 17,000 chartered flights; and nearly 31,000 bus trips each year.

So yeah, not so much making America great again as making America super-broke. As both Hillary Clinton and the #NeverTrump set begin looking ahead to the general election, the implausibility of all this will, no doubt, emerge as a frequent talking point. And yet, if primary season has taught us anything, it's that fact-checking and number-crunching hasn't worked so far to bring Trump down.

Print Citations

CMS: Lapowsky, Issie. "Even Conservatives Say Trump's Immigration Plan Is Dystopian." In *The Reference Shelf: Campaign Trends and Election Law*, edited by Betsy Maury, 121-22. Ipswitch, MA: Salem Press, 2016.

MLA: Lapowsky, Issie. "Even Conservatives Say Trump's Immigration Plan Is Dystopian." *The Reference Shelf: Campaign Trends and Election Law*. Ed. Betsy Maury. Ipswitch: Salem Press, 2016. 121-22. Print.

APA: Lapowsky, I. (2016). Even conservatives say Trump's immigration plan is dystopian. In Betsy Maury (Ed.), *The reference shelf: Campaign trends and election law* (pp. 121-122). Ipswitch, MA: Salem. (Original work published 2016)

Supreme Court's Split Elevates Immigration as Election Issue

By Mike Dorning
Bloomberg Politics, June 23, 2016

The Supreme Court's deadlock on President Barack Obama's immigration plan pushes one of the year's most divisive political issues to the forefront, with Latino voter registration already surging in an apparent reaction to Donald Trump's campaign.

The court split evenly, 4-4, on Obama's plan to shield as many as 4 million undocumented immigrants from deportation, effectively killing the initiative for the rest of his presidency. The decision is likely to further energize Latino voters already mobilized by the anti-immigrant rhetoric of Trump, the presumptive Republican nominee.

Obama called the deadlock "heartbreaking" for undocumented immigrants and their families and said he believes he is out of options on the issue. "I don't anticipate that there are any additional executive actions that we can take," he told reporters Thursday after the court announced the tie vote.

The 4-4 split means that an appeals court ruling against the plan will stand, as will a trial judge's order preventing the administration from implementing the program. Political strategists said the deadlock may further motivate voters on both sides of the issue.

"Demographic Problem"

"It's going to create a renewed sense of panic and fear," said Fernand Amandi, a principal at Bendixen & Amandi, a Miami-based market research firm that did work for Obama's 2012 campaign. "You're not just voting for president: You're voting on whether friends, family, neighbors or colleagues get to stay in the country."

Republicans, meanwhile, "have a big demographic problem," said John Feehery, a Republican strategist and lobbyist who backs Trump. "We have to expand our base to be competitive in future elections. But for this particular election I can see scenarios where it helps both sides. There's a bigger untapped pool of white voters who resent immigration, and they will flock to Trump."

Crucial Constituency

Obama made passing reference to Trump in his remarks without naming him.

"Pretending that we can deport 11 million people or build a wall without spending tens of billions of taxpayers' money is abetting what's not correct," he said. "It's not going to work. It's a fantasy."

Latinos are a crucial constituency in states including Florida, Nevada and Colorado that are battlegrounds in the presidential election. They widely perceive Trump's campaign rhetoric as fanning hostility toward them, alienating even ethnic groups such as Cubans and Puerto Ricans for whom immigration policy isn't directly relevant, Amandi said.

"This will be a flash-point focal issue in the Hispanic community," Amandi said.

Obama said that U.S. immigration enforcement under his administration would continue to focus on "criminals," "gang-bangers" and people who have recently entered the country. "What we don't do is to prioritize people who've been here a long time, who are otherwise law-abiding, who have roots and connections in their communities," he said.

Marginal Impact

Given the intensity of feelings on immigration and the focus on the issue in the Republican primary, the Supreme Court's deadlock may have only a marginal additional impact, said Charles Cook, editor and publisher of the non-partisan *Cook Political Report*.

"The battle lines are drawn and the coalitions are formed," Cook said.

"You have increasing numbers of minority voters who believe the Republican party is of, by and for whites and looks down on anybody else," Cook said. "It is very, very clear where most working-class whites are: they see trade and immigration as threats to their jobs and their lifestyles."

> **Trump won the Republican presidential primary with promises to deport all undocumented immigrants and build a wall on the southern border to reduce unauthorized immigration from Latin America.**

While the mass shooting in Orlando recently propelled terrorism and gun control to the center of political debate, passions surrounding immigration have figured prominently in the political campaign, especially on the Republican side.

Southern Border

Trump won the Republican presidential primary with promises to deport all undocumented immigrants and build a wall on the southern border to reduce unauthorized immigration from Latin America.

When Gallup pollsters asked Americans the single most important challenge for the next president to address, immigration outstripped all other issues except the economy.

Immigration was cited by 14 percent, behind 19 percent who said the economy, according to the May 18-22 poll. Among Republicans and Republican-leaning independents, 17 percent called immigration the most important issue in the election.

"In the end, it is my firm belief that immigration is not something to fear," Obama said.

Registration Surge

There are signs that Trump is stoking a surge in Latino voter registration and citizenship application by immigrants.

In Georgia, Hispanic voter registration soared 19 percent from October 13 to April 26, the deadline to register in order to vote in this year's primary, according to the Secretary of State's office. Should many new Latino voters show up to vote in November, Democrat Hillary Clinton's chances of winning states like Colorado, Arizona and even Georgia would be significantly improved.

Clinton has said she would expand on Obama's immigration plan to include the parents of undocumented immigrants brought into the country as youth.

"I believe that President Obama acted well within his constitutional and legal authority," Clinton said in a statement after the decision was announced.

U.S. citizenship applications in the first quarter rose 28 percent from the same quarter last year. Though citizenship applications typically rise in presidential election years, there was only a 19 percent increase in 2012.

"Now we've got a choice about who we're going to be as a country, what we want to teach our kids, and how we want to be represented in Congress, and in the White House," Obama said. "These are all the questions that voters now are going to have to ask themselves and are going to have to answer in November."

Print Citations

CMS: Dorning, Mike. "Supreme Court's Split Elevates Immigration as Election Issue." In *The Reference Shelf: Campaign Trends and Election Law*, edited by Betsy Maury, 123-25. Ipswitch, MA: Salem Press, 2016.

MLA: Dorning, Mike. "Supreme Court's Split Elevates Immigration as Election Issue." *The Reference Shelf: Campaign Trends and Election Law*. Ed. Betsy Maury. Ipswitch: Salem Press, 2016. 123-25. Print.

APA: Dorning, M. (2016). Supreme court's split elevates immigration as election issue. In Betsy Maury (Ed.), *The reference shelf: Campaign trends and election law* (pp. 123-125). Ipswitch, MA: Salem. (Original work published 2016)

Simmering for Decades, Anger About Trade Boils Over in '16 Election

By Binyamin Appelbaum
The New York Times, **March 29, 2016**

The United States is in the midst of one of the longest economic expansions in its history. Even American factories have lately added hundreds of thousands of jobs.

Meanwhile, the rest of the world is stumbling. Even China.

Yet at perhaps the least likely moment in the last several decades, misgivings about globalization are playing a starring role in the presidential election. Why now?

Anger about unbalanced trade has helped to fuel the rise of Donald J. Trump, the Republican front-runner, and the success of Senator Bernie Sanders of Vermont in his bid for the Democratic nomination. The manifest anger also has pushed their principal rivals, Republican Senator Ted Cruz and the Democratic front-runner, Hillary Clinton, to toughen their own trade rhetoric.

It is a situation that has surprised many experts because polls show voters' concern about the overall health of the American economy has declined significantly in recent years.

Yet many Americans are just taking stock of the transformations wrought by global trade. In two dozen conversations with voters across the country, only two said they had heard of the proposed new trade deal, the Trans-Pacific Partnership, involving the United States and a host of Pacific Rim nations.

Instead, the concerns they expressed were about changes in their own lives and communities over the last couple of decades.

"When we first did that big trade agreement I thought it was a good idea, but now I'm getting a little more conservative about it," said Phyllis Arthur, a 74-year-old Republican from Walnut Creek, California "I think we're being overwhelmed by the goods coming in. That's practically all that's available in the stores."

Kevin White, a 47-year-old Democrat from Dayton, Ohio, said it was hard to find a job. He used to work at a hospital; now he gets federal disability payments.

"The jobs went overseas," lamented Mr. White. "Then people couldn't afford their mortgages and we had a crash and nobody was able to buy anything."

Douglas Irwin, an economist at Dartmouth College who studies trade, said the impact of China's economic rise had become more visible in recent years, even though the worst effects of its rise may already be in the past.

Between 2000 and 2011, imports from China grew to equal 2.6 percent of

American economic output, up from around 1 percent. That "unprecedented shock" was much larger than that from the increase in Japanese imports in the 1980s or Mexican imports in the 1990s, Mr. Irwin said. China's rise, fueled in part by currency manipulation to make its exports cheaper, played a key role in the loss of roughly five million American manufacturing jobs.

Those losses, however, were offset and obscured during the housing boom by a rise in construction jobs. Now, both the factory jobs and the construction jobs have gone away.

Rationally, said Mr. Irwin, "It's too late to get upset about China."

The United States is no longer losing factory jobs. It has added 600,000 over the last five years. Beijing is no longer suppressing its currency; it's now trying to prop up the value.

Politically, however, it appears that the moment is perfectly ripe.

Ahead of another Rust Belt primary next Tuesday in Wisconsin, Mr. Trump is pressing for "fair trade" with foreign countries, while Mr. Cruz has adopted similar language. "We're going to see millions and millions of new high paying jobs," Mr. Cruz told a crowd at an Oshkosh plastics factory on Monday, "coming back to America, coming back from China, coming back from Mexico."

Personalities also appear to be playing a role. Mr. Trump has proved an unusually effective spokesman for concerns among Republican voters. "You look at those empty factories all over the place, and nobody hits that message better than me," he said after winning the Republican primary in Michigan this month.

Mr. Sanders has connected with a Democratic base whose support for President Obama may have damped longstanding concerns about trade.

Mr. Trump and Mr. Sanders have also succeeded in focusing anger on trade as an explanation for broader economic problems afflicting many Americans. Trade flows make up a small part of America's economic activity. The primary explanations for the stagnation of middle-

> **Mainstream economists regard the evidence as unequivocal that trade has produced significant benefits for the American economy and the average household.**

class incomes are necessarily domestic.

"They are following in the footsteps of politicians of all stripes who have found it convenient to blame the boogeyman of unfair trade for domestic economic problems," said Eswar Prasad, a Cornell economist. "Tough talk on trade is an easy way to distract attention from taking on difficult domestic challenges."

Mainstream economists regard the evidence as unequivocal that trade has produced significant benefits for the American economy and the average household.

Yet much of the American public has long been skeptical. A recent *New York Times*/CBS News poll found that 61 percent of respondents favored more trade restrictions to protect domestic industry, just as a majority of respondents has favored increased restrictions in every such poll since 1988.

Charles Shank began to change his mind about foreign trade in the early 2000s as he carried the pieces of Pennsylvania factories south to the Mexican border to be reassembled there.

Mr. Shank, then working as a truck driver, supported the expansion of trade with Mexico and Canada. A registered Republican, Mr. Shank said he subscribed to the party's position that trade deals would open new markets for American companies.

But Mr. Shank, now retired, said the politicians made a mistake. He said he planned to vote in Pennsylvania's coming presidential primary for a candidate who would "go back and renegotiate" better deals with the nation's trading partners.

"I think our trade deals were good ideas with good intentions, but I don't think it had enough controls to protect the United States," said Mr. Shank, 65. "The fact that the factories are leaving, there's something wrong with that whole system right there."

At the same time, Mr. Shank has personally benefited from globalization. He spent years driving imported goods to market. Trade reduced the price of his television and his clothing and increased the variety of food available at the local grocery store.

Like many Americans, Mr. Shank said he would still rather pay more for American goods. A recent Bloomberg poll conducted by Selzer & Company found just 13 percent of respondents said they wanted goods at the lowest price, while 82 percent of respondents said they wanted goods made in America.

But do they?

Mr. Shank said he has always driven Dodge trucks.

He paused.

"Actually," he said, "this year, I bought a Mazda."

Economists and politicians understated the costs of globalization, which tend to be more concentrated than the benefits. Everyone gets a discount; some people lose their jobs. Moreover, the United States has lagged significantly behind other developed countries in providing support for those left behind.

Linda Young lost a good job in 1998 when Munekata America, which made plastic cases for televisions and other electronics, closed its factory in Dalton, Georgia, because most of the companies it served had moved to Mexico. Ms. Young worked until the factory's final day, packing equipment so it, too, could be shipped to Mexico.

Ms. Young, 62, ran a restaurant for a few years. She now cares for her grandchildren.

Her children have navigated globalization with greater success. Her son works for an electric motor company that once served the carpet factories that dominated Dalton but now focuses on construction equipment. Her son-in-law lost his job at one of those carpet plants last year, after 26 years, but, a few months later, he found work at the new Volkswagen plant in nearby Chattanooga, Tennessee.

Ms. Young said she knew globalization had improved the lives of millions around the world. But she was thinking about Dalton's decline when she decided to vote for Mr. Trump in Georgia's Republican primary.

"I don't see their future being better than mine," Ms. Young said of her grandchildren. "I understand we have to help others, but I think we should be a little more astute about helping ourselves."

Giovanni Russonello contributed research.

Print Citations

CMS: Appelbaum, Binyamin. "Simmering for Decades, Anger About Trade Boils Over in '16 Election." In *The Reference Shelf: Campaign Trends and Election Law*, edited by Betsy Maury, 126-29. Ipswitch, MA: Salem Press, 2016.

MLA: Appelbaum, Binyamin. "Simmering for Decades, Anger About Trade Boils Over in '16 Election." *The Reference Shelf: Campaign Trends and Election Law*. Ed. Betsy Maury. Ipswitch: Salem Press, 2016. 126-29. Print.

APA: Appelbaum, B. (2016). Simmering for decades, anger about trade boils over in '16 election. In Betsy Maury (Ed.), *The reference shelf: Campaign trends and election law* (pp. 126-129). Ipswitch, MA: Salem. (Original work published 2016)

Why the Conditions Were Perfect for Bernie's Socialist Crusade

By Robert Kuttner
The American Prospect, March 31, 2016

Once again, Bernie Sanders has demonstrated, with a trifecta of big wins in Hawaii, Alaska, and Washington State, that he has broad and enthusiastic support, especially among the young. Equally astonishing is the large percentage of voters who say they are attracted rather than repelled by Sanders's embrace of socialism.

But if you'd bother to conduct your own focus group among Americans under 40, neither phenomenon should be surprising. Except for those graduating from elite universities, with either full scholarships or wealthy tuition-paying parents, this is the stunted generation—young adults venturing into a world of work, loaded with student debt, unable to find stable jobs or decent careers.

This is also the post-Cold War generation, for whom Soviet communism is a distant memory (along with reliable jobs). For this generation of Americans, capitalism is not exactly a good word, nor is socialism a bad one.

And this is the generation that finds employer-paid health insurance hard to find; often the "Bronze" version of the Affordable Care Act, with its high out-of-pocket payments, is all they can afford; a generation paying too much of unreliable incomes in rent, and putting off the dream of homeownership and having children.

> **Jobs that used to pay decently are being turned into inferior jobs, whether in the manufacturing economy or the service economy.**

So, when a candidate comes along calling for free college education and free universal health care, and far higher minimum wages, it sounds pretty fine. And if capitalism means the 1 percent making off with everything that isn't nailed down, then maybe Sanders-style socialism is worth a try. So say the young.

Private frustrations and longings have at last become politicized. And well they should be. Because the reality of the rules of the game turning brutally against the young has nothing to do with technology or the immutable realities of the digital economy—and everything to do with who gets to write the rules.

The policy wonk types like to point out that the Sanders program would require a huge tax increase.

And indeed it would. But as long as the tax hike is on the upper brackets, that only adds to the appeal of the program. During and after World War II, the top marginal tax rate was north of 90 percent, and this was the era of a record economic boom.

At the heart of this generational revolution is the vanishing good job. Until recently, the claims of a new, on-demand economy, made up of short-term gigs, was challenged by economists, even liberal ones.

It was kind of a new category that didn't show up in the data. You could debate whether Uber and Task Rabbit and kindred companies were good or evil, but they just didn't affect that many workers.

Now, belatedly, this shift is being confirmed. The economists are right—most of the unreliable jobs are not on-demand gigs. Rather, they are other forms of lousy "contingent" work. That category includes temping, contract work, on-call workers, workers hired by staffing agencies, workers with no job security, and inferior forms of conventional employment like adjunct college professors who can make less than minimum wage, Ph.D.'s and all. (So much for the education cure.)

Jobs that used to pay decently are being turned into inferior jobs, whether in the manufacturing economy or the service economy. Yes there is an uptick in entrepreneurship, but for every young person who creates a company like Amazon, there are tens of thousands working in its warehouses.

The Wall Street Journal, of all places, reports a 60 percent increase since 2005 in the proportion of U.S. workers who have these inferior forms of employment.

The Labor Department, denied adequate funding to update its numbers, had not revised its count of contingent workers. So two eminently mainstream economists, Lawrence Katz of Harvard and Alan Krueger of Princeton (one of the very people carping about the cost of Sanders' program) hired the Rand Corporation to do what the Labor Department should be doing—surveying actual current workers.

Katz and Krueger analyzed the results. And guess what? They confirmed in rich detail what your local 28-year-old could tell you: Real jobs are getting harder and harder to find. No wonder the uptick in GDP growth is not impressing voters, especially younger ones.

So Sanders is likely to continue making off with the youth vote. Even if he falls short of the nomination, this is bad news for Hillary Clinton. Whatever her other virtues, most young Americans don't see her speaking to the realities of their condition.

This also presents a real conundrum for mainstream, moderate liberal economists like Katz and Krueger. Altering these trends will require radical reforms, not adjustments at the margins.

Sanders's program may cost a lot of money. It may be socialistic. And it may require congressional majorities that will be a long time coming. But Sanders has the loyalty of the kids because he is speaking the truth.

Print Citations

CMS: Kuttner, Robert. "Why the Conditions Were Perfect for Bernie's Socialist Crusade." In *The Reference Shelf: Campaign Trends and Election Law*, edited by Betsy Maury, 130-31. Ipswitch, MA: Salem Press, 2016.

MLA: Kuttner, Robert. "Why the Conditions Were Perfect for Bernie's Socialist Crusade." *The Reference Shelf: Campaign Trends and Election Law*. Ed. Betsy Maury. Ipswitch: Salem Press, 2016. 130-31. Print.

APA: Kuttner, R. (2016). Why the conditions were perfect for Bernie's socialist crusade. In Betsy Maury (Ed.), *The reference shelf: Campaign trends and election law* (pp. 130-131). Ipswitch, MA: Salem. (Original work published 2016)

Election 2016 Is Propelled by the American Economy's Failed Promises

By Jon Hilsenrath and Bob Davis
The Wall Street Journal, July 7, 2016

When U.S. economic leaders in April 2000 gathered in the White House to mark a decade long expansion, the consensus was clear. Trade, technology and a wise central bank had helped fuel an era of rising prosperity.

Stick to that model, Alan Greenspan, then Federal Reserve Chairman, told the assembly, and "I do not believe we can go wrong."

Much did go wrong. The economic stability and robust growth the U.S. enjoyed in the previous decade proved to be in its final throes. After 2000, the economy would experience two recessions, a technology-bubble collapse followed by a housing boom, then the largest financial crisis in 75 years and a prolonged period of weak growth.

The past decade and a half has proved so turbulent and disappointing it has upended basic assumptions about modern economics and our political system. This string of disappointments has resulted in one of the most unpredictable and unconventional political seasons in modern history, with the rise of Donald Trump and Bernie Sanders.

Median household income, accounting for inflation, has dropped 7% since 2000, and the income gap widened between the wealthy and everyone else. Even though official measures of unemployment have receded from post-recession peaks, seven in 10 Americans believe the nation is on the wrong track, the most recent *Wall Street Journal*/NBC poll found.

The 2016 election is shaping up in large part as a referendum on an economic model that is widely seen as failing. Messrs. Trump and Sanders argue that policies celebrated 16 years ago no longer work for most Americans, a message that is resonating widely among those who have most suffered the consequences. Mr. Trump confounded expectations to win his party's presumptive nomination. Mr. Sanders, though losing his, will take his message to the convention and has yanked his party to the left.

The Promise

America had an economic model that wouldn't fail.

The Reality

American median household incomes, adjusted for inflation, have fallen 7% since 2000. In the process, a persistent majority of individuals have come to believe the country is on the wrong track.

This article begins a series examining the economic roots of that disillusionment and its social and political consequences.

The disappointments are many and deep seated. China, whose vast market seemed to promise prosperity for U.S. exporters, itself became a giant exporter, dealing blows to U.S. communities far more damaging than earlier import waves from Japan and Mexico.

Technology delivered gadgets and software but didn't produce the anticipated economic growth or jobs, especially for those without advanced education. Central bankers, once deified globally, couldn't foresee or manage the financial storms that eventually leveled the global economy.

Economic maelstroms deepened social problems, as working-class communities especially were challenged by drugs, out-of-wedlock births, a dearth of employment opportunities, suicides and fraying social institutions. The problems are scrambling Democrats and Republicans, sending them to new populist frontiers and forcing party leaders to grapple with their purpose and values.

Contributing to the rethink is a sense that Washington, because of gridlock, venality or incompetence, is itself broken and can't fix what ails America.

Workers have come out short-handed. In 2000, they collected 66% of national income through wages, salaries and benefits. That dropped to 61% after the recession and has only recently partially recovered. Profits have risen to 12% of income from 8%.

I do not believe we can go far wrong if we maintain a consistent, vigilant, noninflationary monetary policy...a trade policy that fosters international competition...and an education policy that ensures all Americans can acquire the skills needed to participate in what may well be the most productive economy ever.

—Alan Greenspan, April 2000

In the process, 30 years of established wisdom about how to manage capitalism has been upended by events and challenged by Mr. Trump and Mr. Sanders—the most serious challenge thus far to the post-Cold War economic consensus. Red states and blue states are being redefined along new lines: haves and have-nots.

A recent Pew Research Center poll found 61% of Trump supporters and 91% of Sanders supporters see the economic system as tilted toward powerful interests. Both embrace a new nationalism that rejects global integration and the influence of what they describe as moneyed interests.

It isn't just the public rethinking the old model. Among policy makers and leading economists themselves, the desultory results of the past decade and a half have prompted soul-searching and a re-evaluation of some central tenets of what drives prosperity.

"I went back to square one and asked, 'Where did I miss it and why?' " Mr. Greenspan says. He was wrong about his faith that markets on balance acted rationally, he says. "I had presumed that irrational behavior on the whole was essentially random and produced nothing of value."

Instead, he says, bouts of fear and greed are systematic, leading markets to overshoot and undershoot.

"We've all had to get a dose of humility," says Martin Baily, chairman of President Bill Clinton's Council of Economic Advisers in 2000 and an attendee at that celebratory White House reception.

The Promise

Central banks can manage the balance between growth and inflation and the fallout from financial bubbles.

The Reality

The Fed didn't deliver the growth it expected, consistently undershot its own inflation objective, and missed the buildup of financial excesses which caused the 2007-2009 financial crisis.

The economic rethinking under way is far from complete and echoes the reexamination that occurred after the Great Depression. A new army of economists is investigating what went wrong. Their work will shape how the U.S. deals with trade, monetary policy, technology, the workforce and fiscal policy for decades, though their conclusions aren't always in line with the populism embraced in the political arena.

Mark Gertler, a New York University economics professor, is rewriting models for central banking and the macroeconomy, filling gaps in how economists thought financial markets and monetary policy affected the economy.

For Fed officials in the early 2000s, an article of faith was that manipulating a single interest rate—an overnight-lending bank rate called the federal-funds rate—could keep the economy on an even keel. Mr. Gertler's research partner, Princeton professor and future Fed chairman Ben Bernanke, argued central banks helped create a "Great Moderation" of stable growth and low inflation.

We have had a Federal Reserve that has focused on elongating this economic expansion and has also emphasized appropriate regulation of our banking institutions.
—Abby Joseph Cohen, Goldman Sachs analyst, April 2000

The moderation turned out to be a mirage.

"There certainly was a lot of hubris about the ability to stabilize the economy," says Mr. Gertler.

Mr. Gertler is seeking new ways to account for the risks of financial crises, collapsing banks and other unstable financial institutions. Yet many central-banking dilemmas the last crisis uncovered remain unresolved. Among them: Central bankers aren't at all sure better regulation, the preferred tool of Mr. Gertler and Mr. Bernanke, can prevent another crisis.

Perhaps most vexing, central banks themselves might spark crises by pushing rates down in a quest for growth. "We're stuck," says Raghuram Rajan, the Reserve Bank of India's governor. "We cannot admit the tools we have are less and less powerful than we predicted and may have perverse effects."

The Promise

Technology would lead to rising incomes and broadly shared prosperity.

The Reality

Productivity and output growth have slowed and technology has been polarizing the workforce.

At the Massachusetts Institute of Technology, Erik Brynjolfsson is looking at unexpected ways technology has reshaped the economy by sharply reducing jobs and adding to the pool of disillusioned workers. In the 1990s, he was among the first economists to show computer technology was finally boosting worker productivity, a crucial ingredient in economic growth.

> **U.S. leaders in 2000 anticipated an era of rising prosperity. Much went wrong in ways few foresaw, laying groundwork for Donald Trump and Bernie Sanders.**

His view about workers' gains from technology has turned gloomier. Measured productivity growth has slowed dramatically. He and co-author Andrew McAfee, an MIT business-technology specialist, found that as computing power transforms society, it swallows more jobs—a development they say is accelerating.

Software investment doubled to 1.6% of GDP in the 1990s, as factories and offices added computers that helped firms manage with fewer workers. The shift started hurting workers whose skills computers could replace.

Information technology today represents only 10% of American jobs, but is responsible for 30% of our economic growth...rifling through every sector of our economy, increasing the power of American firms and individuals to share broadly in its prosperity.
—Bill Clinton, April 2000

For a time, those with bachelors' degrees in science seemed safe from automation-prompted layoffs—their knowledge was tough for computers to duplicate—as did less-educated workers in personal service, such as home health aides. Economists argued more education was crucial to future success.

That advice, says Mr. McAfee, turned out to be "way too narrow."

Between 2000 and 2012, estimates Harvard economist David Deming, the hollowing-out of work spread to professions including librarians and engineers. Those with the right skills came out ahead, a big reason the income gap widened. The top 20% of American families accounted for 48.9% of total income in 2014, Census figures show, versus 44.3% in 1990.

The U.S. is on the cusp of a new innovation wave, Mr. Brynjolfsson says, represented by Google's self-driving car. Look for demand for Uber and taxi drivers to expand, he says, then crash, eliminating another job with a middle-class salary—adding still more workers to the ranks feeling betrayed by old economic models.

THE GREAT UNRAVELING

Most presidential elections turn on voter perceptions of the economy, from Ronald Reagan's 1980 invocation of a "misery index," which combined readings of inflation and unemployment, to Barack Obama's call for a powerful government response to the 2008 financial-sector collapse.

Something similar is happening today, only more dramatically. Until Mr. Trump's successful primary run, Republicans cast themselves as the champions of free markets and low marginal-tax rates. Democrats have been the party of activist government that tries to tweak the economy so it shifts in a desired direction.

The economy's long underperformance has scrambled the debate. Old prescriptions, such as tax cuts by Republicans in the early 2000s and government spending by Democrats, haven't delivered prosperity, leading voters to cast about for alternatives.

Those alternatives narrowed to Mr. Trump, who promised to rip up trade deals and deport millions of illegal immigrants, and Mr. Sanders, who would break up big banks, tax stock trading and match Mr. Trump as an opponent of free-trade deals.

China, more than any other issue, shows the disillusionment with globalization.

At the 2000 White House conference, President Clinton said expanded trade with China would "open their markets to our goods and services."

The Promise

Trade with China and other nations would have a net positive impact on the economy as it would expose the world's largest population to U.S. goods and services, while those hurt by trade in America would adapt and be supported.

The Reality

Trade with China turned out to be a bigger shock to the economy than anybody expected, and the adjustment of the workforce slower.

Reality has been rougher on American workers. Hillary Clinton, who pushed a Pacific Rim trade deal as secretary of state, now positions herself as tough on China and opposes that same trade deal.

Mr. Trump has made China-bashing a campaign centerpiece. Of America's 100 counties with industries most exposed to Chinese imports, 89 voted for him in

Republican primaries. Of the 100 least-exposed counties, before all of his competitors dropped out, 28 gave him the nod. Mr. Sanders takes a tough line on China.

Economists long recognized import competition hurt some workers but generally dismissed the costs as small relative to benefits such as cheaper goods. Research from widening trade with countries such as Japan and Mexico confirmed that theory, despite activists' targeting the North American Free Trade Agreement as a job-killer.

Economists were blinded, though, to the scale of potential downsides, says Gordon Hanson, a University of California at San Diego economist. His work shows how soaring Chinese imports, which picked up after Beijing joined the World Trade Organization in 2001, magnified technology's impact on jobs. "We were the high priests protecting free trade," he says. "There was a little bit of intellectual insularity."

We in this country have to worry about those who have been left behind in this country, and we have to worry about our role in the world and the vote in China in the next several months will be a crucial test of our country's international sentiment.
—Lawrence Summers, Treasury Secretary, April 2000

Chinese competition, goosed partly by a currency China kept cheap, had far greater effects on U.S. manufacturing than any country since World War II—a finding MIT labor economist David Autor has helped make mainstream with Mr. Hanson and David Dorn of the University of Zurich. The trio studied 722 communities around the country and how they responded to import competition.

Their conclusion overturned conventional wisdom. China was simply different, they found in a 2013 paper. Its workforce was so vast, wages so low and productivity rising so fast, it caused greater disruptions in the American labor market than any country before.

"Washington and we in the establishment spent too much time celebrating the efficiency gains of trade," says Timothy Adams, U.S. Treasury undersecretary under President George W. Bush, "and not enough time thinking about the people who were impacted."

Between 2000 and 2007, import competition from China accounted for 982,000 manufacturing jobs lost, about one-fourth of all manufacturing job losses. Between 1999 and 2011, work published this year found, China accounted for 2.4 million jobs lost, including manufacturing and service jobs.

That loss might have been less damaging if U.S. workers were shifting from declining industries and towns and into growing ones, as they once did. However, fewer workers are willing to move, Mr. Autor and his co-authors wrote. Moreover, America is producing fewer fast-growing startups.

Surveying U.S. economic prospects, former Clinton Treasury Secretary Lawrence Summers invokes a Depression-era idea, "secular stagnation," to argue a dearth of investment opportunities is holding back spending and growth while the income gap has created an overabundance of savings pushing down interest rates.

In the slow-growth world he foresees, global trade becomes more fraught as competitors grab for pieces of a pie that isn't growing rapidly. Tensions over currency policies mount. Central banks have limited tools to cushion blows, putting pressure on fiscal policy—taxes and spending to boost investment—to spur demand.

That wasn't what Mr. Summers argued at the 2000 White House conference, where he said the private sector was so abundant "with staggering high quality investment opportunities" it was the government's job to get out of the way.

Today he says the government must help. "The world has changed," he says. "So my views have changed."

Print Citations

CMS: Hilsenrath, Jon, and Bob Davis. "Election 2016 Is Propelled by the American Economy's Failed Promises." In *The Reference Shelf: Campaign Trends and Election Law*, edited by Betsy Maury, 132-38. Ipswitch, MA: Salem Press, 2016.

MLA: Hilsenrath, Jon, and Bob Davis. "Election 2016 Is Propelled by the American Economy's Failed Promises." *The Reference Shelf: Campaign Trends and Election Law*. Ed. Betsy Maury. Ipswitch: Salem Press, 2016. 132-38. Print.

APA: Hilsenrath, J., & B. Davis. (2016). Election 2016 is propelled by the American economy's failed promises. In Betsy Maury (Ed.),*The reference shelf: Campaign trends and election law* (pp. 132-138). Ipswitch, MA: Salem. (Original work published 2016)

4
Campaign Messaging: Language, Social Media, Video

Robyn Beck / AFP/Getty Images

Attendees at a town hall for digital content creators and social media influencers with Hillary Clinton (not in photo) listen as a question is asked of the presumptive Democratic president nominee, June 28, 2016 in Hollywood, California.

News and Information in
the 2016 Campaign

The importance of the media in American politics, and international politics, cannot be overstated. For centuries, print (and later televised) media have helped to inform voters on key issues, to lobby for and against specific legislative proposals or political candidates, and to investigate the truth behind political statements and initiatives. In the first US presidential election, between Thomas Jefferson and John Adams (with Washington having run unopposed for both terms in office), the campaign teams for Jefferson and Adams fought a fierce battle in the press, and it was in the 1796 race that the now venerable tradition of "mudslinging"—publishing insults, political "dirt," and exaggerated or false stories about rival candidates—became a part of American campaigns.[1] In the 2010s, the influence of the traditional press has waned, with campaign messaging increasingly focused on a plurality of sources, including a vast array of social media sites, rather than on the traditional mix of newspapers, magazines, and television.

In general, digital media democratized mass communication and made American politics more participatory for millions of Americans. However, historians and political analysts are divided over whether or not the Internet and social media has been good for politics as a whole, or has diluted and confused the process of disseminating information. Some argue that, in the age of social media, soundbytes and controversial, often uncontextualized, comments have been elevated to the level of national news stories and that this attention to minor detail, with candidates more often communicating in 140 word Tweets than through full speeches, has only served to complicate and obscure the transmission of legitimate news and information. Theorists are essentially asking whether digital media has helped or simply cluttered the political process.

In the 2008 election, analysts believe that Facebook was essential to Barack Obama's victory as Obama's campaign was the first to make effective use of the medium.[2] While Facebook dominated the social media environment in the 2008 and 2012 elections, and remains the most used social media outlet in 2016, during the ensuing years, Twitter eclipsed Facebook in popularity with younger users and became an important political tool. One of the primary differences between Twitter and Facebook is that Twitter is more interactive, providing the perception that consumers are interacting directly with candidates and/or celebrities. Heading into 2016, some media analysts speculated that it would be Twitter that would determine the winners and losers of the 2016 race.

Social Media in 2016

A poll in January of 2016 found that at least 44 percent of Americans were getting at least some information about the campaign from social media. For the first time in history, social media outpaced all of the major news outlets, whether online, televised, or in print, in terms of consumer reach. A Pew Research study in July, found that, although Clinton's campaign produced as many tweets and posts as Trump's campaign, Trump received far more media attention. However, media analysts were uncertain whether Twitter's reach translated into the ability to legitimately reach undecided voters. Megan McArdle, of *Bloomberg News*, believes that because social media outlets curate content, providing users with more of the kind of content they seem to "like," social media feeds become increasingly one-sided, reflecting a voter's own desires rather than a realistic view of the campaign.[3]

Donald Trump arguably used social media more effectively than any other candidate in the 2016 race, but it remains to be seen whether Trump's use of Twitter and Facebook was good or bad for his campaign. Though Trump's social media persona certainly attracted the lion's share of media attention, many of the candidate's inflammatory posts and comments also arguably helped to make Trump one of the least popular presidential candidates in history, with a disapproval rate of over 60 percent in August. For instance, when Trump's insulting Tweet criticizing the parents of Muslim Army Capt. Humayun Khan, killed by a suicide bomber in Iraq, for speaking against him at the Democratic National Convention, garnered Trump widespread attention, though most of the attention was negative. The Veterans of Foreign Wars and House Republican Speaker Paul Ryan, though typically conservative supporters, took to social media to criticize Trump's controversial comments.

Digital videos of Trump's rallies in Ohio and Pennsylvania, disseminated through social media, produced further controversy. In August, for instance, Trump insinuated in a filmed rally that Clinton would abolish the Second Amendment if elected (which media outlets noted was fundamentally speculative and not based on Clinton's voting history) and stated that, if she was elected, perhaps the "Second Amendment people" could do something about it. A media firestorm ensued, with some accusing Trump of implicitly supporting violent action against Clinton. Trump claimed that these allegations were due to media misinterpretation and bias, but the United States Secret Service claimed to have contacted the Trump campaign about the remark.[4]

Trump's tendency to use Twitter as a platform for issuing insults and controversial statements has made the candidate enormously popular. As of August, 2016, Mr. Trump had 22.7 followers on Facebook, Twitter, and Instagram, while Clinton had earned closer to 15 million. Trump referred to his domination of social media as representing a "Twitter army" supporting his candidacy. Numerous articles theorized about the potential significance of Trump's social media popularity, however, experts in the field were careful to point out that having a follower is not the same as having a supporter. Trump is more active on Twitter and is not shy about tweeting simple, personal messages or reactions to various events or incidents, while Clinton's tweets are more formal, and reminiscent of campaign soundbytes. But, the question remains: Is Trump actually winning anything by dominating the Twitter conversation? With so many of Mr. Trump's tweets and posts reprinted in the media or retweeted to highlight their controversial tone or message, analysts are unsure what percentage of the "Twitter Army" follow him because they support him and what percentage of his followers are actually his critics and opponents or simply follow him because he offers a more entertaining feed.

Even supposing that Trump's Twitter followers are also supporters, the impact of Trump's "Twitter Army," as well as the impact of the followers of the other candidates, may be far less than some media outlets have speculated. An analysis of Twitter statistics on the political website *FiveThirtyEight,* shows that at least 8 percent of Trump's Twitter followers, and 7 percent of Clinton's, are actually fake accounts, with the likelihood that the actual number of fake accounts is considerably higher.[5] In 2008, and to a lesser extent in 2012, the candidate (in both cases Obama) who was able to marshal social media had a better line of communication with young voters. Since then, the demographics of social media have changed, with a higher percentage of older consumers using Twitter and Facebook, while the mainstream media increasingly covers Twitter commentary as news. Unlike campaign donations or attending rallies, following someone on social media requires little effort, little commitment, and little thought. For all these reasons, though the political social media revolution continues to be big news, time will determine how media popularity translates into votes.

Bias and Trust

A September 2015 Gallup Poll found that American trust in mass media had hit a historic low, with only 40 percent of Americans saying that they have either "a great deal" or "a fair amount" of trust in mass media to be accurate and fair. By contrast, in 1997, 53 percent of Americans expressed trust in mainstream media's accuracy. The Iraq War was a turning point for American trust in the media as the controversial GOP military agenda created a deeper divide in American public opinion and ideological reporting became far more common. In 2004, for the first time, a minority (44 percent) said they trusted the media. Since then, despite some transient upticks in media confidence, Americans' trust in the media has continued to erode.[6]

The erosion of trust in the media has been, in part, influenced by persistent campaigning to convince the American public that various news outlets should not be trusted. Such campaigning exists on both sides of the conservative/liberal divide. Studies have repeatedly shown that the conservative news outlet Fox News and the liberal news outlet MSNBC, dedicate less time to factual reporting than they do to news commentary and opinion, and both networks do so with strong ideological and political bias. A study from Fairleigh Dickinson University in 2012 asked NPR, Fox News, MSNBC, CNN, and talk radio listeners/viewers to submit to a test of their political knowledge. The same questions were posed to respondents who did not consume any political or news media and relied on family and friends for news and information. NPR listeners were found to be the most well-informed media consumers, while those who reported watching "only Fox News," could answer fewer questions correctly than individuals who never watched/listened to any news media.[7] Some sources show that conservative Trump supporters have begun to turn against Fox News due to the outlets' continued attacks on Trump's campaign. The candidates February 2016 Tweet, "@FoxNews is so biased it is disgusting. They do not want Trump to win. All negative!," was retweeted 30,899 times.[8]

While the majority of Americans agree that the major news outlets are not trustworthy, what about social media? According to a 2016 Pew report, 38 percent of Americans get most of their news online. The percentage is higher for younger consumers, with 50 percent of those 18–29 and 49 percent of those 30–49 getting most of their news from Internet sources. Internet news is more popular with those who prefer reading news to televised news programs. In addition, social media news is more popular with consumers who like to stay current while on the go, with 72 percent of Americans using mobile devices to read or watch news items. The study also found that social media outlets were the least trusted source for news. Pew found that US consumers trusted social media less than all national or local news outlets, and less than getting news through family, friends, and acquaintances.[9]

Micah L Issitt

Works Used

"American Presidential Candidates and Social Media." *Economist*. Economist Newspaper. Feb 29 2016. Web. 18 Aug 2016.

Beaujon, Andrew. "Survey: NPR's Listeners Best-Informed, Fox Viewers Worst-Informed." *Poynter*. The Poynter Institute. May 23 2012. Web. 18 Aug 2016.

Bialik, Carl. "Everyone Has Fake Twitter Followers, But Trump Has the Most. Sad!" *Fivethirtyeight*. *Five Thirty Eight*. Apr 14 2016. Web. 18 Aug 2016.

Goodtimes, Johnny. "A Brief History of Campaign Mudslinging, From 1796 to Today." *Philadephila Magazine*. Metro Corp. Oct 24 2012. Web. 18 Aug 2016.

"How Social Media Inflates Our Perception of Our Choice Presidential Candidate." *NPR*. National Public Radio. Apr 16 2016. Web. 18 Aug 2016.

"How the Presidential Candidates Use the Web and Social Media." *Pew Research*. Pew Research Center. Aug 15 2012. Web. 18 Aug 2016.

Krieg, Gregory. "Donald Trump's 27-day Spiral: From Convention Bounce to Campaign Overhaul." *CNN*. Cable News Network. Aug 18 2016. Web. 18 Aug 2016.

Mitchell, Amy, Gottfried, Jeffrey, Barthel, Michael, and Elisa Shearer. "The Modern News Consumer." *Pew Research Center*. Jul 7 2016. Web. 18 Aug 2016.

Riffkin, Rebecca. "Americans' Trust in Media Remains at Historical Low." *Gallup*. Sep 28 2015. Web. 18 Aug 2016.

Webley, Kayla. "How the Nixon-Kennedy Debate Changed the World." *Time*. Time Inc. Sep 23 2010. Web. 18 Aug 2016.

Notes

1. Goodtimes, "A Brief History of Campaign Mudslinging, from 1796 to Today."
2. "How the Presidentail Candidates Use the Web and Social Media," *Pew Research*.
3. "How Social Media Inflates Our Perception of Our Choice Presidential Candidate," *NPR*.
4. Krieg, "Donald Trump's 27-day Spiral: From Convention Bounce to Campaign Overhaul."
5. Bialik, "Everyone Has Fake Twitter Followers, But Trump Has the Most. Sad!"
6. Riffkin, "Americans' Trust in Media Remains at Historical Low."
7. Beaujon, "Survey: NPR's Listeners Best Informed, Fox Viewers Worst-Informed."
8. "American Presidential Candidates and Social Media," *Economist*.
9. Mitchell, Gottfried, Barthel, and Shearer, "The Modern News Consumer."

The Rhetorical Brilliance of Trump the Demagogue

Jennifer Mercieca
The Conversation, December 11, 2015

Donald Trump's December 7 Statement on Preventing Muslim Immigration has attracted worldwide disdain. Nearly 500,000 Britons have signed a petition asking their government to prevent Trump from entering their country. In the US, Trump's comments have been denounced by Democrats, Republicans, the media and religious groups.

Yet a recent poll has found that 37% of likely voters across the political spectrum agree with a "temporary ban" on Muslims entering the US.

Trump possesses an arrogance and volatility that makes most voters recoil. So how has he maintained a grip on a segment of the Republican base that—at least, for now – seems unshakable?

And how has his support persisted, despite the fact that some have called him a demagogue and a fascist, or that political observers have found parallels between him and polarizing figures like George Wallace, Joseph McCarthy, Father Coughlin – even Hitler?

As a scholar of American political rhetoric, I write about and teach courses on the use and abuse of rhetorical strategy in public discourse. Scrutinizing Trump's rhetorical skills can partially explain his profound and persistent appeal.

The Rhetoric of Demagoguery

The Greek word "demagogue" (demos = people + agōgos = leader) literally means "a leader of the people." Today, however, it's used to describe a leader who capitalizes on popular prejudices, makes false claims and promises, and uses arguments based on emotion rather than reason.

Donald Trump appeals to voters' fears by depicting a nation in crisis, while positioning himself as the nation's hero – the only one who can conquer our foes, secure our borders and "Make America Great Again."

His lack of specificity about how he would accomplish these goals is less relevant than his self-assured, convincing rhetoric. He urges his audiences to "trust him," promises he is "really smart" and flexes his prophetic muscles (like when he claims to have predicted the 9/11 attacks).

Trump's self-congratulating rhetoric makes him appear to be the epitome of hubris, which, according to research, is often the least attractive quality of a potential leader. However, Trump is so consistent in his hubris that it appears authentic: his greatness is America's greatness.

So we can safely call Trump a demagogue. But one fear of having demagogues actually attain real power is that they'll disregard the law or the Constitution. Hitler, of course, is a worst-case example.

Amazingly, one of Trump's very arguments is that he won't be controlled.

On the campaign trail, he's harnessed his macho businessman persona – crafted through social media and years spent on TV (where he was often the most powerful person in the room) – to make his case for the presidency. It's a persona that rejects restraints: he speaks of not being constrained by his party, media, other candidates, political correctness, facts – anything, really. In a sense, he's fashioning himself as an uncontrollable leader.

Using Speech to Demolish Detractors

But most voters would never want an uncontrollable president. So why do so many remain adamant in their support?

First, Trump draws on the myth of American exceptionalism. He depicts the United States as the world's best hope: there is only one chosen nation and, as president, all of his decisions work toward making America great. By tying himself to American exceptionalism – while classifying his detractors as "weak" or "dummies" – he's able to position his critics as people who don't believe in, or won't contribute to, the "greatness" of the nation.

Trump also uses fallacious and divisive rhetorical techniques that prevent him from being questioned or backed into a corner.

He often uses *ad populum* arguments, which are appeals to the wisdom of the crowd ("polls show," "we're winning everywhere").

When opponents question his ideas or stances, he'll employ *ad hominem* attacks – or criticisms of the person, rather than the argument (dismissing his detractors as "dummies," "weak" or "boring"). Perhaps most famously, he derided Carly Fiorina's appearance when she started to go up in the polls after the first Republican debate ("Look at that face!" he cried. "Would anyone vote for that? Can you imagine that, the face of our next president?").

Finally, his speeches are often peppered with *ad baculum* arguments, which are threats of force ("when people come after me they go down the tubes").

Because demagogues make arguments based on false claims and appeal to emotion, rather than reason, they'll often resort to these devices. For example, during his 1968 presidential run, George Wallace declared, "If any demonstrator ever lays down in front of my car, it'll be the last car he'll ever lay down in front of" (*ad baculum*). And Senator Joseph McCarthy resorted to an *ad hominem* attack when he derided former Secretary of State Dean Acheson as a "pompous diplomat in striped pants with a phony British accent."

Trump will also employ a rhetorical technique called paralipsis to make claims that he can't be held accountable for. In paralipsis, the speaker will introduce a topic or argument by saying he doesn't want to talk about it; in truth, he or she wants to emphasize that very thing.

For example, in New Hampshire on December 1, he said, "But all of [the other candidates] are weak and they're just weak – I think that they are weak generally if you want to know the truth. But I don't want to say that because I don't want to…I don't want to have any controversies, no controversies, is that okay? So I refuse to say that they are weak generally, okay?"

Trump's Ultimate Fallacy

Let's return to Trump's December 7 2015 statement about Muslims to analyze which rhetorical techniques are in play:

Without looking at the various polling data, it is obvious to anybody the hatred is beyond comprehension. Where this hatred comes from and why we will have to determine. Until we are able to determine and understand this problem and the dangerous threat it poses, our country cannot be the victims of horrendous attacks by people that believe only in Jihad, and have no sense of reason or respect for human life. If I win the election for President, we are going to Make America Great Again.

In this statement, Trump immediately makes two things axiomatic (or unquestionable): American exceptionalism and Muslims' hatred for America. According to Trump, these axioms are supported by the wisdom of the crowd (*ad populim*); they are "obvious to anybody."

He also defines Muslims in essential terms as people who believe only in jihad, are filled with hatred and have no respect for human life. Trump uses Reification – the treatment of objects as people and people as objects – to link his axioms together and support his case: "Our country cannot be the victims of horrendous attacks by people that believe only in jihad."

Here, he personifies "our country" by presenting the nation as a person. Meanwhile, he uses "that" rather than "who" to signal that Muslims are not people, but objects.

His underlying logic is that our nation is a victim of these "objects." Objects need not be treated with the same amount of care as people. Therefore we are justified in preventing Muslims from entering the country.

> **He often uses *ad populum* arguments, which are appeals to the wisdom of the crowd ("polls show," "we're winning everywhere").**

Finally, it's worth noting that Trump's use of evidence is incomplete and biased toward his point of view. His announcement cites a survey of American Muslims "showing 25% of those polled agreed that violence against Americans here in the United States is justified."

The polling data came from the Center for Security Policy (CSP), which the Southern Poverty Law Center has called an "anti-Muslim think tank." Furthermore, Trump fails to report that in the same survey, 61% of American Muslims agreed that "violence against those that insult the prophet Muhammad, the Qur'an, or Islamic faith" is not acceptable. Nor does he mention that 64% didn't think that "violence against Americans here in the United States can be justified as part of the global jihad."

Unfortunately, like a true demagogue, Trump doesn't seem all too concerned with the facts.

Print Citations

CMS: Mercieca, Jennifer. "The Rhetorical Brilliance of Trump the Demagogue." In *The Reference Shelf: Campaign Trends and Election Law*, edited by Betsy Maury, 146-49. Ipswitch, MA: Salem Press, 2016.

MLA: Mercieca, Jennifer. "The Rhetorical Brilliance of Trump the Demagogue." *The Reference Shelf: Campaign Trends and Election Law*. Ed. Betsy Maury. Ipswitch: Salem Press, 2016. 146-49. Print.

APA: Merieca, J. (2016). The rhetorical brilliance of Trump the demagogue. In Betsy Maury (Ed.), *The reference shelf: Campaign trends and election law* (pp. 146-149). Ipswitch, MA: Salem. (Original work published 2015)

Who's Influencing Election 2016?

By William Powers
Medium, **February 23, 2016**

With Super Tuesday just around the corner, we know one thing about this election: it's the most riveting in years. But why? What makes it so different from everything that came before?

The obvious answer is the surprising line-up of final contenders. A year ago, the idea that a Donald Trump or a Bernie Sanders could have a serious shot at the White House was unthinkable, especially to the "experts" working off twentieth-century playbooks. Now here we are, and the real question is how the dynamics of public opinion—and influence, in particular—have changed to make this new kind of politics possible.

What is influence? Voters have long formed opinions about candidates in two basic ways: directly, by watching and listening to them through debates, interviews and other campaign events carried on radio and TV, as well as political advertising; and indirectly, by consuming news stories, opinions and other election information offered up by journalists and commentators in the public sphere, along with family, friends and co-workers.

Just a few decades ago, it was easy to say who were the key influencers: the powerful political and media players—both organizations and individuals—who orchestrated and largely defined the election conversation.

What has changed? A few things. Thanks to the digital revolution, the old behemoths of political influence, the two major parties and the traditional media, have lost their former dominance. The parties are still hugely powerful and will wind up nominating two final candidates, one of whom it's very likely will be the next president. But each party is now contending with a magnetic renegade they didn't see coming.

This occurred largely through the media, but not just the traditional media. There's no question the old outlets still exert major influence. When the Pew Research Center recently asked American adults to name the election information source they find most helpful, the number one answer was cable news. Yet only 24% gave that answer. The rest cited sources spread widely among ten other categories of information. Tied for second place after cable were an odd couple: local TV—a longtime influencer in communities across the country—and social media, which have been steadily gaining influence over the last several elections.

In short, the old influence hierarchy has been shattered, replaced by a new mosaic of influence in which social media play a growing role.

So who's influencing Election 2016? For the last year, our research group, the Laboratory for Social Machines, which is part of the MIT Media Lab, has been capturing and saving all the election news published by a basket of influential media outlets. We also have access to the entire Twitter archive, plus the full "firehose" of about 500 million new tweets each day. We have been crawling this data, pulling the election-related tweets and classifying them in various ways. By applying algorithms to both data sets, journalism and Twitter, we were able to identify the election influencers who loom large at the intersection of news and social media. (For more details about how we did the analysis, see the FAQs at the end.)

Below are the top 150 influencers, as calculated by presence and impact in the election news coverage and the Twitter conversation since last August. In this social media age, individuals have voices on the same platforms as huge organizations, so we have combined them all in a single list.

Some Things to Note:

- Trump took the number-one influencer spot by scoring highest in all four of the metrics used to construct the list, two for news influence and two for Twitter influence. Further confirmation that he is the master of both domains.

- After Trump, the top of the list is unsurprisingly dominated by other presidential candidates, both those still in the race and some who have exited. However, non-candidates also appear in the upper ranks. For instance, Daniel Scavino Jr., Trump's social media director, is influencer number eighteen, beating out eight former presidential candidates including Martin O'Malley and Rick Santorum.

- Fox News comes in at number twelve (just ahead of Bill Clinton) as the most influential news organization. And Fox's Megyn Kelly, famous for sparring with Trump, is the most influential journalist.

- Just because you're an influencer doesn't mean your views are carrying the day. Jeb Bush is ranked number 4 even though he just withdrew from the race. That's because over the nearly seven-month period covered by our data, he played a very prominent role in the conversation. The popular fascination with his withdrawal confirms this.

- Some influencers aren't active participants in the conversation. Russian premier Vladimir Putin and ex-president Ronald Reagan, who's deceased, made the list by figuring in the election news coverage (both have been mentioned often in presidential debates). Reagan is also one of a handful of people on the list who are shown without a Twitter handle, because they are not on Twitter (accounts about these people don't count).

- This is by no means a definitive list of election influencers, but rather an attempt to illuminate an important piece of the new influence landscape. Big-money campaign donors didn't appear often enough in our data to make the list, though arguably they have more election influence than anyone. No newspaper or magazine journalists made it, though many produce highly influential work. Reason: When their work is passed around online via links, the bylines tend not to be mentioned, so their individual influence wasn't captured. However, *The New York Times, The Washington Post* and *Time* all made the list as organizations.

- The analysis surfaced numerous people who have appeared now and then in election news and social chatter, but it was hard to gauge their impact without data. Now we have it. Examples: Ivanka Trump, Chelsea Clinton, #BlackLivesMatter activist and Baltimore mayoral candidate DeRay Mckesson, Cher and Pope Francis.

- The "Other" category includes many whose influence is entirely Twitter-centric, including political activists of both right and left. It also includes some people and organizations that made it through humor and parody, such as The Onion, @LOLGOP and @weknowwhatsbest, a conservative parody of the White House press secretary.

How does influence look by category? Below is a chart showing how it stacks up, followed by break-out lists for all the categories.

INFLUENCE BY CATEGORY

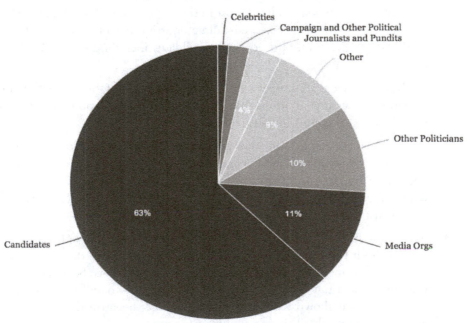

Distribution of influence across the top 150 election influencers

1.	Donald Trump, @realdonaldtrump		16.	Mike Huckabee, @govmikehuckabee
2.	Hillary Clinton, @hillaryclinton		17.	Scott Walker, @scottwalker
3.	Bernie Sanders, @berniesanders		20.	Martin O'Malley, @martinomalley
4.	Jeb Bush, @jebbush		21.	Rick Santorum, @ricksantorum
5.	Ted Cruz, @tedcruz		23.	Bobby Jindal, @bobbyjindal
6.	Ben Carson, @realbencarson		24.	Lindsey Graham, @lindseygrahamsc
7.	Marco Rubio, @marcorubio		45.	George Pataki, @governorpataki
9.	Rand Paul, @randpaul		81.	Jim Webb, @jimwebbusa
10.	Carly Fiorina, @carlyfiorina		122.	Jim Gilmore, @gov_gilmore
11.	Chris Christie, @chrischristie		129.	Lincoln Chafee, @lincolnchafee
14.	John Kasich, @johnkasich			

Candidates

8.	Barack Obama, @barackobama		78.	John Kerry, @johnkerry
13.	Bill Clinton, @billclinton		82.	Harry Reid, @senatorreid
15.	Joe Biden, @joebiden		95.	Nikki Haley, @nikkihaley
25.	Mitt Romney, @mittromney		106.	Elizabeth Warren, @senwarren
30.	Paul Ryan, @speakerryan		118.	Trey Gowdy, @tgowdysc
31.	George W. Bush		121.	Allen West, @allenwest
34.	Rick Perry, @governorperry		135.	Ron Paul, @ronpaul
38.	John Boehner, @speakerboehner		139.	Michael Bloomberg, @mikebloomberg
40.	Sarah Palin, @sarahpalinusa		141.	Newt Gingrich, @newtgingrich

Other Politicians

18.	Daniel Scavino Jr., @danscavino		85.	Ivanka Trump, @ivankatrump
27.	GOP, @gop		108.	The Democrats, @thedemocrats
72.	Corey Lewandowski, @clewandowski_		126.	Debbie Wasserman Schultz, @dwstweets
77.	Reince Priebus, @reince		148.	Cheryl Mills
79.	Josh Earnest, @presssec		150.	Chelsea Clinton, @chelseaclinton

Campaigns and Other Political

12.	Fox News, @foxnews	74.	ABC News Politics, @abcpolitics
19.	CNN, @cnn	84.	Slate, @slate
22.	The Hill, @thehill	87.	Fox & Friends, @foxandfriends
29.	Drudge Report News, @drudge_report_	91.	Mother Jones, @motherjones
33.	Politico, @politico	98.	The Daily Caller, @dailycaller
35.	CNN Politics, @cnnpolitics	100.	The Associated Press, @ap
36.	The New York Times, @nytimes	103.	National Review, @nro
43.	Washington Post, @washingtonpost	104.	Think Progress, @thinkprogress
44.	Time.com, @time	111.	CNN Breaking News, @cnnbrk
53.	Huffington Post, @huffingtonpost	112.	Vox, @voxdotcom
54.	ABC News, @abc	113.	Washington Examiner, @dcexaminer
58.	Salon.com, @salon	114.	NBC News, @nbcnews
60.	MSNBC, @msnbc	116.	Drudge Report, @drudge_report
61.	Fox Business, @foxbusiness	120.	Raw Story, @rawstory
66.	Huffpost Politics, @huffpostpol	127.	NYT Politics, @nytpolitics
68.	The Daily Show, @thedailyshow	137.	CBS News, @cbsnews
71.	Breitbart News, @breitbartnews	142.	Mashable, @mashable
73.	TheBlaze.com, @theblaze		

Media Orgs

48.	James Woods, @realjameswoods	124.	Bill Maher, @billmaher
55.	Patton Oswalt, @pattonoswalt	130.	Michael Moore, @mmflint
101.	Cher, @cher	136.	Jimmy Fallon, @jimmyfallon
119.	Stephen Colbert, @stephenathome		

Celebrities

28.	Megyn Kelly, @megynkelly	89.	Greta Van Susteren, @greta
42.	Sean Hannity, @seanhannity	90.	Mark Levin, @marklevinshow
51.	Ben Shapiro, @benshapiro	102.	Bill O'Reilly, @oreillyfactor
56.	Laura Ingraham, @ingrahamangle	123.	Chris Wallace
57.	Jake Tapper, @jaketapper	133.	John Fugelsang, @johnfugelsang
65.	Wayne Dupree, @waynedupreeshow	134.	Howard Kurtz, @howardkurtz
70.	Jorge Ramos, @jorgeramosnews	146.	Glenn Beck, @glennbeck
75.	Bret Baier, @bretbaier	147.	Chuck Todd, @chucktodd
76.	Hugh Hewitt, @hughhewitt		

Journalists and Pundits

26.	Bill Mitchell, @mitchellvii	93.	Nation Of Immigrants, @immigrantnacion
32.	Viral Buzz News, @viralbuzznewss	94.	Diamond and Silk, @diamondandsilk
37.	The Progressive Mind, @libertea2012	96.	People For Bernie, @people4bernie
39.	Lolgop, @lolgop	97.	The Baxter Bean, @thebaxterbean
41.	Vladimir Putin, @putinrf_eng	99.	Slone, @slone
46.	The Daily Edge, @thedailyedge	105.	Janie Johnson, @jjauthor
47.	Daniel John Sobieski, @gerfingerpoken	107.	Ricky Vaughn, @ricky_vaughn99
49.	Ronald Reagan	109.	Dinesh D'Souza, @dineshdsouza
50.	DeRay Mckesson, @deray	110.	Dr. Marty Fox, @drmartyfox
52.	Troy Osinoff, @yo	115.	RockPrincess, @rockprincess818
59.	WH Press Secretary (Parody), @weknowwhatsbest	117.	The Briefing, @thebriefing2016
62.	Pope Francis, @pontifex	125.	Carmine Zozzora, @carminezozzora
63.	Beau Biden, @beaubiden	128.	The Onion, @theonion
64.	Chuck Nellis, @chucknellis	131.	God, @thetweetofgod
67.	Hannah K, @hannahkauthor	132.	Kim Davis
69.	Feisty Floridian, @peddoc63	138.	Planned Parenthood, @ppact
80.	AJ+, @ajplus	140.	Judy Stines, @jstines3
83.	Cloyd Rivers, @cloydrivers	143.	** Trump **, @housecracka
86.	Bipartisan Report, @bipartisanism	144.	Issa, @twaimz
88.	Frank Luntz, @frankluntz	145.	Media Matters, @mmfa
92.	Roger Stone, @rogerjstonejr	149.	Jennifer, @brownjenjen

Other

It's important to remember that the technologies disrupting the public sphere are still evolving, so influence will remain a moving target. We hope that this effort to quantify it in a new way (see below for an explanation of our method) will inspire others to try their own approaches.

Technology aside, influence is by nature always shifting—that's part of what makes it interesting. By the fall when the election is nearing, the list might look quite different. We'll let you know!

William Powers is a research scientist at the Laboratory for Social Machines and author of the *New York Times* bestseller *Hamlet's BlackBerry*.

Eric Chu, a graduate student at the Laboratory for Social Machines, developed the analytics and visualizations for this post. Lisa Conn, a student at the MIT Sloan School of Management, also made significant contributions to the project.

FAQs

(Prepared with Eric Chu, Soroush Vosoughi and Prashanth Vijayaraghavan, all of the Laboratory for Social Machines)

How Exactly Did You Measure Influence?

We wanted to identify election influencers from both news and social media. Some people and organizations figure prominently in the news, but not so much in social media, while for others it's the reverse. So we started with two "gates" for becoming a candidate for the list, the news gate and the Twitter gate.

On the news side, you had to be mentioned at least 25 times in the election news coverage we've captured since last August 1, or at least three times per month during that same period. We settled on these numbers after testing different thresholds to ensure we got a healthy number of prospective influencers. About 1,200 met these criteria and made it through the news gate.

On the Twitter side, we developed algorithms that allow us to identify and save only tweets that are about the election and also compile a list of those who authored them. So we began by isolating all of those election commenters, many millions of people and organizations. We then multiplied the number of election tweets from each person or organization by the number of people following them. So someone who tweeted frequently about the race but had a relatively small following could potentially make it in, as could a celebrity who only tweeted once but reached millions with that tweet. The 10,000 people and organizations with the highest scores made it through the Twitter gate.

We then took everyone who made the first cut (news or Twitter) and rated them for four different influence metrics: 1) total mentions in election news, 2) election news centrality, 3) total Twitter mentions in election tweets, 4) total number of retweets on election tweets. We weighted these equally at 25% each. The 150 top scorers made the list.

What Is Centrality?

Centrality is a kind of network analysis. It's a way of measuring the degree to which a person or other entity within a network is connected to others in the same network. For instance, the PageRank algorithm that drives Google measures the centrality of web pages.

Identifying the most influential people within a human network is a classic use of centrality. In our analysis, news centrality is the degree to which each of our influencer candidates appeared in election news coverage along with other influential people or organizations.

How Do Retweets Show Influence?

To be a true influencer, it's not enough just to make a lot of noise about the election. There has to be evidence that other people are listening to this person or organization, that their voice is rippling, having impact. Retweets are an indicator of that.

Is This Analysis Part of a Larger Project?

Yes, our group has built an election analytics machine called The Electome. Funded in part by a grant from the Knight Foundation, the project aims to further public understanding of how politics and news are changing in the digital age, and to show how campaign journalism can move beyond the traditional "horse race" coverage. We have several partners with whom we'll be collaborating on projects. We've already done one analysis with *The Washington Post* and are planning more. We're also publishing pieces on our own, by our colleague Andrew Heyward about how we're tracking what we call the Horse Race of Ideas.

Some on the list are not exactly household names. Did you check the identities and credentials of the people behind them?

We did not investigate the backgrounds of the influencers. Some of the Twitter accounts are clearly not under real names. Some have content we found offensive. We didn't eliminate anyone on these bases. This is not a list of "good" influencers or a seal of approval for anyone's views. Whatever they've been saying about the election, if their voice is being heard widely according to our metrics, they were deemed influential and made the list.

Additional thanks to Andrew Heyward, Raphael Schaad and Sophie Chou.

Print Citations

CMS: Powers, William. "Who's Influencing Election 2016?" In *The Reference Shelf: Campaign Trends and Election Law*, edited by Betsy Maury, 150-57. Ipswitch, MA: Salem Press, 2016.

MLA: Powers, William. "Who's Influencing Election 2016?" *The Reference Shelf: Campaign Trends and Election Law*. Ed. Betsy Maury. Ipswitch: Salem Press, 2016. 150-57. Print.

APA: Powers, W. (2016). Who's influencing election 2016? In Betsy Maury (Ed.), *The reference shelf: Campaign trends and election law* (pp. 150-157). Ipswitch, MA: Salem. (Original work published 2016)

Here's How Social Media Will Impact the 2016 Presidential Election

By Rohan Ayyar
Adweek, February 17, 2016

So far, the run up to the 2016 elections has been, at various times, amusing or weird, but mostly interesting, thanks to social media. If not for these ever flexible platforms, we wouldn't have seen this hilarious Snap of Hillary chillin', the world wouldn't be the same without those odd Trump-isms on Twitter, or worse, we wouldn't have known what Scott Walker is eating!

If we are to believe the figures estimated by Borrell Associates, politicians will be allocating over 9 percent of media budget towards digital and social media— this comes to an estimated $1 billion. And don't we all know for whom this budget is allocated?

Long story short, the efforts of electoral candidates and their social media agencies seem to be concentrated towards winning the affection of millennials (25 to 34 year olds), and although no one can say today which candidate is going to win the elections later this year, one thing is clear: social media is winning the elections today.

The Elections and Social Media

One interesting thing to note here is it's not only candidates who are showing an affinity towards social media; websites like Facebook, Google, Twitter and Snapchat are doing their bit to warm up to politicos too.

Twitter, for instance, shut down two apps that showed tweets that politicians had deleted – if ever a social network pandered to political advantage, this was it. Twitter later formed an agreement with Politwoops. They even hosted a breakfast event in Washington rolling out the proverbial red carpet for election candidates. And they went on to partner with Square so people could tweet their donations to their preferred parties and candidates.

Eric Laurence, Facebook's head of U.S. Industry for Politics and Government, once cited the benefits of their video advertising saying it was a "great way to reach and mobilize supporters and voters that candidates need to win elections." He further added that "those voters are on Facebook," which is not far off the mark, counting the 200 million U.S. citizens actively using Facebook. The company has a dedicated team which meets candidates and offers assistance with Facebook's advertising services.

Even the fairly new entrants like Snapchat are proffering filters and 10-second video ads catered to political campaigns. The first few candidates to run ads on this platform were John Kasich, Rand Paul and Scott Walker. Snapchat even hired ex-Google leader Rob Saliterman, who led political ad sales during the George W. Bush administration.

Coming to the giant now, Google is a leader when it comes to 2016 elections. From sponsored links in Google searches, YouTube video ads and the new-fangled programmatic display ads on online publishing websites such as the *New York Times,* presidential candidates have a lot of scope to reach out to the right audience through Google.

Lee Dunn, who is heading the election campaign management team at Google told *Glamour* that YouTube will help candidates to target people based on their geographical locations, language, etc. 2016 will become known for being the campaign of video content. People want authenticity and directness from candidates, and the best platform to provide that without a filter from the media is YouTube.

Clearly, the 2016 election candidates have woken up to social media and the social networks have woken up to the amount of cash at stake.

Now the question isn't who is using social media, the question is who is using social media most effectively. People are watching candidates with hawk eyes, waiting for one wrong tweet…

> **Now the question isn't who is using social media, the question is who is using social media most effectively.**

What's worse, candidates are continuously up to odd antics, trying to be "cool" so as to impress millennials. In fact, this might be taking them away from the precious presidential hot seat.

So the question that President Obama changed from "Can presidential candidates gain from social media?" to "How do presidential candidates gain from social media?" is now more like "How do candidates and parties ride this huge, big wave that has come out of nowhere and has changed the shape of elections and politics?"

Winning Strategies from Social Media Experts

A lot of consultants and agencies seem to be finding the answer and I have rounded up some of these strategies and solutions here.

Erin Lindsay from Precision Strategies, a consulting firm founded by people behind Obama's campaign, told *The Hill*: Authenticity is a big thing in social media. I think the candidates that are the most successful are the ones that are clearly the most comfortable.

I think what Lindsay is trying to say is that you should adjust your tone depending on various platforms: on Reddit, be ready to answer any questions; on Twitter, be ready to handle impromptu debates; on Facebook, show concern and warmth.

The dos and don'ts for various social media platforms are endless. But the basic mantra is same – be authentic at all times.

Another gem of advice comes from Jim Walsh, co-founder of DSPolitical: When Walsh tried to persuade politicians about the effectiveness of targeted reach and precision using digital media in 2012, he had a hard time fighting traditional media like print and TV. Today, his company has expanded to almost double their size with half the need for persuasion, and is serving some of the best political parties.

So do they have a magic wand?

The magic wand that agencies like DSPolitical have is – data and tools. Companies like DSPolitical, CampaignGrid and Targeted Victory use analytics tools to narrow down every one of the 190 million registered voters and target personalized messages at them using their browsing history, real estate and tax records.

Further, data firms like Data Trust, i360 and TargetSmart track, compile and analyze social data which help candidates in their social media campaigns.

When it comes to the agencies helping them out, it is not only big data exchanges such as the above, but also various other social listening and collaboration tools that come in handy. For instance, Quintly can be used for benchmarking competition, monitoring and analyzing campaigns, and finding influencers. The same goes for Wrike, which allows marketing teams to seamlessly collaborate on campaigns while saving major chunks of their time. Since campaigners need to respond quickly and in real time, SaaS (Software as a Service) tools like these can prove to be very useful.

And the Winner Is...

I know you're wondering why I haven't used the T-word yet. No article on the presidential elections is complete without commenting on the antics of The Donald. However, I wanted you to read what I had to say before going off on tangents chasing @realDonaldTrump. To say Donald Trump has won the social media battle is a serious understatement. He could very well be the first president who rewrote the rules on social media.

Brigitte Majewski, research director at Forrester, cautions against making assumptions based on follower count, though: Just because you have a follower doesn't mean you have a vote. It just means that you have caught their ear. It's a good signal, but at the end of the day, a signal is not a vote.

Agreed, but when you dig into the share of voice and do some sentiment analysis on all those posts, it becomes clear that The Donald is well ahead of the others in the race to the White House.

And to trump that, he appears to need no apprentice!

Print Citations

CMS: Ayyar, Rohan. "Here's How Social Media Will Impact the 2016 Presidential Election." In *The Reference Shelf: Campaign Trends and Election Law*, edited by Betsy Maury, 158-60. Ipswitch, MA: Salem Press, 2016.

MLA: Ayyar, Rohan. "Here's How Social Media Will Impact the 2016 Presidential Election." *The Reference Shelf: Campaign Trends and Election Law*. Ed. Betsy Maury. Ipswitch: Salem Press, 2016. 158-60. Print.

APA: Ayyar, R. (2016). Here's how social media will impact the 2016 presidential election. In Betsy Maury (Ed.), *The reference shelf: Campaign trends and election law* (pp. 158-160). Ipswitch, MA: Salem. (Original work published 2016)

2016 Presidential Election Circus: Is Social Media the Cause?

by Marissa Lang
The San Francisco Chronicle, April 5, 2016

In 12 months, the country has collectively spent more than 1,284 years reading about Donald Trump on social media.

The Republican presidential candidate's reach is unprecedented, according to the latest data from SocialFlow, a social media management company whose software handles news dissemination for many of the country's top media organizations, including the *New York Times, Washington Post* and *Wall Street Journal.*

If he sought similar attention by buying ads, Trump's social reach would cost $380 million. Instead, he's getting it for free in tweets, likes and shares—although not all of it is positive. Social media's influence in this presidential election is stronger than it has ever been, experts said, and the information cycle it has created will shape campaigns for years to come.

There are many reasons social media has become such a powerful influence.

More people than ever get their news mainly from social networks like Facebook, Twitter and Snapchat. Candidates have discovered the quickest way to make news is to put out a statement or comment in a social media post.

"It's really opened the floodgates of candidates being able to tap into this ecosystem of voters and news consumers who are getting information about these candidates 24/7," said Patrick Ruffini, Republican political strategist and founder of Engage, a digital media firm. "This election cycle is the first I've seen (where) candidates realize social media is their direct pipeline into mainstream media coverage and to voters."

This creates what Ruffini calls a "feedback loop," wherein candidates' posts on social media make news, and then those news stories get circulated through social media, building momentum and generating even more chatter.

"This is the first true social media election," said Frank Speiser, SocialFlow's co-founder and chief product officer. "Before it was an auxiliary method of communication. But now (candidates) can put messages out there and get folks on social media to act on your behalf by just sharing it around. You don't have to buy access to reach millions of people anymore."

Facebook now boasts nearly 1.6 billion monthly active users, up 60 percent from

2012, the year of the last election, when it crossed the 1 billion mark. Twitter today has 385 million monthly active users, up from 185 million in 2012.

The way politicians use social media is also markedly different.

In 2012, they tended to favor short, calculated statements—maybe once a day—that were highly controlled and sanitized, Ruffini said. They would retweet followers or thank supporters. But it was hardly the first place they went to espouse an opinion or issue a policy proposal.

"Four years ago," Ruffini said, "social media politics was really boring."

Social Media Strategy

Today, social media has evolved from afterthought to strategy, he said, thanks largely to Trump's habitual social-media-first proclamations. Candidates have begun using sites like Twitter and Facebook as a direct line to voters.

It seems to be paying off, particularly among younger voters.

Among 18- to 29-year-olds, nearly two-thirds said social media is the most helpful means of learning new things about politics, according to a study released last year by the Pew Research Center. By contrast, only half of Gen-Xers and 40 percent of Baby Boomers agreed with that statement.

Overall, Pew found, 44 percent of American adults said they had learned something new in the past week about the election from social media.

"That's a pretty large share," said Jesse Holcomb, the associate director of research at Pew. "Our data suggest that social media is a critical gateway to information about the campaign—particularly for younger adults."

Other candidates, like Democratic hopefuls Hillary Clinton and Bernie Sanders, have ramped up their social media presence to compete for time and eyeballs. But research shows they are falling far short of the reach Trump has amassed.

> **Candidates have discovered the quickest way to make news is to put out a statement or comment in a social media post and avoid paying for ad space.**

Clinton has garnered just shy of $100 million in free exposure via social media by SocialFlow's estimate. The only area where she trumps the Republican front-runner is in her rate of engagement—how many people like, share or click through to stories about the former secretary of state, where she runs marginally ahead.

Convoluted Messages

Since the beginning of the election, SocialFlow said, the nation has spent roughly 874 years on social media reading about Sanders and Clinton combined—a third less than the time people have devoted to Trump on the same networks.

The reason for this, Speiser said, likely lies in Trump's bombast and convoluted messaging.

"One thing that Trump does is he will combine two or three issues in a single statement or proposal. Now, he may be muddling them, but it doesn't matter because it activates groups that are interested in all of the above," Speiser said. "Like how he'll conflate crime and gun violence with immigration. It may not be true, but the fact that he says it excites groups whose top issues are crime or guns or immigration."

In December, when Trump announced his proposal to ban all Muslims from entering the United States, the news generated more social media engagement than any other news about the election since the race began, SocialFlow said. (While Trump made the remarks in a speech in South Carolina, not on social media, they nonetheless immediately found a home online.) Trump's comments remain the single most-responded-to news event since then with roughly 230,000 likes—more than 788 times the average number Trump-related stories tend to receive.

By January, SocialFlow said, Trump had become the most talked-about person on the planet.

"Trump, by himself, has eclipsed all the conversation around (the Islamic State), terrorism, the economy and other important issues," Speiser said. "The conversation around him is greater than the top 10 other election issues combined."

The data SocialFlow collects don't indicate whether the comments being made are positive or negative—or whether people "favorite" or "like" a story because they actually like it, or if they're simply noting it. Some people even ironically "hate-like" social media posts.

SocialFlow's analysis also doesn't take into account posts by citizens that do not link to a news story or the candidates' own posts—unless those posts generate press coverage.

"Story of the election"

If researchers took those elements into account, Ruffini and Speiser said they would expect that Trump's recorded reach would grow.

"It's just going to get bigger in the main election," Ruffini said. "The amount of free media exposure given to Trump—whether that's on social media or more traditional news media—I think is absolutely the story of the election. We've just never seen anything like it before."

Print Citations

CMS: Lang, Marissa. "2016 Presidential Election Circus: Is Social Media the Cause?" In *The Reference Shelf: Campaign Trends and Election Law*, edited by Betsy Maury, 161-63. Ipswitch, MA: Salem Press, 2016.

MLA: Lang, Marissa. "2016 Presidential Election Circus: Is Social Media the Cause?" *The Reference Shelf: Campaign Trends and Election Law*. Ed. Betsy Maury. Ipswitch: Salem Press, 2016. 161-63. Print.

APA: Lang, M. (2016). 2016 presidential election circus: Is social media the cause? In Betsy Maury (Ed.), *The reference shelf: Campaign trends and election law* (pp. 161-163). Ipswitch, MA: Salem. (Original work published 2016)

Digital Video Plays Critical Role in 2016 Election

By Philip Rosenstein
MediaPost, July 8, 2016

The field of political marketing in the 2016 election cycle has seamlessly adopted the tech advancements. One particular medium that has seen significant use within campaigns is digital video.

Candidate campaigns and super PACs have focused heavily on digital video advertising, on mobile, desktop and to a lesser extent, connected TV. The main draws for digital video include cross-screen capabilities and interactivity, two facets of modern marketing strategies that are increasingly important and effective.

Millennials and Hispanic voters are particularly prone to being influenced by online video, per a national study by Tremor Video and Cygnal, the research and advertising firm.

The study showed that while Hispanic voters are less likely than the average American to consume political news daily, they are 24% more likely to use online video to consume information about candidates and issues. A key finding: Hispanic voters are twice as likely to be motivated to register to vote by online video when compared to the general population.

A key finding: Hispanic voters are twice as likely to be motivated to register to vote by online video when compared to the general population.

These numbers are even greater for millennials.

They are 2.5x more likely to register to vote after watching an online video than the general population, and they are twice as likely to be influenced to vote for a candidate or issue by an online video.

Mobile also has a particular role to play.

"Both millennials and Hispanics have interacted heavily with candidate information on their phones. We have been astonished by the time these groups have spent learning about the 2016 campaign through digital channels," Monica Seebohm, national director of politics and advocacy at Tremor Video, told *Red, White & Blog*.

Seebohm also noted that the best video advertising ROI in politics is found on mobile.

Still, digital video faces some challenges. The global ad tech firm Brightcom held a roundtable in June focused on video ad spending around the 2016 cycle, where a number of interested parties discussed the role of video.

Michele DeVine, programmatic sales manager at Vox Media, explained that she anticipates "issues in terms of scale for video when it comes to publishers. We are starting to look at other options: in-banner videos, custom execution that can include video players."

The importance of turnout for certain demographic groups, in particular millennials and Hispanics, will increase the necessity for campaigns and causes to utilize digital video to deliver their message.

Print Citations

CMS: Rosenstein, Philip. "Digital Video Plays Critical Role in 2016 Election." In *The Reference Shelf: Campaign Trends and Election Law*, edited by Betsy Maury, 164-65. Ipswitch, MA: Salem Press, 2016.

MLA: Rosenstein, Philip. "Digital Video Plays Critical Role in 2016 Election." *The Reference Shelf: Campaign Trends and Election Law*. Ed. Betsy Maury. Ipswitch: Salem Press, 2016. 164-65. Print.

APA: Rosenstein, P. (2016). Digital video plays critical role in 2016 election. In Betsy Maury (Ed.), *The reference shelf: Campaign trends and election law* (pp. 164-165). Ipswitch, MA: Salem. (Original work published in 2016)

Foul-Mouthed and Proud of It on the '16 Campaign Trail

Matt Flegenheimer and Maggie Haberman
The New York Times, November 27, 2015

Donald J. Trump pledged to bomb the, uh, stuffing out of the Islamic State.

Senator Rand Paul called any proposed trade-off between safety and liberty nothing but "bull," before adding a syllable.

Even Jeb Bush, the stern patrician of the Republican race, has shown a growing fondness for some gentler four-letter words, at times adding them to prepared remarks that had called for something meeker.

"We're Americans, damn it!" he shouted recently at a New Hampshire barbecue, though no one had suggested otherwise.

A little more than two months before the voting begins, the candidates have charged into what appears to be the inaugural profanity primary, wrought by an overstuffed field of competitors vying for attention and the specter of a foul-mouthed Manhattanite perched atop the polls.

The reasons for saltiness seem varied— a play for machismo, perhaps, particularly as national security becomes a chief focus, or a signal of vitality, rawness, a willingness to break through the din. Across both parties, female candidates in the race— Carly Fiorina and Hillary Rodham Clinton— have little reputation for using such language.

"Are you allowed to use profanity?" Mr. Paul asked, after doing so on Nov. 19, to raucous cheers during remarks at George Washington University.

It would appear so.

Yet the outbursts make clear the extent to which Mr. Trump, the election's clear pacesetter in vulgarity, continues to dictate the tenor of the race. (Though in recent days, his most provocative remarks, by most accounts, have been perfectly printable— like claiming, against all evidence, that he saw thousands of Muslims in New Jersey celebrating the Sept. 11, 2001, terrorist attacks in New York.)

Candidates hoping to outswear Mr. Trump are almost certainly overmatched. He has appraised the friendship between Mr. Bush and Senator Marco Rubio as "political BS," without abbreviating, and twice told an Ohio crowd "you bet your ass" he would revive the interrogation technique known as waterboarding.

A recent interview about Mr. Trump's Twitter habits ended with this warning: "Treat us fairly," he said. "Otherwise I'll tweet the"— er, daylights— "outta you."

Mr. Trump's advisers see his influence in his rivals' choice of words, noting Mr. Paul's expletive this month and an email to supporters using that word.

"Rand totally admires and worships Mr. Trump and copies anything he says," said Corey Lewandowski, the Trump campaign manager, in an email. ("Claiming Rand is imitating Trump? Now that's really"— ahem, a farce— retorted Doug Stafford, Mr. Paul's main adviser, who in fact repeated the out-of-bounds noun his boss had used at GWU)

There have, of course, been indecorous moments in presidential politics before. George W. Bush, on the trail in 2000, was caught swearing into a live microphone while assessing a reporter from *The New York Times*. Senator John McCain, the 2008 Republican presidential nominee and a Navy veteran, could be quite coarse.

The reasons for saltiness seem varied— a play for machismo, perhaps, particularly as national security becomes a chief focus, or a signal of vitality, rawness, a willingness to break through the din.

And this election season was robbed of perhaps its most colorful imprecatory prospect when Vice President Joseph R. Biden Jr. decided against a run. (His masterpiece: calling the president's health care law a "big deal," with a two-syllable modifier in between, during what he thought was a private aside.)

But those moments became public by accident. Such frequent, deliberate cursing by presidential candidates addressing campaign audiences in this election cycle seems to be without modern precedent. It is a striking departure for a party whose 2012 nominee, Mitt Romney, let fly expressions like "H-E-double-hockey-sticks" when he wanted to be puckish.

Republican officials have strained to adjust, questioning whether the moment will last.

"He does it because he needs attention and can't control himself," Stuart Stevens, who was Mr. Romney's chief strategist, said of Mr. Trump. "Both are not qualities in demand in a president."

Henry Barbour, a Republican National Committee member, said it was all "just part of this strange reality-TV era we are suffering through."

Some milder adjectives appear to be bipartisan. In the first Democratic debate, Senator Bernie Sanders of Vermont memorably declared that America was tired of hearing about Hillary Rodham Clinton's "damn emails."

Lower-polling candidates in the Republican field have gravitated instead toward a Trump-like tactic: Insult rivals, add a dash of profanity, end with a rhetorical question.

"You've got the No. 2 guy tried to kill somebody at 14, and the No. 1 guy is high-energy and crazy as hell," Senator Lindsey Graham said on MSNBC last month, referring to Ben Carson, who has said he tried to stab a friend as a teenager, and Mr. Trump. "How am I losing to these people?"

Even the mellow Mr. Carson has participated, gingerly.

"This is a bunch of crap," he said at the debate in Boulder, Colorado, last month, discussing government regulations.

Some candidates seem to relish the shift in decorum. When Mr. Trump offered his colorful assessment of the Bush-Rubio relationship in September, Mr. Bush was asked to respond generally to the slight. "I will not answer that question until I hear exactly what he said and the terminology he used," he said, feigning a dodge until the reporter, Dana Bash of CNN, obliged.

"I just wanted to hear it," he said with a smirk.

For news organizations, style guidelines generally dictate that obscenities should not be printed unless they are newsworthy.

A bleepworthy Mr. Bush, for instance, would not be afforded a literal rendering. But a President Bush? Hot damn.

Michael Barbaro contributed reporting.

Print Citations

CMS: Flegenheimer, Matt, and Maggie Haberman. "Foul-Mouthed and Proud of It on the Campaign Trail." In *The Reference Shelf: Campaign Trends and Election Law*, edited by Betsy Maury, 166-68. Ipswitch, MA: Salem Press, 2016.

MLA: Flegenheimer, Matt, and Maggie Haberman. "Foul-Mouthed and Proud of It on the Campaign Trail." *The Reference Shelf: Campaign Trends and Election Law*. Ed. Betsy Maury. Ipswitch: Salem Press, 2016. 166-68. Print.

APA: Flegenheimer, M., & M. Haberman. (2016). Foul-mouthed and proud of it on the campaign trail. In Betsy Maury (Ed.), *The reference shelf: Campaign trends and election law* (pp. 166-168). Ipswitch, MA: Salem. (Original work published 2015)

What Google and Twitter Can Tell Us About 2016

By Daniel White
Time, February 22, 2016

If you were trying to figure out who would win the South Carolina primary on Saturday, you could have read the polls. Or you could have checked Google data.

The Internet search giant predicted Donald Trump would win the South Carolina primary (an admittedly easy call) as well as a close race between Florida Senator Marco Rubio and Texas Senator Ted Cruz for second place, based on searches by people in the Palmetto State. Google also correctly forecast that day that interest in Vermont Senator Bernie Sanders would spike, though not enough to edge out former Secretary of State Hillary Clinton in the notoriously hard-to-poll Nevada caucuses.

But don't think that means Google has now replaced Gallup, the esteemed polling company that no longer tracks the presidential horserace. Experts inside and outside Google think it's premature to start relying on search trends to see who's going to win the election. Instead, they see it and social-media outlet Twitter serving as a complement to traditional polling, enriching the raw data with new insights.

"When there's a lot of information, this sort of 'who's winning, who's losing' narrative is a … cue to who I should pay attention to," Shannon McGregor, a researcher at the University of Texas' Twitter Research Group, told *Time*. "So in some ways social-media metrics, to the extent that the public is being exposed to them, can help them in that way. It's more information that they have about what's going on out there in terms of the election and in terms of how other people are feeling about it."

Data from Google and Twitter has a couple of advantages over traditional polls. For one, it's faster, which means it can pick up late-breaking surges for candidates further back in the pack. For example, local Twitter data picked up a surge of interest in Cruz just before the Iowa caucuses, while local Google searches showed Ohio Governor John Kasich's last-minute momentum heading into the New Hampshire primary.

Companies like Google and Twitter have been eager to share this data with the public, campaigns and journalists, according to Daniel Kreiss, an assistant professor of media and journalism at the University of North Carolina at Chapel Hill. Elections present a high-profile opportunity for web analytics to present themselves as a public service and not just a private company.

"They sort of want to be that underlying infrastructure that will help campaigns connect with voters, help voters learn more about candidates, help people get involved," Kreiss told *Time*. "Really sort of serve as that base level of being a key player in the electoral process ... companies want to be part of infrastructure for democracy."

Another social-media platform that's looking to get involved in the election is Facebook, which encourages users to post about watching presidential debates and voting. Facebook releases data on user conversation ahead of primaries but is usually not predictive of the final results. This is because the site is not as public as Twitter and Google, with a lot of user information available only to friends and connections.

McGregor argues that all of the companies' increasing political involvement can have a beneficial side effect, helping generate more interest among the public.

"To the extent that people encounter politics in these personal spaces, it can help broaden the reach of politics, and it can help bring more people into politics by encountering them in these relatively informal and personal spaces," she said.

While social-media posts are publicly expressive, engaging in conversation with other users, data from search engines can signal latent attitudes, according to Joe DiGrazia, a Neukom fellow at Dartmouth University focusing on computational methodologies in the social sciences. Instead of answering a question from a pollster, entering a search on a site like Google or Bing is honest and immediate— your search history doesn't lie.

This is the new focus group— instead of pooling a small, limited group of voters to watch a debate, media-savvy analysts can just watch user responses on social media, according to Chris Kerns, vice president of research and insights at social-media marketing platform Spredfast.

"What social data does for us is it gives you not only a huge panel of people talking about either a show, or in the case of this weekend's primaries and caucuses, issues and candidates, but it also gives it to you in seconds," he said. "That panel is still going to be skewed based on the people that are on Twitter and the people that are talking about politics, it's still 1,000 times better than the old model."

Sometimes the focus group gets it right and sometimes it can be way off, according to DiGrazia. Like, if a candidate were involved in a scandal, you might see a surge in interest or chatter that does not indicate increased support.

"They're often predictive, because they measure interest in a candidate, and interest is often correlated with support. These things are often predictive of election outcomes," DiGrazia told *Time*. "But at the same time you can have situations where they will lead you astray."

For example, interest in Jeb Bush spiked on Google over the weekend because the former Florida governor dropped out of the race.

Some researchers argue that the data is most useful when limited to a geographic location, like a metropolitan area, and ordered along a period of time. For instance in New Hampshire, search interest in Kasich spiked on Google on the day of the primary, correctly indicating that he would earn a surprising second-place finish.

The sheer utility of the data when compared with polling makes it invaluable to DiGrazia, offering quick public-opinion analysis that would normally take a polling outfit a longer period of time and a deep research budget. "It's fast and it's cheap. You can get it quickly and in real time, and you don't have to spend any money commissioning a poll," he said.

Starting with John McCain's 2000 presidential campaign and culminating in Barack Obama's 2008 race to the White House, campaigns have made use of web data to fine-tune their strategies to appeal to and communicate with voters, according to Kreiss, who is the author of *Taking Our Country Back*, a history of online politics from 2004 to present.

Data, says Kreiss, "helps campaigns orient themselves"— helping them find what works and what doesn't, but isn't an end-all, be-all to campaigning in the digital age. "A lot of this data is messy. It's often unclear the volume of activity going on around some particular issue and how that translates to things like vote share, how that relates to donations."

> **Experts inside and outside Google think it's premature to start relying on search trends to see who's going to win the election. Instead, they see it and social-media outlet Twitter serving as a complement to traditional polling, enriching the raw data with new insights.**

There are pitfalls of relying on data— especially when it comes to those who think it will replace polling outright. The age-old Twitter adage applies: retweets do not equal endorsements.

Just because someone mentions a candidate online is not an indicator of support, and it's likely that they may not even be saying anything positive at all. Former Google data scientist Seth Stephens-Davidowitz says researchers need more time to establish a methodology for pulling data from the web.

"Polls took a while to figure out, it wasn't just overnight. People knew proper polling methodology. We don't know proper methodology to weight tweets and Google searches," he said. "It's been established, without a doubt, that there are important insights that couldn't be found anywhere else in this data."

Print Citations

CMS: White, Daniel. "What Google and Twitter Can Tell Us About 2016." In *The Reference Shelf: Campaign Trends and Election Law*, edited by Betsy Maury, 169-71. Ipswitch, MA: Salem Press, 2016.

MLA: White, Daniel. "What Google and Twitter Can Tell Us About 2016." *The Reference Shelf: Campaign Trends and Election Law*. Ed. Betsy Maury. Ipswitch: Salem Press, 2016. 169-71. Print.

APA: White, D. (2016). What Google and Twitter can tell us about 2016. In Betsy Maury (Ed.), *The reference shelf: Campaign trends and election law* (pp. 169-171). Ipswitch, MA: Salem. (Original work published 2016)

Facebook to Provide "Political Bias" Training for Employees

By Rob Bluey

The Daily Signal, June 22, 2016

Facebook is adding a training program for its employees to address concerns that the company has a bias against conservatives.

Sheryl Sandberg, Facebook's chief operating officer, announced the addition of a "political bias" section to the company's managing unconscious bias class during a Wednesday event at the American Enterprise Institute.

"We have a managing bias class that all of our leaders and a lot of our employees have taken that I was part of helping to create. And we focused on racial bias, age bias, gender bias, national bias, and we're going to add in a scenario now on political bias," Sandberg said. "So as we think about helping people understand different points of view and being open to different points of view, we're dealing with political bias as well going forward."

Sandberg's announcement comes six weeks after a former Facebook contractor accused the company of suppressing conservative news on the platform. Since that Gizmodo report on May 9, Facebook has revamped how it operates the Trending Topics feature. The company also hosted more than a dozen conservative leaders, including Heritage Foundation President Jim DeMint, at its Menlo Park, California, headquarters on May 18 to address the fallout.

American Enterprise Institute President Arthur Brooks, who attended the May 18 meeting, called the addition of "political bias" training both "interesting and encouraging."

Sandberg used her appearance at AEI to articulate Facebook's commitment to all points of view.

"Facebook is a platform for all ideas and all voices," she said. "We have 1.6 billion people using the platform, which means all ideas have to be able to be expressed."

She acknowledged, however, that Facebook and other tech companies are perceived to be liberal.

"That's a pretty important accusation and it's one we take seriously," Sandberg said. "It's also one which frankly rang true to some people because there is concern that Silicon Valley companies have a liberal bias. And so we took it very seriously and did a thorough investigation, and we didn't find a liberal bias."

Those perceptions about Facebook are at least partly fueled by donations Facebook employees have made to political causes. According to a Reuters analysis of campaign finance data, 79 percent of Facebook employee contributions in 2016 have supported Democrats. Those employees donated more than $114,000 to Democrat Hillary Clinton—nearly $100,000 more than to the closest Republican, Sen. Marco Rubio, before he dropped out of the presidential race, according to The Hill.

Even though Facebook's investigation found "no systematic bias," Sandberg said the company decided to take steps to improve.

"We think a lot about diversity at Facebook. It's something our industry has struggled with, we've struggled with," she said. "We think to build a product that 1.6 billion people use, you need diversity. And what you really want is cognitive diversity … intellectual diversity."

> **Even though Facebook's investigation found "no systematic bias," Sandberg said the company decided to take steps to improve.**

Sandberg noted that Donald Trump has almost as many Facebook fans as Clinton and Sen. Bernie Sanders—combined. She also praised Rep. Elise Stefanik, R-N.Y., as a model example of a member of Congress who is using the platform effectively.

In her role as a leader at Facebook, Sandberg said, she encourages employees to speak up and disagree with her. She shared with Brooks two examples of how that played out at the company and why employees were rewarded as a result.

"You need people with different opinions and you need an environment where people can express those opinions," she told the packed room at AEI's 12th floor conference center in downtown Washington.

"People are not going to speak truth to power unless you make that apparent," she added. "And that's how we get not just different voices into the company but make sure we're listening to different voices."

At a time when publishers of all ideological perspectives use Facebook as a distribution platform, Brooks pressed Sandberg on the company's role in the dissemination of news. But Sandberg dismissed the notion that Facebook wanted to be a media company.

"We're clear about the industry we're in and the company we're in: We're a tech company, we're not a media company," she said. "We're not trying to hire journalists and we're not trying to write news."

Print Citations

CMS: Bluey, Rob. "Facebook to Provide 'Political Bias' Training for Employees." In *The Reference Shelf: Campaign Trends and Election Law*, edited by Betsy Maury, 172-73. Ipswitch, MA: Salem Press, 2016.

MLA: Bluey, Rob. "Facebook to Provide 'Political Bias' Training for Employees." *The Reference Shelf: Campaign Trends and Election Law*. Ed. Betsy Maury. Ipswitch: Salem Press, 2016. 172-73. Print.

APA: Bluey, R. (2016). Facebook to provide "political bias" training for employees. In Betsy Maury (Ed.), *The reference shelf: Campaign trends and election law* (pp. 172-173). Ipswitch, MA: Salem. (Original work published 2016)

The Polls Are All Wrong: A Startup Called Civis Is Our Best Hope to Fix Them

Garrett M. Graff
Wired, August 22, 2016

During primary season, when they were still mainly just spectators to the 2016 presidential race, Dan Wagner and David Shor had a routine they liked to observe on election nights. The two men—the CEO and senior data scientist, respectively, of a startup called Civis Analytics—would stay late at work, drinking bourbon and watching returns come in. Their office, a repurposed industrial space in Chicago's West Loop, would rattle every time the L train rumbled by.

As much as Wagner and Shor were following the political horse race itself, they were also watching to see how the race's oddsmakers were doing. The US polling industry has been suffering a crisis of insight over the past decade or so; its methods have become increasingly bad at telling which way America is leaning. Like nearly everyone who works in politics, Wagner and Shor knew the polling establishment was liable to embarrass itself this year. It wasn't a question of if, but when—and how badly.

It didn't take long to find out. About 10 days before the Iowa caucuses in February, two major polls came out: One put Hillary Clinton ahead by 29 points; the other, as if it were tracking an entirely different race, showed Bernie Sanders leading by eight. In the Republican contest, Donald Trump topped the state's final 10 polls and averaged a seven-point advantage. On the night of the caucus itself, the Civis office in Chicago was crowded with staffers gathered around a big flatscreen TV for a viewing party. They all watched as Clinton—and Ted Cruz—won the state.

But the biggest polling train wreck came a few weeks later, when the Michigan primary rolled around. In early March, every single poll gave Clinton at least a five-point lead; some had her ahead by as many as 20 points. Even ace statistician Nate Silver's *FiveThirtyEight*—a go-to site ever since he correctly predicted outcomes in 49 out of 50 states in the 2008 presidential race—gave Clinton a greater than 99 percent chance of winning.

Polling is misrepresentative: An elderly white woman is 21 times more likely to answer a phone poll than a young Hispanic male.

By the night of the primary itself, the crowd at Civis had dwindled to just Wagner and Shor in front of a single TV. Early returns in Wayne County, home of Detroit, confirmed what Wagner had already suspected: The polls were way off. "Someone made a terrible mistake," he thought. Despite unanimous predictions to the contrary, Sanders walked away with the state. "It was just poor measurement," Wagner says.

He and Shor weren't without sympathy for the pollsters in this case. Michigan, Shor explains, is one of the hardest states for any researcher to survey. For pollsters in an election season, it's like the moment in the stress test that causes the already-ailing patient to collapse on the treadmill. First of all, pollsters in Michigan have to contend with the same methodological problems that have turned polling into such a crapshoot nationwide. The classic pollster's technique known as random digit dialing, in which firms robo-dial phone after phone, is failing, because an ever-dwindling number of people have landlines. By 2014, 60 percent of Americans used cell phones either most or all of the time, making it difficult or impossible for polling firms to reach three out of five Americans. (Government regulations make it prohibitively expensive for pollsters to call cell phones.) And even when you can dial people at home, they don't answer; whereas a survey in the 1970s or 1980s might have achieved a 70 percent response rate, by 2012 that number had fallen to 5.5 percent, and in 2016 it's headed toward an infinitesimal 0.9 percent. And finally, the demographics of participants are narrowing: An elderly white woman is 21 times more likely to answer a phone poll than a young Hispanic male. So polling samples are often inherently misrepresentative.

In Michigan, all these systemic problems are compounded by a uniquely dire local crisis of data collection. The state's official list of registered voters—known in industry parlance as a voter file, typically a roster of names, addresses, and voting histories—is a mess. The economic collapse has driven many Michiganders to change addresses and phone numbers, a churn that disproportionately affects black voters. That made the polls for the contest between Sanders and Clinton particularly susceptible to atrocious sampling error. "A lot of the polling was showing Sanders doing unrealistically badly with African Americans," Shor says.

Wagner and Shor knew all this about Michigan because that's their business—they are two of the most revered numbers guys in American politics—but also from hard-won firsthand experience. Four years ago, when they both worked for President Obama's reelection campaign, they helped narrowly avoid an expensive debacle in the Great Lakes State by convincing their team to completely ignore the public polls.

Back in 2012, Wagner, a bespectacled former economic consultant, and Shor, a math prodigy who started college at 13, were the driving forces behind the Obama campaign's 54-member analytics team, which worked in an area nicknamed the Cave and became famous for bringing *Moneyball*-style analysis to politics. Their signature product was the *Golden Report,* a daily rundown of the presidential race reflecting the team's 62,000 nightly computer simulations of how the electoral map might unfold in November.

Wagner and Shor were the driving forces behind Obama's analytics team, famous for bringing *Moneyball*-style analysis to politics.

The *Golden Report* was the campaign's most precious secret, delivered straight to the campaign manager and a small number of other leaders. They even kept the

Cave physically segregated to ensure that no other staff knew the internal predictions. Obama's strategists based nearly all their tactical decisions on the report's probabilistic estimates of which states were in play, using them to figure out where to allocate staff and advertising dollars.

Going into the summer of 2012, Michigan had been a solidly safe state for Obama. But that June, public polling showed him dropping by 10 points, putting Michigan within Romney's reach. Romney's campaign responded by pouring millions of dollars into the state. But the Cave's models, based on historical data and daily voter contacts by campaign volunteers, found support for the president had dropped only slightly; the public polls, they calculated, were undercounting Democrats.

The Obama campaign faced an agonizing decision: scramble or hold steady. The brass were prepared to spend as much as $20 million on advertising and get-out-the-vote efforts, but Wagner's team recommended against that. "It was a big, strategic campaign decision," Shor recalls. "Should we trust our polls? We're right and everyone else is wrong?" Ultimately the campaign listened. "We ended up being right. That single decision paid for the entire analytics department," Shor says. "People generally talk about polling problems as the margin of error of plus or minus 3 percent. No, the difference between good polling and bad is wasting millions in a state that's not competitive."

Many legislators think their constituents are more conservative than they really are—Republicans overestimate by 20 percentage points.

Those are the stakes for a campaign. For the country, the stakes are more diffuse but arguably even bigger. It's not just political polls that are ailing. The very same methodological crisis that handicaps them now afflicts all kinds of survey-based research—from the General Social Survey, which undergirds vast amounts of social sci-

> **Traditionally, the most efficient way for a campaign to gather strategic intelligence on a slice of the electorate has been to conduct its own internal polls, effectively using the same methods public pollsters use. But those don't really work anymore.**

ence on public attitudes, to the US government's official barometers of poverty, health, and consumer spending. The result is that America is simply not as predictable as it once was (a fact that's easy to appreciate in a year that's seen the rise of Trump). Today's polling landscape appears so fraught that Gallup, long the industry leader, opted out of presidential horse-race polls this year; the reputational risk of being wrong was simply too high. Civis, on the other hand, promises a paradigm that could rescue American politics from confusion. The startup—which works closely with the Democratic Party—didn't play much of a role during the primaries, but now it intends to help the Democrats wage the most data-intensive campaign in history. In fact, if Wagner's models are correct, the firm might have the greatest insight into America that anyone has ever had. As he puts it, "We offer an incredibly scarce resource: How do people really feel about the country?" But of course that knowledge won't be available to the general public—only to those who can afford it.

Dan Wagner didn't set out to transform modern political campaigns. He started out as a volunteer for Obama in 2007, phone banking and helping translate mailings into Spanish, which he'd learned while doing his thesis research on Chilean fiscal policy. The campaign soon realized his statistical and computational skills could be put to better use and transferred him to Des Moines to be deputy manager of the Iowa voter file. It was a $2,500-a-month job that required transposing information from cards voters had filled out to a database that tracked nascent support for the freshman senator. Despite the long hours and tedious work, it still beat his previous job, crunching economic forecasts for Harley-Davidson. And, of course, it put him in the thick of a campaign that would become famous for using data in politics.

As it turned out, Wagner had arrived at Obama for America just as Democratic campaigns in general were beginning to undergo a seismic shift. Until that point, campaigns had organized themselves around traditional polls. A traditional poll is basically a kind of spot check—a dipstick dropped into one part of an engine at one particular moment in time. But even back in 2007, sampling errors and nonresponse rates were beginning to make those spot checks chronically inaccurate. Now the dipstick wasn't just a momentary reading; it didn't even tell you how much oil you had left. The rise of data analytics in campaigning suggests a model that's more like an engine that is monitored continuously, with sensors collecting a record of performance over time. Getting to that kind of continuous monitoring, however, means building long-term databases of information about voters that can be refreshed and crunched a bunch of different ways. That has been a very long process—one that the Democratic Party embarked on more than 10 years ago.

For decades, knitting together the nation's disparate voter rolls and gleaning large-scale political data on voters had been nearly impossible. Too many voter lists were available only on paper, scattered among town clerks' offices and city halls. Even at their best, voter files rarely contained more than a handful of categories. When Terry McAuliffe took office as chair of the Democratic National Committee in 2001, he was horrified to find that the party possessed a national email list of just 70,000 people. McAuliffe and his successor, Howard Dean, both accelerated the party's investment in databases, analytic tools, and email lists to better identify and communicate with potential voters.

Then, in 2006, veteran politico Harold Ickes joined forces with one of McAuliffe's techies, Laura Quinn, to go private. They built an $11 million not-for-profit data warehouse for Democrats called Catalist, recruiting talent from companies like Amazon and assembling more than 450 commercial and private data layers on each adult American. For the first time, they could link voters to a unique, seven-digit identifier—a kind of lifetime political passport number—that would follow them across the country no matter how many times they moved. (Those efforts weren't matched by the Republican side, which failed to institutionalize the data and knowledge it had collected during George W. Bush's two campaigns. Since then, the Democratic advantage in data analytics has been huge.)

From its earliest days in 2007, Obama's campaign put data at the center of its strategy, A/B testing nearly everything, harvesting details from interactions with voters and supporters both online and in person, then trying to meld it together in databases to form a unified picture of supporters. Obama's 2012 presidential campaign crunched poll numbers and voter data to determine a proprietary 0-to-100 "persuadability score" for every voter, which indicated the likelihood that person would choose Obama. In between the elections, Wagner stayed with the DNC, refining critical voter models and creating more and more accurate tools. During the 2010 special election to fill Ted Kennedy's Senate seat for Massachusetts, Wagner correctly warned that Democrat Martha Coakley was poised to lose to Republican Scott Brown, even as party heavyweights and Coakley's pollsters remained confident. That embarrassing loss was part of what encouraged Obama's reelection leadership to take Wagner's modeling as all but gospel. When Election Day 2012 rolled around, Wagner gave a presentation to major supporters at campaign headquarters in Chicago, outlining how he expected the day to unfold. It was a tour de force of data and charts, all pointing to the inescapable conclusion that Mitt Romney was about to lose.

"We offer an incredibly scarce resource: How do people really feel about the country?"

By night's end, the analytics team proved to be precisely correct—Obama won by the Cave's predicted 126 electoral votes. Even more impressive, the Cave was accurate down to individual precincts. In Ohio, for instance, it had forecast Obama would receive 57.68 percent of the vote in Cincinnati's Hamilton County; the final number was 57.16 percent.

Google chair Eric Schmidt was among the supporters listening to Wagner's presentation. That evening Schmidt asked Wagner what he was doing next. Their conversation led to a personal loan from the tech executive. Later he made a venture capital investment that enabled Wagner to found Civis in 2013 and keep his core team together. "It didn't take a rocket scientist to realize we'd built something special," Wagner says.

Political campaigns have always been among the strangest of startups: Backed by venture funding from hundreds or thousands or, in rare cases, even millions of donors, they scale up quickly—Hillary Clinton's campaign will likely go through roughly a billion dollars in barely two years—in an effort to capture a specific market share on a specific Tuesday: 50 percent plus one vote. Limited time and money force candidates to coldly focus on what works. There's no graceful pivot to plan B if your campaign loses.

Traditionally, the most efficient way for a campaign to gather strategic intelligence on a slice of the electorate has been to conduct its own internal polls, effectively using the same methods public pollsters use. But those don't really work anymore. Bad internal polling convinced Romney's team right up until Election Day that the former Massachusetts governor was on a path to victory.

Today, campaigns realize they have to look elsewhere for their intelligence, which has caused a major change in how the political industry functions. In the past, an entire campaign's data and infrastructure would go poof after Election Day. Now Civis and similar firms are building institutional memory with permanent information storehouses that track America's 220 million-odd voters across their adult lives, noting everything from magazine subscriptions and student loans to voting history, marital status, Facebook ID, and Twitter handle. Power and clients flow to the firms that can build and maintain the best databases of people's behavior over time.

BlueLabs, started by other Obama alums, has been Clinton's lead data team—one founder, Elan Kriegel, has been embedded with her campaign in Brooklyn for over a year. On the GOP side, Ted Cruz worked with Cambridge Analytica, a British firm that specializes in behavioral analytics, targeting voters based on their personality types. Sanders, true to his nature as a small-donor, grassroots politician, relied on a large group of tech volunteers organized through Reddit and Slack chat rooms, complete with a bot that helped direct new volunteers to needed tasks. And Trump, true to his nature as an orange-faced Shiva, Destroyer of Conventional Politics, employed no internal pollsters at all for the primaries and used public poll results less as predictive tools than as cudgels and fodder for boasting.

Wagner and the Civis team sat out the primary, but when they swing into action for the general election, they won't be rusty. The startup has built up a large roster of corporate and nonprofit clients, including the College Board, the Gates Foundation, Boeing, and Airbnb; it presents itself as being in the business of helping clients drive individuals to take action, whether that's voting, donating to a nonprofit, or buying a product. The company has grown to a staff of 110, with Wagner's messy desk smack in the middle of rows of developers. They have spent the past three years crafting what they see as a newer, better marriage of data analysis and activism.

As it happens, that marriage does not involve completely abandoning the use of the telephone as a research tool. The key, Civis says, is to use what you already know about a population—all the information in your database—to help you make the right phone calls. It's an approach that Civis calls list-based sampling. Say you want to find out how Hispanic millennials feel about a candidate. Instead of randomly dialing 350,000 telephone numbers in order to finally reach your target sample size of 1,000 people in your demographic (if you're lucky), firms like Civis start by plucking from their master database all the people who seem like they might be Hispanic millennials. Then they start either dialing them up or contacting them through online surveys. It's not perfect: It might take 60,000 calls to get those 1,000 responses. But that's better than 350,000, and it beats back the problem of sampling error. Then you can draw stronger inferences from the information you do glean—because you can analyze how it correlates with all the other information in your database.

Here's one example of how Civis has mixed database and phone research. Soon after the passage of the Affordable Care Act, Civis was tapped by Enroll America—a nonprofit set up by the Obama administration to boost the program's enrollment—to figure out how to identify who didn't have health insurance. To do this, Civis started in 2013 by making a relatively small number of random phone calls to people who were already in its database. In those phone surveys, it asked 10,020 people just one simple question: "Are you currently covered by a health insurance plan?"

Civis and others are building data storehouses that track America's 220 million-odd voters across their adult lives.

Comparing those answers to other information in its databases, Civis figured out which variables were likely predictors that someone wasn't covered—factors like voting history, geography, consumer history, and the length of time someone has lived at a given address. Next, to validate the model, Civis withheld portions of the data set from its model algorithms, allowing it to see if the model accurately predicted outcomes that its algorithms hadn't seen before. Finally, Civis used that model to create a 0-to-100 "uninsured score" for all 180 million American adults under the age of 65, predicting the likelihood that each was uninsured.

In the end, Civis used its predictive model to generate zip-code-based maps that Enroll America used to plan enrollment events and place follow-up calls. The result: The nation's uninsured rate dropped from 16.4 percent in 2013 to 10.7 percent in 2015, with huge gains in particular for young people, blacks, Hispanics, and rural Americans.

These methods aren't easy. Civis employs six physicists, a number of linguistics PhDs, and other academic types who had experience working with large data sets. But these kinds of backroom political operatives stand to define the 2016 presidential campaign. Heading into the November election, Civis hopes the thousands of data points in the party's files and its models add up to the most accurate understanding of the American electorate anyone has ever had. "Data's taking over the world," Wagner says, "and anyone who isn't building toward that is going to be left behind." As he sees it, the American population is just too large, too diverse, and too complicated to understand with sampling technology pioneered during the 1930s. "The distance between observation and truth is just getting larger and larger," he says.

Of course, accurately measuring the American electorate isn't everything in a political campaign. You do actually have to persuade people. (Ted Cruz and Jeb Bush probably had better data about Republican voters than their leading opponent did; still, it was Donald Trump who made the sale.) But as it happens, the data science practiced by Civis and other firms is also designed to help candidates know what to say, and to whom, in order to be most persuasive.

What to Watch for in the Fall Campaign

The race will be hard to follow, given the poor quality of political polls. "Chill," advises Dan Wagner, CEO of Civis Analytics. "Stay away from the day-to-day polls." Candidates have access to better data than the rest of us, so watch where their campaigns are adding staff; those are the states that will be the most competitive. Here are some other telling signals.

High Hispanic Turnout

Against Donald Trump, that is. Minorities are a growing part of the electorate—now as much as 30 percent. If Hispanic voters turn out in droves to oppose Trump's immigration rhetoric, Clinton will be able to pick off traditional battleground states like Nevada and Florida. If her campaign expands into red states like Arizona and Georgia, she's angling for a landslide.

Clinton Playing Defense

Democrats have an electoral base of about 242 of the needed 270 votes—they can lose Ohio and Florida and still win the presidency. On the other hand, Trump, whose voters are overwhelmingly white, must win in traditionally Democratic rust-belt states like Pennsylvania, Michigan, and Wisconsin. If Clinton starts moving to defend those states, expect a closer race.

Republican Defectors

Conservative suburban communities packed with upper-income working women and business types who find Trump's antitrade stance abhorrent might deliver states like Virginia and New Hampshire to Clinton. In that case, it might also mean the Senate will end up going Democratic. If so, get ready for a slightly more expedited Supreme Court confirmation process.

Recently the US arm of the UN High Commissioner for Refugees enlisted Civis to help figure out what messages would elicit American support for aiding Syrian refugees fleeing ISIS. Civis' team was surprised to find that the group's messaging—explaining that refugees underwent thorough security checks and that none had been found to be terrorists—actually caused a backlash. "It probably encouraged the idea that there was something to fear about the refugees," explains Christine Campigotto, who oversees Civis' work with nonprofits and NGOs. "They'd be better off not saying anything at all." However, when Republicans were told that more than 50 percent of refugees were children, that message saw a 7 percent swing in increased support.

That scenario proves all too common: It turns out that seasoned media and political professionals aren't all that good at understanding what will resonate with the public. For decades, veteran strategists have made critical choices based on gut instinct and historical tradition. The new algorithms and models are finding that gut instinct, even if honed by years of experience, is actually a very bad way to make decisions. "People want to believe their work is effective and their smartness is perceptive," Shor says. "In a lot of cases, it's just not true—and it's increasingly less true."

Academic research affirms that politicians aren't that skilled at understanding what their constituents want. One 2013 study, by UC Berkeley's David E. Broockman and the University of Michigan's Christopher Skovron, found both Democratic and Republican legislators believe their constituents to be more conservative than they actually are—with Republicans overestimating their constituents' conservatism by 20 percentage points.

Other new data-driven firms back up that research. Echelon Insights, launched by GOP consultant Patrick Ruffini in 2014 with pollster Kristen Soltis Anderson, is working to advance what the field calls unstructured listening, mining the vast streams of online conversation on Twitter and Facebook to see what the public cares about that might not be on politicians' radar. Ruffini has found there are three separate conversations online: liberals, conservatives, and Beltway insiders.

What matters inside Washington doesn't necessarily translate outside of it and vice versa; Ruffini says that last year such research helped identify that both Ted Cruz and Bernie Sanders would outperform their low public polling numbers, since each had a clear base of online supporters. "For a long time, Bernie was ignored by the Beltway," he says.

"Data's taking over the world, and anyone who isn't building toward that is going to be left behind."

More broadly, Civis' work is uncovering an uncomfortable truth for many horse-race pollsters: Public opinion just isn't that dynamic. Political support shifts slowly and subtly, generally over months and years rather than in response to the day-by-day, headline-blaring gyrations the media trumpets as breaking news. "In public polling, you see a lot of big swings," Campigotto says. "That movement is driven more by poor sampling methods and bias in the response. They're making a headline out of statistical noise. Not that many people change their minds between Wednesday and Friday."

The lesson for news junkies is a simple one: As Election Day approaches, don't pay attention to the headlines about what the polls say—these won't be rigorous enough or accurate enough to detect what's really happening. As Shor says, "Campaigns have access to high-quality polling, and the public generally doesn't." Instead, watch what the candidates are actually doing on the ground. It's like boxing: Sophisticated observers know that the sparring up top matters less than the footwork, which predicts when and where a punch will land.

Shor points back to the Michigan example from 2012. "The fact that the Obama campaign wasn't spending money, that kind of speaks for itself. Look at where they're spending. Look at where they're adding staff. That's where they think they'll be competitive." In other words, if Donald Trump tells you he's going to have a "yuuuggge" victory in a state like New York or Pennsylvania, check whether Hillary Clinton is moving staff there before you take him at his word. The data might not back it up.

Print Citations

CMS: Graff, Garrett M. "The Polls Are All Wrong: A Startup Called Civis Is Our Best Hope to Fix Them." In *The Reference Shelf: Campaign Trends and Election Law*, edited by Betsy Maury, 174-82. Ipswitch, MA: Salem Press, 2016.

MLA: Graff, Garrett M. "The Polls Are All Wrong: A Startup Called Civis Is Our Best Hope to Fix Them." *The Reference Shelf: Campaign Trends and Election Law*. Ed. Betsy Maury. Ipswitch: Salem Press, 2016. 174-82. Print.

APA: Graff, G.M. (2016). The polls are all wrong: A startup called Civis is our best hope to fix them. In Betsy Maury (Ed.), *The reference shelf: Campaign trends and election law* (pp. 174-182). Ipswitch, MA: Salem. (Original work published 2016)

Bibliography

"2016 Campaign: Strong Interest, Widespread Dissatisfaction." *Pew Research*. Pew Research Center. Jul 7 2016. Web. 16 Aug 2016.

"American Presidential Candidates and Social Media." *Economist*. Economist Newspaper. Feb 29 2016. Web. 18 Aug 2016.

Barasch, Emily. "The Twisted History of Gerrymandering in American Politics." *Atlantic*. Atlantic Monthly Group. Sep 19 2012. Web. 15 Aug 2016.

Barnes, Robert and Ann E. Marimow. "Appeals Court Strikes Down North Carolina's Voter-ID Law." *The Washington Post*. Jul 29 2016. Web. 20 Aug 2016.

Bates, Laura. 'Spanking' Hillary Clinton Is Grotesque Misogyny." *Time*. Time Inc. Feb 8 2016. Web. 19 Aug 2016.

Beaujon, Andrew. "Survey: NPR's Listeners Best-Informed, Fox Viewers Worst-Informed." *Poynter*. The Poynter Institute. May 23 2012. Web. 18 Aug 2016.

"Beyond Distrust: How Americans View Their Government." *Pew Research*. Pew Research Center. Nov 23 2015. Web. 16 Aug 2016.

Bialik, Carl. "Everyone Has Fake Twitter Followers, But Trump Has the Most. Sad!" *Fivethirtyeight*. FiveThirtyEight. Apr 14 2016. Web. 18 Aug 2016.

Blake, Aaron. "Is 2016 the Anger Election? Not Quite." *The Washington Post*. Jan 26 2016. Web. 16 Aug 2016.

Blumenthal, Paul. "On Campaign Finance, Republicans and Democrats Could Not Be Further Apart." *The Huffington Post*. Jul 19 2016. Web. 19 Aug 2016.

Boak, Josh. "Why It Matters: Income Inequality." *U.S. News*. U.S. News and World Report. Aug 18 2016. Web. 18 Aug 2016.

Bouie, Jamelle. "How Trump Happened." *Slate*. Slate Media Group. Mar 13 2016. Web. 18 Aug 2016.

Bult, Laura. "McDonald's CEO Gets 368% Pay Raise." *Daily News*. New York Daily News. Apr 16 2016. Web. 17 Aug 2016.

Bump, Philip. "Donald Trump Is Getting ZERO Percent of the Black Vote in Polls in Pennsylvania and Ohio." *The Washington Post*. Nash Holdings. Jul 13 2016. Web. 16 Aug 2016.

"Campaign Exposes Fissures Over Issues, Values and How Life Has Changed in the U.S." *Pew Research*. Pew Research Center. Mar 31 2016. Web. 18 Aug 2016.

Chait, Jonathan. "Sorry, Obama: Donald Trump Is a Populist, and You're Not." *New York*. New York Media LLC. Jun 30 2016. Web. 17 Aug 2016.

"Changing Attitudes on Gay Marriage." *Pew Research*. Pew Research Center. May 12 2016. Web. 24 Aug 2016.

"Chinese Immigration and the Chinese Exclusion Acts." *Office of the Historian*. U.S. Department of State. 2016. Web. 18 Aug 2016.

Chotiner, Isaac, "Is Donald Trump a Populist? Or, Is He Just Popular?" *Slate*. Slate Monthly Group. Feb 24 2016. Web. 16 Aug 2016.

"Citizens Don't Like Gerrymandering; Study Offers Alternative Redistricting Methods." *UVA Today*. University of Virginia. Weldon Cooper Center for Public Service. Jun 30 2014. Web. 16 Aug 2016.

Confessore, Nicholas and Megan Thee-Brenan. "Poll Shows Americans Favor an Overhaul of Campaign Financing." *New York Times*. New York Times Company. Jun 2 2015. Web. 13 Aug 2016.

Cressman, Derek. "End Court-Ordered Corruption." *US News*. U.S. News and World Report. Jan 29 2016. Web. 16 Aug 2016.

Davis, Bob. "The Thorny Economics of Illegal Immigration." *Wall Street Journal*. Dow Jones & Co. Feb 9 2016. Web. 17 Aug 2016.

Desilver, Drew and Patrick Van Kessel. "As More Money Flows into Campaigns, Americans Worry About Its Influence." *Pew Research*. Pew Research Center. Dec 7 2015. Web. 19 Aug 2016.

Domke, Todd. "Commentary: How Did Trump Happen?" *WBUR*. WBUR Radio. Jun 28 2016. Web. 18 Aug 2016.

"Donald Trump Calls for 'Extreme Vetting' of Immigrants to US." *BBC News*. BBC. Aug 16 2016. Web. 18 Aug 2016.

Drezner, Daniel W. "Does the 2016 Campaign Provide a Mandate Against TPP?" *Washington Post*. Nash Holdings. Jun 23 2016. Web. 19 Aug 2016.

Elliott, Philip and Sam Frizell. "Why It's Easy to Forget Hillary Clinton Is Making History." *Time*. Jun 6 2016. Web. 17 Aug 2016.

"Exclusive: Trump Supporters More Likely to View Blacks Negatively – Reuters/Ipsos Poll." *Reuters*. Reuters. Jun 28 2016. Web. 17 Aug 2016.

"Favorability: People in the News." *Gallup*. Gallup. Aug 19 2016. Web. 19 Aug 2016.

Frum, David. "The Great Republican Revolt." *The Atlantic*. Atlantic Monthly Group. Jan/Feb 2016. Web. 18 Aug 2016.

Fuller, Jaime. "From George Washington to Shaun McCutcheon: A Brief-ish History of Campaign Finance Reform." *The Washington Post*. Nash Holdings. Apr 3 2014. Web. 15 Aug 2016.

Goldberg, Michelle. "The Hillary Haters." *Slate*. The Slate Group. Jul 24 2016. Web. 20 Aug 2016.

Goodtimes, Johnny. "A Brief History of Campaign Mudslinging, From 1796 to Today." *Philadelphia Magazine*. Metro Corp. Oct 24 2012. Web. 18 Aug 2016.

Hamilton, Alec. "A Brief History of Campaign Finance (and Why It Matters)." *WNYC*. New York Public Radio. Dec 21 2010. Web. 15 Aug 2016.

Hanson, Gordon H. "Immigration, Productivity, and Competitiveness in American Industry." *AEI*. American Enterprise Institute. 2011. Pdf. 18 Aug 2016.

"How Social Media Inflates Our Perception of Our Choice Presidential Candidate." *NPR*. National Public Radio. Apr 16 2016. Web. 18 Aug 2016.

"How the Presidential Candidates Use the Web and Social Media." *Pew Research*. Pew Research Center. Aug 15 2012. Web. 18 Aug 2016.

Koran, Laura and Ryan Browne. "Can Trump Be the First to Go Directly From Corner Office to Oval Office?" *CNN*. Cable News Network. Aug 12 2016. Web. 18 Aug 2016.

Krieg, Gregory. "Donald Trump's 27-day Spiral: From Convention Bounce to Campaign Overhaul." *CNN*. Cable News Network. Aug 18 2016. Web. 18 Aug 2016.

Krugman, Paul. "A Country Is Not a Company." *HBR*. Harvard Business Review. Jan-Feb 1996. Web. 19 Aug 2016.

LoBianco, Tom and Ashley Killough. "Trump Pitches Black Voters: 'What the Hell Do You Have to Lose?'." *CNN*. Cable News Network. Aug 19 2016. Web. 18 Aug 2016.

Maloy, Simon. "Trump's Economic Speech: Lots of Goodies for the Rich, With a Hearty Dose of Gaffes." *Salon*. Salon Media Group, Ltd. Aug 9 2016. Web. 16 Aug 2016.

Matthews, Chris. "Donald Trump Says Hillary Clinton Is Corrupt—Is He Right?" *Fortune*. Fortune Inc. Jun 13 2016. Web. 19 Aug 2016.

McCarthy, Justin. "In U.S., 65% Dissatisfied with How Gov't System Works." *Gallup*. Gallup Inc. Jan 22 2014. Web.

McDaniel, Jason and Sean McElwee. "Trump Supporters Have Cooler Feelings Towards Many Groups, Compared to Supporters of Other Candidates." *The New West*. Western Political Science Association. May 16 2016. Web. 19 Aug 2016.

McLaughlin, Dan. "History Is Not on the Democrats' Side in 2016." *The Federalist*. FDRLST Media. Sep 4 2014. Web. 19 Aug 2016.

"Michael Froman: Where the TPP Stands." *Wall Street Journal*. Dow Jones & Company. Jun 19 2016. Web. 24 Aug 2016.

"Minimum Wage Mythbusters." *DOL*. United States Department of Labor. 2015. Web. 17 Aug 2016.

Mitchell, Amy, Gottfried, Jeffrey, Barthel, Michael, and Elisa Shearer. "The Modern News Consumer." *Pew Research Center*. Jul 7 2016. Web. 18 Aug 2016.

Narayanswamy, Anu, Cameron, Darla, and Matea Gold. "Money Raised as of July 31." *Washington Post*. Nash Holdings. Jul 31 2016. Web. 21 Aug 2016.

Nyhan, Brendan. "Voter Fraud is Rare, but Myth is Widespread." *New York Times*. New York Times Company. Jun 10 2014. Web. 20 Aug 2016.

O'Connor, Lydia and Daniel Marans. "Here Are 13 Examples of Donald Trump Being Racist." *Huffington Post*. Huffington Post. Feb 29 2016. Web. 17 Aug 2016.

"On Views of Race and Inequality, Blacks and Whites Are Worlds Apart." *Pew Research*. Jun 27 2016. Web. 16 Aug 2016.

Page, Susan. "For Clinton, Sisterhood is Powerful – and Trump Helps." *USA Today*.

Panagopoulos, Costas. "Public Awareness and Attitudes About Redistricting Institutions." *Journal of Politics and Law*. Vol 6, No 3; 2013. Pdf. 15 Aug 2016.

Parini, Jay. "Why Do They Hate Hillary Clinton So Much?" *CNN*. Cable News Network. Mar 21 2016. Web. 19 Aug 2016.

Patton, Leslie. "McDonald's $8.25 Man and $8.75 Million CEO Shows Pay Gap." *Bloomberg*. Bloomberg Business. Dec 11 2012. Web. 25 Aug 2016.

Peri, Giovanni. "The Economic Benefits of Immigration." *CLAS Berkeley*. Center for Latin American Studies. University of California, Berkeley. Fall 2013. Web. 18 Aug 2016.

Ratha, Dilip. "The Impact of Remittances on Economic Growth and Poverty Reduction." *MPI Policy Brief*. Migration Policy Institute. Sep 2013. Web. 18 Aug 2015.

"Republicans' Early Views of GOP Field More Positive Than in 2012, 2008 Campaigns." *Pew Research*. May 19 2015. Web. 19 Aug 2016.

Riffkin, Rebecca. "Americans' Trust in Media Remains at Historical Low." *Gallup*. Sep 28 2015. Web. 18 Aug 2016.

Robinson, Eugene. "The Rock-Star Appeal of Bernie Sanders." *The Washington Post*. Nash Holdings. Oct 1 2015. Web. 19 Aug 2016.

Saad, Lydia. "Half in U.S. Support Publicly Financed Federal Campaigns." *Gallup*. Gallup Inc. Jun 24 2013. Web. 12 Aug 2016.

Saad, Lydia. "Trump Leads Clinton on Top-Ranking Economic Issues." *Gallup*. Gallup. Jun 2 2016. Web. 24 Aug 2016.

Sahadi, Jeanne and Tal Yellin. "Hillary vs. Bernie: Their Money…and Yours." *CNN Money*. Cable News Network. Aug 18 2016. Web. 18 Aug 2016.

Sanchez, Gabriel and Alan L. Abramowitz. "Hillary Clinton's Lead in the Polls May Be Larger Than it Seems. Here's Why." *The Washington Post*. Nash Holdings. Jun 20 2016. Web. Aug 17 2016.

Scott, Eugene. "Judge Upholds Controversial North Carolina Voter ID Law." *CNN*. Cable News Network. Apr 26 2016. Web. 21 Aug 2016.

Sherman, Erik. "San Francisco Restaurant Jobs Grow Then Fall After Minimum Wage Jump." *Forbes*. Forbes Inc. Jan 15 2016. Web. 17 Aug 2016.

Smith, Noah. "Finally, an Answer to the Minimum Wage Question." *Bloomberg*. Bloomberg LP. May 27 2015. Web. 17 Aug 2016.

Stebenne, David. "Re-mapping American Politics: The Redistricting Revolution Fifty Years Later." *OSU*. Oregon State University. Vol 5, Iss 5, Feb 2012. Web. 15 Aug 2016.

Strachan, Maxwell. "U.S. Economy Lost Nearly 700,000 Jobs Because of NAFTA, EPI Says." May 12 2011. Web. 25 Aug 2016. *Huffington Post*.

Swanson, Ana. "The Myth and the Reality of Donald Trump's Business Empire." *The Washington Post*. Feb 29 2016. Web. 18 Aug 2016.

Wasik, John. "Voter Fraud: A Massive, Anti-Democratic Deception." *Forbes*. Forbes Inc. Nov 6 2012. Web. 20 Aug 2016.

Webley, Kayla. "How the Nixon-Kennedy Debate Changed the World." *Time*. Time Inc. Sep 23 2010. Web. 18 Aug 2016.

"Weighing Pros and Cons of the Proposed Trans-Pacific Partnership." *Stanford Economics*. Stanford University School of Economics. Nov 12 2015. Web. 24 Aug 2016.

Weiser, Wendy R. and Lawrence Norden. "Voting Law Changes in 2012." *Brennan Center*. Brennan Center for Justice. 2011. Pdf. 19 Aug 2016.

Williams, Vanessa and Scott Clement. "Three in Four Voters of Color 'Strongly'

Dislike Trump." *The Washington Post*. Nash Holdings. Jun 20 2016. Web. 17 Aug 2016.

Winter, Tom. "Trump Bankruptcy Math Doesn't Add Up." *NBC News*. National Broadcasting Company. Jun 24 2016. Web. 18 Aug 2016.

Wolf, Richard and Gregory Korte. "Supreme Court Strikes Blow Against Gerrymandering." *USA Today*. Gannett Company. Jun 29 2015. Web. 15 Aug 2016

Wolf, Richard. "Supreme Court Upholds Virginia Redistricting." *USA Today*. May 23 2016. Web. 15 Aug 2016.

"Women and Leadership." *Pew Research*. Pew Research Center. Jan 14 2015. Web. 19 Aug 2016.

Worstall, Tim. "$15 Minimum Wage Threatens 5.3 Million US Manufacturing Jobs." *Forbes*. Forbes, Inc. Sep 2 2015. Web. 16 Aug 2016.

Zong, Jie and Jeanne Batalova. "Frequently Requested Statistics on Immigrants and Immigration in the United States." *MPI*. Migration Policy Institute. Apr 14 2016. Web. Aug 17 2016.

Websites

Ballotopedia
www.balletopedia.org

Ballotopedia is an online encyclopedia covering local, state, and federal politics. The website provides thousands of articles on both broad and specific political issues like the TPP proposal, LGBT rights, and immigration, and describes the positions of candidates on each issue. The searchable database also provides detailed results from local and national elections.

Crowdpac
www.crowdpac.com

Nonpartisan website that allows users to create crowdsourcing campaigns for various political issues and also provides articles and analysis of key issues in 2016 and a description of how each candidate stands on the issues. With each political issue presented through the site, user-created crowdsourcing campaigns are presented and explained to visitors.

Donald Trump Campaign
www.donaldjtrump.com

Official website for the campaign of Donald Trump and Mike Pence. Website provides links to media promoting Trump's presidential campaign as well as brief descriptions of the candidate's stance on key issues, and links to donate to the Trump campaign.

Donald Trump Facebook Page
https://www.facebook.com/DonaldTrump/

Official Facebook page for the candidacy of Donald Trump. Contains links to media detailing aspects of the Trump campaign and allows users to comment on statements made by Trump and others on the page.

Election Central
www.pbseduelectioncentral.com

Election Central is a website from the Public Broadcasting Service Learning Media department that provides simple introductory videos and articles explaining the electoral process and a variety of topics related to political campaigns, debates, and the roles of various organizations involved in the process, such as election foundations and political parties. *Election Central* is a useful website for young learners as well as for adults looking to refresh their knowledge of the political process.

Fact Check

www.factcheck.org

Nonpartisan website provides analysis of claims made by political candidates and spokespeople for political campaigns. *Fact Check* provides analysis of political ads, speeches, and social media posts. *Fact Check* also notes when a candidate had made repeated false claims on a topic and describes relevant data on the issue.

FiveThirtyEight

www.fivethirtyeight.com

FiveThirtyEight, owned by ESPN, is a political and sports information site that provides a wealth of statistical data about the 2016 presidential race including interactive charts, detailed analyses of opinion poll data, and a running predictor (updated daily) on the probability for each candidate to win specific states and the national election.

Hillary Clinton

www.hillaryclinton.com

Official website for the campaign of Hillary Clinton and Tim Kaine. Contains links to news and media related to the campaign and descriptions of Clinton's stance on key issues. Also provides links for supporters wishing to volunteer or donate to the campaign.

Hillary Clinton Facebook Page

https://www.facebook.com/hillaryclinton

Official Facebook page for the Hillary Clinton presidential campaign. Contains statements from Clinton, links to news reports and other media, and allows supporters or critics to post comments on various topics discussed on the page.

New York Times Election Tracker

http://www.nytimes.com/interactive/2016/us/elections/2016-presidential-candidates.html

New York Times interactive website that provides live coverage of 2016 campaign issues, news, and polling results. The website also links to numerous articles published through *New York Times* as well as other media agencies. The election tracker provided by *New York Times* also links to another interactive website detailing how the candidates for the 2016 presidential election stand on specific issues like immigration, gun control, climate change, and Syrian refugees.

Political Communication Lab Stanford University

www.pcl.stanford.edu

The Political Communication Lab at Stanford University provides an archive of political video from 1994 to 2016 that includes official campaign advertisements and recordings of endorsements for candidates. For the 2016 campaign, the PCL contains a collection of ads run in support of both Trump and Clinton.

Politifact

www.politifact.com

The Pulitzer Award-winning website provides analysis of political truthfulness by fact checking statements made by politicians and political candidates. Provides coverage of all candidates in the 2016 presidential race.

Pollster

www.elections.huffingtonpost.com/pollster

Pollster is an interactive website created by the *Huffington Post* that provides detailed analysis of public opinion polls related to the election. On specific issues, *Pollster* provides a combined chart indicating the broad consensus from an analysis of specific polls while also providing links to the polls used to compile each analysis.

RealClearPolitics

www.realclearpolitics.com

Nonpartisan political website that provides information on polls and studies related to political campaigns. *RealClearPolitics* also covers legislative issues in the executive and congressional branches and the website posts opinion pieces and news articles written from both sides of the political divide.

RockTheVote

www.rockthevote.com

Nonprofit organization promoting political participation towards the nation's emerging voting-age population. The website provides celebrity and professional commentary and helps direct voters to information on state voting laws and procedures. *Rockthevote* also allows users to register to vote online and links to state voter registration offices.

White House
www.whitehouse.gov

Official website for the executive branch of the United States government. Provides links to President Obama's speeches and press releases as well as coverage of current legislative proposals initiated by the Obama administration.

Index

Acheson, Dean, 149
Adams, Timothy, 139
Amandi, Fernand, 124
Atwater, Lee, 12
Autor, David, 113, 139
Baily, Martin, 136
Bash, Dana, 172
Bernanke, Ben, 136
Biden, Joe, 61
Biden, Joseph R. Jr., 171
Boehner, John, 13, 24
Broockman, David E., 187
Brooks, Arthur, 86, 177
Brynjolfsson, Erik, 137
Bush, George H. W., 12
Bush, Jeb, ix, 21, 38, 64, 83, 84, 85, 87,
    88, 89, 97, 119, 153, 170, 174, 186
Carson, Ben, 68, 86, 88, 97, 171
Clinton, Bill, xii, 37, 41, 58, 67, 75, 76,
    82, 113, 136, 137, 153
Clinton, Hillary, ix, xi, xii, xiii, 36, 37,
    39, 45, 48, 49, 50, 51, 53, 64, 70, 71,
    72, 73, 74, 75, 77, 82, 90, 98, 110,
    119, 120, 123, 126, 127, 132, 138,
    141, 165, 173, 178, 180, 184, 188,
    189, 190, 191, 192, 196
Cook, Charles, 125
Cruz, Ted, 20, 31, 48, 56, 64, 97, 127,
    173, 180, 185, 186, 188
Daley, David, 9
Dean, Howard, 183
Deming, David, 137
DeVine, Michele, 169
DiGrazia, Joe, 174
Dukakism, Michael, 12, 82
Dunn, Lee, 161
Durbin, Dick, 31
Elias, Marc, 28
Feehery, John, 124
Fiorina, Carly, 86, 98, 149, 170
Fulop, Steven, 19

Gao, Shaofen "Lisa", 20
Garcia, Ann, 120
Gertler, Mark, 136
Ginsberg, Ben, 12
Graham, Lindsey, 171
Greenspan, Alan, 134, 135
Hanson, Gordon, 113, 139
Hill, Steven, 23–200
Huckabee, Mike, 20, 81, 86
Ickes, Harold, 183
Irwin, Douglas, 127
Kaptur, Marcy, 24
Kasich, John, 68, 120, 161, 173
Kerns, Chris, 174
Kessler, Fred, 23
Koch, Charles and David, 16, 33
Kreiss, Daniel, 173
Kucinich, Dennis, 24
Laurence, Eric, 160
Leahy, Patrick, 26
Levdansky, David, 9
Lewis, John, 12, 26
Lindsay, Erin, 161
Lioz, Adam, 30
Lott, Trent, 51
Lycan, Eric, 20
Majewski, Brigitte, 162
McAfee, Andrew, 137
McAuliffe, Terry, 183
McCain, John, 86, 171, 175
McCarthy, Joseph, 56, 148, 149
McGregor, Shannon, 173
McKinnon, Mark, 33
Murray, Charles, 63, 72, 92
Palin, Sarah, 61
Paul, Rand, 161, 170
Perry, Rick, 24, 86
Prasad, Eswar, 128
Putin, Vladimir, 153
Quinn, Laura, 183
Raskin, Jamie, 24

Reagan, Ronald, 24, 36, 62, 89, 101, 138, 153
Republican, 59
Rob Richie, 23
Romney, Mitt, 21, 61, 65, 71, 85, 86, 87, 89, 171, 184
Rubio, Marco, 21, 66, 84, 85, 88, 97, 170, 173, 178
Ruffini, Patrick, 164, 187
Sandberg, Sheryl, 177
Sanders, Bernie, ix, xi, xiii, 4, 31, 36, 45, 62, 66, 74, 75, 89, 95, 98, 100, 110, 127, 131, 134, 137, 152, 165, 171, 173, 178, 180, 188, 192
Sarbanes, John, 31
Scavino, Daniel Jr., 153
Schmidt, Eric, 184
Seebohm, Monica, 168
Shor, David, 180
Skovron, Christopher, 187
Speiser, Frank, 164

Stephens-Davidowitz, Seth, 175
Stevens, John Paul, 33
Stevens, Stuart, 87, 171
Summers, Lawrence, 139
Sumner, Charles, 53
Trump, Donald, v, ix, x, xiii, 36, 38, 45, 46, 48, 49, 51, 58, 60, 62, 63, 64, 70, 71, 77, 80, 86, 89, 92, 97, 98, 99, 100, 107, 108, 109, 110, 119, 122, 124, 134, 137, 144, 146, 147, 148, 152, 162, 164, 173, 178, 180, 186, 188, 189, 190, 191, 192, 195
Wagner, Dan, 180, 186
Walker, Scott, 62, 85, 87, 160, 161
Wallace, George, 36, 101, 148, 149
Wallace, Lurleen, 39
Walsh, Jim, 162
Webb, Jim, 98, 120
Weintraub, Ellen, 22, 29
Wertheimer, Fred, 16
Wolgin, Philip E., 120